CENTRAL
EUROPE
PHRASEBOOK

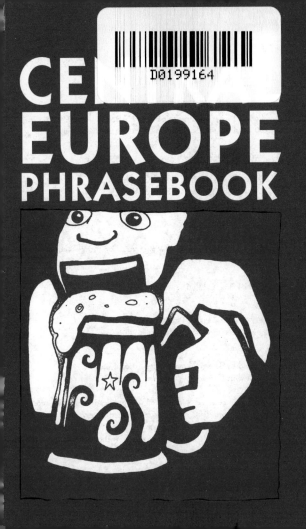

Central Europe phrasebook
2nd edition – February 2001

Published by
Lonely Planet Publications Pty Ltd ABN 36 005 607 983
90 Maribyrnong St, Footscray, Victoria 3011, Australia

Lonely Planet Offices
Australia Locked Bag 1, Footscray, Victoria 3011
USA 150 Linden St, Oakland CA 94607
UK 10a Spring Place, London NW5 3BH
France 1 rue du Dahomey, 75011 Paris

Cover illustration
'So... this Dwarf walks into a bar, and...' by Patrick Marris

ISBN 1 86450 226 6

text © Lonely Planet Publications 2001
cover illustration © Lonely Planet 2001

Printed by The Bookmaker International Ltd
Printed in China

About the Authors

Katarina Steiner updated the Czech chapter which was originally written by Richard Nebeský. She also wrote and updated the Slovakian chapter based on the second edition of Lonely Planet's *Eastern Europe phrasebook*. Katarina is a Sydney based freelance translator and interpreter of the languages of Czech, German and Slovak.

German was updated by Gunter Mühl. From Hannover, Germany, Gunter teaches German at the University of Canterbury in Christchurch, New Zealand, and works as a freelance translator. This chapter was based on Lonely Planet's *German phrasebook*, written by Franziska Buck and Anke Munderloh.

Katalin Koronczi wrote and updated Hungarian. A Budapester born and bred, Katalin Koronczi has worked in the tourism profession for 23 years. She also finds time to run her own translation bureau.

Krzysztof Dydyński wrote the Polish chapter. He was born and raised in Warsaw, Poland. He travelled extensively in Asia and lived in South America for nearly five years before settling in Australia, where he currently resides and works. He's the author of several Lonely Planet guidebooks, including *Poland, Kraków, Colombia* and *Venezuela*.

Slovenian was updated by Miran Hladnik who is a professor of Slovene literature at the University of Ljubljana, Slovenia. Once upon a time he was a Slovene lecturer in the US and, using his teaching experience, he wrote a phrasebook, *Slovene for Travelers*. The original chapter was written by Draga Gelt.

From the Authors

Katalin Koronczi would like to thank all those who helped her in compiling the Magyar section, especially her young son Peter who gave her just enough peace and quiet to complete the work to deadline.

Warmest thanks from Krzysztof Dydyński to Angela Melendro, Ela Lis, Beata Wasiak, Basia Meder, Tadek Wysocki, Kuba Leszczyński, Majka and Marek Bogatek, and Grażyna and Jacek Wojciechowicz for help with the Polish chapter.

Miran Hladnik wishes you a joyful start in acquisition of the Slovene language and a pleasant stay in Slovenia.

From the Publisher

One of our many high-calibre designers, Patrick Marris, illustrated both the book and its cover. Patrick, together with Yukiyoshi Kamimura and Brendan Dempsey, designed and laid out these beautiful pages. Fabrice Rocher supervised all this and Natasha Velleley provided the map. Lou Callan edited from a distance and Vicki Webb and Karin Vidstrup Monk co-edited, while Fleur Goding, Haya Husseini and Emma Koch proofed. As usual, Karin Vidstrup Monk pulled everything together, Sally Steward initiated the project and got sick, Peter D'Onghia did layout checks and got sick. Karin still has some hair left.

CONTENTS

INTRODUCTION

The Central European languages covered in this book include Czech, German, Hungarian, Polish, Slovak and Slovene. These languages come from three different language families.

Slavonic languages, which originated north of the Carpathians. They are now divided into three subgroups. Czech, Polish and Slovak belong to the West Slavonic subgroup, while Slovene is a South Slavonic language.

German, a close relative of English, belongs to the West Germanic group of languages, while Hungarian, a Finno-Ugric language, is unique in Europe. It's closest European relative is Finnish, although today the two languages are no longer mutually intelligible.

Transliterations

Simplified transliterations have been provided in red throughout the book. Italics is used to indicate where to place stress in a word.

Arthur or Martha?

When there are both masculine and feminine forms of a word, they are indicated in either of two ways, with the masculine form always appearing first:

- with a slash separating the masculine and feminine word within a sentence:

    What are your favourite games?
    yah-key hrih maash raad/   *Jaké hry máš rád/*
    raa-dah   *ráda?* (m/f)

- when the distinction between masculine and feminine is more complex, each word is given in full:

    business   üz-let-em-ber   *üzletember* (m)
    person   üz-let-as-sony   *üzletasszony* (f)

German gender is indicated slightly differently, see pg 85.

CENTRAL EUROPE

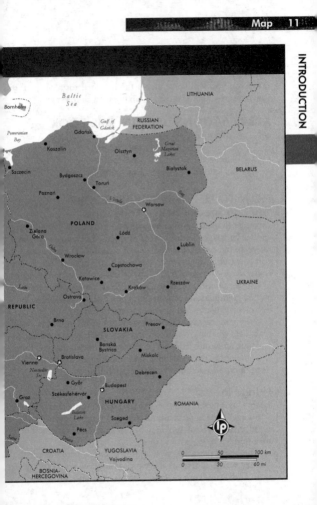
Map 11

INTRODUCTION

INTRODUCTION

Polite Forms

When a language has polite and informal forms of the singular pronoun 'you', the polite form has been used in most cases. However, you will come across the informal form of 'you' in some phrases, such as those for talking with children.

ABBREVIATIONS USED IN THIS BOOK

col	colloquial	n	neuter
f	feminine	pl	plural
inf	informal	pol	polite
m	masculine	sg	singular

HOW TO USE THIS PHRASEBOOK
You *Can* Speak Another Language

Anyone can speak another language. Don't worry if you haven't studied languages before, or that you studied a language at school for years and can't remember any of it. It doesn't even matter if you failed English grammar. After all, that's never affected your ability to speak English! And this is the key to picking up a language in another country. You don't need to sit down and memorise endless grammatical details and you don't need to memorise long lists of vocabulary. You just need to start speaking.

Once you start, you'll be amazed how many prompts you'll get to help you build on those first words. You'll hear people speaking, pick up sounds from TV, catch a word or two that you think you know from the local radio, see something on a billboard – all these things help to build your understanding.

Plunge In

There's just one thing you need to start speaking another language – courage. Your biggest hurdle is overcoming the fear of saying aloud what may seem to you to be just a bunch of sounds. There are a number of ways to do this.

The best way to start overcoming your fear is to memorise a few key words. These are the words you know you'll be saying again and again, such as 'hello', 'thank you' and 'How much?'.

Here's an important hint though: right from the beginning, learn at least one phrase that will be useful but not essential. Such as 'See you later' or even a conversational piece like 'It's nice today, isn't it?' (people everywhere love to talk about the weather). Having this extra phrase (just start with one, if you like, and learn to say it really well) will enable you to move away from the basics, and when you get a reply and a smile, it'll also boost your confidence. You'll find that people you speak to will like it too, as they'll understand that at least you've tried to learn more of the language than just the usual essential words.

Ways to Remember

There are several ways to learn a language. Most people find they learn from a variety of these, although people usually have a preferred way to remember. Some like to see the written word and remember the sound from what they see. Some like to just hear it spoken in context (if this is you, try talking to yourself in the foreign language, but do it at home or somewhere private, to give yourself confidence, and so others don't wonder about your sanity!). Others, especially the more mathematically inclined, like to analyse the grammar of a language, and piece together words according to the rules of grammar. The very visually inclined like to associate the written word and even sounds with some visual stimulus such as illustrations, TV and general things they see in the street. As you learn, you'll discover what works best for you – be aware of what made you really remember a particular word, and if it sticks in your mind, keep using that method.

Kicking Off

Chances are you'll want to learn some of the language before you go. The first thing to do is to memorise those essential phrases and words. Check out the basics and don't forget that extra phrase. Try the sections on making conversation or greeting people for a phrase you'd like to use. Write some of these words and phrases down on a piece of paper and stick them up around the place: on the fridge, by the bed, on your computer, as a bookmark –

INTRODUCTION

somewhere where you'll see them often. Try putting some words in context – the 'How much is it?' note, for instance, could go in your wallet.

Any Questions?

Try to learn the main question words. Each language chapter contains a box with the most common ones. As you read through different situations, you'll see these words used in the example sentences, and this will help you remember them. So if you want to take a bus, turn to the Bus section in each chapter (use the Index pages to find it quickly). You've already tried to memorise the word for 'which' and you'll see the word for 'bus'. When you come across the sentence 'Which bus goes to ...?', you'll recognise the key words and this will help you remember the whole phrase.

I Have a Flat Tyre

Doesn't seem like the phrase you're going to need? Well, in fact it could be very useful. As are all the phrases in this book, provided you have the courage to mix and match them. We have given specific examples within each section. But the key words remain the same even when the situation changes. So while you may not be planning on any driving during your trip, the first part of the phrase 'I have ...' could refer to anything else, and there are plenty of words in the other phrases that, we hope, will fit your needs. So whether it's 'a ticket' or 'a visa', you'll be able to put the words together to convey your meaning.

Finally

Don't be concerned if you feel you can't memorise words. You'll find the most essential words and phrases on the Quick Reference page at the start of each chapter. You could also try tagging a few pages for other key phrases, or use the notes pages to write your own reminders.

CZECH

CZECH

QUICK REFERENCE

Hello	*dob*-ree-dehn	Dobrý den.
Goodbye.	*nah*-skhleh-dah-noh	Na shledanou.
Yes./No.	*ah*-no/neh	Ano./Ne.
Excuse me.	*zdo*-vo-leh-nyeem	S dovolením.
May I?	*do*-vol-teh-mi?	Dovolte mi?
Sorry.	*pro*-miny-teh	Promiňte.
Please.	*pro*-seem	Prosím.
Thank you.	*dyeh*-ku-yi	Děkuji.
That's fine.	*neh*-nyee zahch.	Není zač.
You're welcome.	*pro*-seem	Prosím.
What time is it?	*ko*-lik-yeh *ho*-dyin?	Kolik je hodin?
Where's ...?	*gdeh*-yeh ...?	Kde je ...?
Go straight ahead.	y*dyeh*-teh *przhee*-mo	Jděte přímo.

Turn left/right	*zah*-to-chteh	Zatočte
at the ...	*vleh*-vo/ *prah*-vo ...	vlevo/vpravo ...
next corner	nah *przhee*-shtyeem *ro*-hu	na příštím rohu

I'd like a ...	*przhaal*/ *przhaa*-lah bikh-si ...	Přál/Přála bych si ... (m/f)
single room	*yeh*-dno-loozh-ko-vee *po*-koy	jednolůžkový pokoj
one-way ticket	*yeh*-dno-smyehr-noh *yeez*-dehn-ku	jednosměrnou jízdenku
return ticket	*spaa*-teh-chnyee *yeez*-dehn-ku	zpáteční jízdenku

I don't understand.		
neh-roh-zu-meem		Nerozumím.
Do you speak English?		
mlu-vee-teh *ahn*-glits-ki?		Mluvíte anglicky?
Where are the toilets?		
gdeh-ysoh *zaa*-kho-di?		Kde jsou záchody?
How do I get to ...?		
yahk-seh *do*-stah-nu k ...?		Jak se dostanu k ...?

1	*yeh*-dna	jedna	6	shehst	šest
2	dvah	dva	7	se*h*-dum	sedm
3	trzhi	tři	8	o-sum	osm
4	*chti*-rzhi	čtyři	9	de*h*-vyeht	devět
5	pyeht	pět	10	*deh*-seht	deset

CZECH

The Czech language belongs to the Slavonic group of Indo-European languages, which is subdivided into East, West and South Slavonic groups. Czech, together with Slovak, Polish and Lusatian, is part of the West Slavonic group. It is the main language of the Czech Republic and is spoken by 10 million people.

Although Czech has several dialects, this phrasebook uses a standardised form of the language, literary Czech (*spisovná čeština*), which is based on the central Bohemian dialect. However, this is no longer associated with a particular social group or territory, and functions as a common language understood by all Czechs. Therefore, you won't have trouble communicating wherever you are in the country.

Some Czech sentences will be phrased differently depending on whether you are male or female, so both forms are given when applicable.

PRONUNCIATION
Czech is spelt as it is spoken, and once you become familiar with the sounds, it can be read easily.

Vowels
An accent over a vowel indicates that it is lengthened.

Short Vowels
a	ah	as the 'u' in 'cut'
e	eh	as the 'e' in 'bet'
ě	yeh	as the 'ye' in 'yet'
i/y	i	as the 'i' in 'bit'
o	o	as the 'o' in 'pot'
u	u	as the 'u' in 'pull'

Long Vowels

á	aa	as the 'a' in 'father'
é	air	as the 'ai' in 'air'
í/ý	ee	as the 'ee' in 'see'
ó	aw	as the 'aw' in 'saw'
ú/ů	oo	as the 'oo' in 'zoo'

Vowel Combinations

aj	ahy	as the 'i' in 'ice'
áj	aay	as 'eye'
au	ow	an 'ow' as in 'clown'
ej	ehy	as the 'ey' in 'hey'
ij, yj	iy	as the 'ee' in 'see' followed by the 'y' in 'year'
íj, ýj	eey	as the 'ee' in 'see' followed by the 'y' in 'year'; pronounced longer than *ij* and *yj*
oj	oi/oy	as the 'oy' in 'boy'
ou	ou/ouh	as the 'o' in 'note' followed by the 'u' in 'pull'
uj	uy	as the 'u' in 'pull', followed by the 'y' in 'year'
ůj	ooi/ooy	ad the 'oo' in 'zoo', followed by the 'y' in 'year'

Consonants

Consonants not described here are pronounced as in English, except *k, p* and *t*, which are pronounced without a puff of breath.

c	ts	as the 'ts' in 'lets'
č	ch	as the 'ch' in 'chew'
ch	kh	as the 'ch' in Scottish 'loch'
g	g	as the 'g' in 'get'
j	y	as the 'y' in 'year'
r	r	a rolled 'r', made with the tip of the tongue
ř	rzh	a rolled 'r' followed by the 's' in 'treasure'
s	s	as the 's' in 'sit', never as in 'rose'
š	sh	as the 'sh' in 'ship'
ž	zh	as the 's' in 'treasure'
ď, ň, ť	dy, ny, ty	pronounced with the tongue touching the roof of the mouth, adding a 'y' sound
d, n, t	dy, ny, ty	when followed by *i, í* and *ě*, pronounced as *ď, ň, ť*

CZECH

Stress

In Czech the first syllable is usually stressed. Vowels are pronounced the same whether they are stressed or not.

SUBJECT PRONOUNS		
SG		
I	jaah	já
you (inf)	tih	ty
(pol)	vih	Vy
he/she/it	ohn/oh-nah/oh-noh	on/ona/ono
PL		
we	mih	my
you	vih	vy
they (m)	oh-nyih	oni
(f)	oh-nih	ony
(n)	oh-nah	ona

CZECH

GREETINGS & CIVILITIES
Top Useful Phrases

Hello./Goodbye.	*dob*-ree-dehn/	*Dobrý den./*
	nah-skhleh-dah-noh	*Na shledanou.*
Yes./No.	*ah*-no/neh	*Ano./Ne.*
Yes. (col)	yo	*Jo.*
Excuse me.	*zdo*-vo-leh-nyeem	*S dovolením.*
May I?	*do*-vol-teh-mi?	*Dovolte mi?*
Do you mind?		
Sorry.	*pro*-miny-teh	*Promiňte.*
(excuse/forgive me)		
Please.	*pro*-seem	*Prosím.*
Thank you.	*dyeh*-ku-yi	*Děkuji.*

Many thanks.
   mots-kraat *dyeh*-ku-yi   *Mockrát děkuji.*
That's fine. You're welcome.
   neh-nyee zahch *pro*-seem   *Není zač. Prosím.*

CZECH

Greetings

Good morning.
   dob-rair *yit*-ro/*raa*-no   *Dobré jitro/ráno.*
Good afternoon.
   dob-rair *ot*-po-lehd-neh   *Dobré odpoledne.*
Good evening.
   dob-ree *veh*-chehr   *Dobrý večer.*
Good night.
   dob-roh nots   *Dobrou noc.*
How are you?
   yahk-seh *maa*-teh?   *Jak se máte?*
Well, thanks.
   dyeh-ku-yi, *dob*-rzheh   *Děkuji, dobře.*

Forms of Address

Madam/Mrs	*pah*-nyee	*Paní*
Sir/Mr	pahn	*Pan*
Miss	*slehch*-nah	*Slečna*
companion/friend	*przhee*-tehl	*přítel* (m)
	przhee-tehl-ki-nyeh	*přítelkyně* (f)

QUESTION WORDS		
How?	yahk?	Jak?
When?	gdi?	Kdy?
Where?	gde?	Kde?
Which?	kteh-ree?	Který?
Who?	gdo?	Kdo?
Why?	proch?	Proč?

SMALL TALK
Meeting People

What's your name?
yahk-seh *ymeh*-nu-yeh-teh? — *Jak se jmenujete?*

My name's ...
ymeh-nu-yi-seh ... — *Jmenuji se ...*

I'd like to introduce you to ...
mo-hu vaas *przheht-*
stah-vit ... — *Mohu vás představit ...*

Pleased to meet you.
tye-shee mnyeh, zheh
vaas *po*-znaa-vaam — *Těší mě, že vás poznávám.*

How old are you?
ko-lik yeh vaam leht? — *Kolik je vám let?*

I'm ... years old.
yeh mi ... let — *Je mi ... let.*

CZECH

Nationalities

Where are you from?
od-kud *po*-khaa-zee-teh? — *Odkud pocházíte?*

I'm from ...	ysehm ...	Jsem ...
Australia	*sow*-straa-li-yeh	z Austrálie
Canada	*skah*-nah-di	z Kanady
England	*sahn*-gli-yeh	z Anglie
Ireland	*sir*-skah	z Irska
New Zealand	*sno*-vair-ho *zair*-lahn-du	z Nového Zélandu
Scotland	zeh *skot*-skah	ze Skotska
the USA	zeh *spo*-yeh-neekh *staa*-too	ze Spojených států
Wales	*zvah*-leh-su	z Walesu

CZECH

Occupations

I'm a/an ...	ysehm ...	Jsem ...
artist	*u*-myeh-lehts	*umělec* (m)
	u-myehl-ki-nyeh	*umělkyně* (f)
business	*op*-kho-dnyeek	*obchodník* (m)
person	*op*-kho-dnyi-tseh	*obchodnice* (f)
computer	*proh*-grah-maa-tor	*programátor* (m)
programmer	*proh*-grah-maa-tor-kah	*programátorka* (f)
doctor	*lair*-kahrzh	*lékař* (m)
	lair-kahrzh-kah	*lékařka* (f)
engineer	*in*-zheh-neer	*inženýr* (m)
	in-zheh-neer-kah	*inženýrka* (f)
farmer	*zeh*-myeh-dyeh-lehts	*zemědělec* (m)
	zeh-myeh-dyehl-ki-nyeh	*zemědělkyně* (f)
journalist	*no*-vi-naarzh	*novinář* (m)
	no-vi-naarzh-kah	*novinářka* (f)
lawyer	*praa*-vnyeek	*právník* (m)
	praa-vnyi-chkah	*právnička* (f)
manual worker	*dyehl*-nyeek	*dělník* (m)
	dyehl-nyi-tseh	*dělnice* (f)
mechanic	*ow*-to-meh-khah-nik	*automechanik* (m)
	ow-to-meh-khah-nich-kah	*automechanička* (f)
nurse	*o*-sheh-trzho-vah-tehl	*ošetřovatel* (m)
	o-sheh-trzho-vah-tehl-kah	*ošetřovatelka* (f)
office worker	*oo*-rzheh-dnyeek	*úředník* (m)
	oo-rzheh-dnyi-tseh	*úřednice* (f)
scientist	*vyeh*-dehts	*vědec* (m)
	vyeht-ki-nyeh	*vědkyně* (f)
student	*stu*-dehnt	*student* (m)
	stu-dehnt-kah	*studentka* (f)
teacher	*u*-chi-tehl	*učitel* (m)
	u-chi-tehl-kah	*učitelka* (f)
waiter	*chee*-shnyeek	*číšník* (m)
	chee-shnyi-tseh	*číšnice* (f)
	(*sehr*-veer-kah)	(*servírka*) (f)
writer	*spi*-so-vah-tehl	*spisovatel* (m)
	spi-so-vah-tehl-kah	*spisovatelka* (f)

What do you do?
tso *dyeh*-laa-teh?

Co děláte?

I'm unemployed.
ysehm neh-zah-myest-
nah-nee/
neh-zah-myest-nah-naa

*Jsem nezaměstnaný/
nezaměstnaná.* (m/f)

Religion

What's your religion?
yah-kair-ho ysteh
naa-bo-zhehn-skair-ho
vi-znaa-nyee?

*Jakého jste náboženského
vyznání?*

I'm not religious.
ysehm behz *vi*-znaa-nyee

Jsem bez vyznání.

I'm ...	ysehm ...	Jsem ...
Buddhist	*bu*-dhi-stah	*buddhista* (m)
	bu-dhist-kah	*buddhistka* (f)
Catholic	*kah*-to-leek	*katolík* (m)
	kah-to-li-chkah	*katolička* (f)
Christian	*krzheh*-styahny	*křesťan* (m)
	krzheh-styahny-kah	*křesťanka* (f)
Hindu	*hin*-du	*hindu* (m/f)
Jewish	zhid	*žid* (m)
	zhi-dof-kah	*židovka* (f)
Muslim	*mu*-slim	*muslim* (m)
	mu-slim-kah	*muslimka* (f)

Family

Are you married?
ysteh *zheh*-nah-tee?/
vdah-naa?   *Jste ženatý/vdaná?* (m/f)

I'm single.
ysehm *svo*-bo-dnee/
svo-bo-dnaa   *Jsem svobodný/*
                              svobodná. (m/f)

I'm married.
ysehm *zheh*-nah-tee/
fdah-naa   *Jsem ženatý/*
                              vdaná. (m/f)

I'm separated.
neh-zhi-yih seh sveem
part-nerehm   *Nežiji se svým partnerem.* (m)
neh-zhi-yih seh svouh
part-ner-kow   *Nežiji se svou partnerkou.* (f)

I'm ...	yaah *ysehm* ...	*Já jsem ...*
a widow	*vdoh*-vah	*vdova*
a widower	*vdoh*-vets	*vdovec*
divorced	roz-veh-deh-nee	*rozvedený* (m)
	roz-veh-deh-naa	*rozvedená* (f)

How many children do you have?
ko-lik *maa*-teh *dyeh*-tyee?   *Kolik máte dětí?*

I don't have any children.
neh-maam *dyeh*-tyi   *Nemám děti.*

I have a daughter/son.
maam si-*nah*/*tseh*-ru   *Mám syna/dceru.*

How many brothers/sisters
do you have?
ko-lik *maa*-teh *brah*-troo/
sehs-tehr?   *Kolik máte bratrů/sester?*

Do you have a boyfriend/
girlfriend?
maa-teh *znaa*-most?   *Máte známost?*

brother	*brah*-tr	bratr
children	*dyeh*-tyi	děti
daughter	*tseh*-rah	dcera
family	*ro*-dyi-nah	rodina
father	*o*-tehts	otec
grandfather	*dyeh*-deh-chehk	dědeček
grandmother	*bah*-bi-chkah	babička
husband	*mahn*-zhehl	manžel
mother	*maht*-kah	matka
sister	*sehs*-trah	sestra
son	sin	syn
wife	*mahn*-zhehl-kah	manželka

Kids' Talk

What's your name?
  yak-seh *yimeh*-nuh-yesh? — *Jak se jmenuješ?*

How old are you?
  koh-lick yeh-tyih let? — *Kolik je ti let?*

When's your birthday?
  gdih maash nah-roh-zeh-nyih-nih? — *Kdy máš narozeniny?*

How many brothers and sisters do you have?
  koh-lick maash brah-troo ah ses-ter? — *Kolik máš bratrů a sester?*

What grade are you in?
  veh *kteh*-reeh ysih trzhee-dyieh? — *Ve které jsi třídě?*

Do you have your own room?
  maash svooi vlast-nyeeh poh-koi? — *Máš svůj vlastní pokoj?*

I share my room.
  dyeh-leem seh oh poh-koi — *Dělím se o pokoj.*

I have my own room.
  maahm poh-koi proh-seh-beh — *Mám pokoj pro sebe.*

What are your favourite games/hobbies?
  yah-keh hrih maash raad/*raa*-daa ? — *Jaké hry máš rád/ráda?* (m/f)

CZECH

collecting things	*zbeeh*-raht vyeh-tsih	*sbírat věci*
making things	*vih*-raab-yet vyeh-tsih	*vyrábět věci*
playing outside	hraat seh *ven*-kuh	*hrát se venku*
sports	spohrt	*sport*
video games	vih-deoh-hrih	*videohry*
watching TV	*dyee*-vat seh nah teh-leh-vih-zih	*dívat se na televizi*

I have a ...	jaah *maahm* ...	*Já mám ...*
mouse	mish-kuh	*myšku*
budgerigar	*ahn*-doohl-kuh	*andulku*
canary	*kah*-naar-kah	*kanárka*
cat	*kotch*-kuh	*kočku*
cow	*kraah*-vuh	*krávu*
dog	psah	*psa*
donkey	os-lah	*osla*
duck	*kakh*-nuh	*kachnu*
frog	*zhaah*-buh	*žábu*
rabbit	zah-yeets	*zajíc*

Feelings

I'm ...		
angry	hnyeh-vaam seh	*Hněvám se.*
cold	yeh mi *zi*-mah	*Je mi zima.*
happy	ysehm *shtyahst*- nee	*Jsem šťastný.* (m)
	ysehm *shtyahst*- naa	*Jsem šťastná.* (f)
hot	yeh mi *hor*-ko	*Je mi horko.*
hungry	maam hlaht	*Mám hlad.*
in a hurry	*spyeh*-khaam	*Spěchám.*
right	maam *prahf*-du	*Mám pravdu.*
sad	ysehm *smut*-nee	*Jsem smutný.* (m)
	ysehm *smut*-naa	*Jsem smutná.* (f)
thirsty	maam *zhee*-zehny	*Mám žízeň.*
tired	ysehm *u*-nah-veh-nee	*Jsem unavený.* (m)
	ysehm *u*-nah-veh-naa	*Jsem unavená.* (f)
well	*mnyeh*-yeh *dob*-rzheh	*Mně je dobře.*
worried	maahm *stah*-rost	*Mám starost.*

I (don't) like ...
   mnyeh *seh*-to *(neh-)*lee-bee ...   *Mně se to (ne)líbí ...*
I'm sorry. (condolence)
   u-przhee-mnoh *soh*-strahst   *Upřímnou soustrast.*
I'm grateful.
   ysehm vaam *vdyehch-* nee   *Jsem vám vděčný.* (m)
   ysehm vam *vdyehch-*naa   *Jsem vám vděčná.* (f)

CZECH

Useful Phrases

Sure!   *yi*-styeh!   *Jistě!*

Just a minute.
   poch-kehy-teh *khvee*-li   *Počkejte chvíli.*
It's important.
   toh-yeh *doo*-le-zhi-tair   *To je důležité.*
It's not important.
   toh *neh*-nyi *doo*-leh-zhi-tair   *To není důležité.*
It's possible.
   to-yeh *mo*-zhnair.   *To je možné.*
It's not possible.
   to *neh*-nyi *mo*-zhnair   *To není možné.*
Wait!
   poch-kehy-teh!   *Počkejte!*
Good luck!
   przheh-yi vaam *mno*-ho   *Přeji vám mnoho štěstí!*
   shtyeh-styee!

BREAKING THE LANGUAGE BARRIER

Do you speak English?
mlu-vee-teh *ahn*-glits-ki?   *Mluvíte anglicky?*

Does anyone speak English?
mlu-vee *nyeh*-gdo
ahn-glits-ki?   *Mluví někdo anglicky?*

I speak a little ...
mlu-veem *tro*-khu ...   *Mluvím trochu ...*

I don't speak ...
neh-mlu-veem ...   *Nemluvím ...*

I understand.
ro-zu-meem   *Rozumím.*

I don't understand.
neh-roh-zu-meem   *Nerozumím.*

Could you speak more
slowly, please?
moo-zheh-teh *mlu*-vit
po-mah-leh-yi?   *Můžete mluvit pomaleji?*

Could you repeat that?
moo-zheh-teh to
o-pah-ko-vaht?   *Můžete to opakovat?*

How do you say ...?
yahk-seh *rzheh*-kneh ...?   *Jak se řekne ...?*

What does ... mean?
tso *znah*-meh-naa ...?   *Co znamená ...?*

CZECH

I speak ...	*mlu*-veem ...	*Mluvím ...*
Dutch	ho-lahn-ski	holandsky
English	*ahn*-glits-ki	anglicky
French	*frahn*-tsoh-ski	francouzsky
German	nye-mehts-ki	německy
Hungarian	mah-dyahrs-ki	maďarsky
Italian	i-tahl-ski	italsky
Russian	rus-ki	rusky
Spanish	shpah-nyehl-ski	španělsky

BODY LANGUAGE

Czech speakers are friendly and knowledgeable about a number of subjects. They have a marvellous sense of humour that can be fully appreciated only in their own language. This might be a good reason for you to try and break the language barrier – it will be worthwhile. Their body language doesn't have any typical gestures which distinguish them from other Central Europeans.

CZECH

SIGNS

INFORMACE	INFORMATION
NOUZOVÝ VÝCHOD	EMERGENCY EXIT
OTEVŘENO/ZAVŘENO	OPEN/CLOSED
TELEFON	TELEPHONE
TEPLÁ/STUDENÁ	HOT/COLD
VCHOD	ENTRANCE
VSTUP VOLNÝ	FREE ADMISSION
VSTUP ZAKÁZÁN	NO ENTRY
VÝCHOD	EXIT
ZÁCHODY/WC/TOALETY	TOILETS
ZADÁNO/RESERVOVÁNO	RESERVED
ZAKÁZÁNO	PROHIBITED
ZÁKAZ KOUŘENÍ	NO SMOKING

CZECH

PAPERWORK

English	Pronunciation	Czech
address	*ah*-dreh-sah	adresa
age	vyehk	věk
birth certificate	*ro*-dnee list	rodný list
car registration	*tehkh*-ni-tskee	technický
	proo-kahz	průkaz
date of birth	*dah*-tum	datum
	nah-ro-zeh-nyee	narození
driver's licence	*rzhi*-dyich-skee	řidičský
	proo-kahz	průkaz
identification	*leh*-gi-ti-mah-tseh	legitimace
identity card	*proo*-kahz	průkaz
	to-to-zhno-styi	totožnosti
marital status	*mahn*-zhehl-skee stahf	manželský stav
name	*ymair*-no	jméno
nationality	*staa*-tynyee	státní
	przhee-slush-nost	příslušnost
next of kin	*nehy*-blizh-shee	nejbližší
	przhee-bu-znee	příbuzný (m)
	nehy-blizh-shee	nejbližší
	przhee-bu-znaa	příbuzná (f)
reason for travel	*oo*-chehl *tsehs*-ti	účel cesty
business	*ob*-khod-nyee	obchodní
	yed-naa-nyeeh	jednání
holiday/tourism	*doh*-voh-leh-naa/	dovolená/
	tuh-ris-tih-kah	turistika
religion	*naa*-bo-zhehn-stvee	náboženství
passport	pahs	pas
passport number	*pah*-su (*chee*-slo)	pas č. (číslo)
place of birth	*mees*-to	místo
	nah-ro-zeh-nyee	narození
profession	*po*-vo-laa-nyee	povolání
sex	*po*-hlah-vee	pohlaví
surname	*przheey*-meh-nyee	příjmení
visa	*vee*-zum	vízum

GETTING AROUND

What time does the ... leave/arrive?	gdi ot-yee-zhdyee/ przhi-yee-zhdyee ...?	Kdy odjíždí/ přijíždí ...?
boat	lody	loď
(inter)city bus	(meh-zi-)myehst-skee ow-to-bus	(mezi)městský autobus
train	vlahk	vlak
tram	trahm-vahy	tramvaj

CZECH

Directions

Where's ...?	gdeh-yeh ...?	Kde je ...?

How do I get to ...?
  yahk-seh do-stah-nu k ...? Jak se dostanu k ...?

Is it far/closeby?
  yeh to dah-leh-ko/blees-ko? Je to daleko/blízko?

Can I walk there?
  do-stah-nu-seh tahm pyehsh-ki? Dostanu se tam pěšky?

Can you show me (on the map)?
  moo-zheh-teh mi-to u-kaa-zaht (nah mah-pyeh)? Můžete mi to ukázat (na mapě)?

Are there other means of getting there?
  mo-hu-seh tahm do-staht yi-nahk? Mohu se tam dostat jinak?

I want to go to ...
  khtsi yeet ... Chci jít ...

Go straight ahead.
  ydyeh-teh przhee-mo Jděte přímo.

It's two blocks down.
  o dvyeh u-li-tseh daal O dvě ulice dál.

Turn left/right at the ...	zah-to-chteh vleh-vofprah-vo ...	Zatočte vlevo/vpravo ...
next corner	nah przhee-shtyeem ro-hu	na příštím rohu
traffic lights	u seh-mah-for-ru	u semaforu
behind	zah	za
in front of	przhehd	před
far	dah-leh-ko	daleko
near	blees-ko	blízko
opposite	nah-pro-tyi	naproti
north	seh-ver	sever
south	yikh	jih
east	vee-khod	východ
west	zaa-pahd	západ

CZECH

SIGNS

AUTOBUSOVÁL/ TRAMVAJOVÁ ZASTÁVKA	BUS/TRAM STOP
CELNICE	CUSTOMS
JÍZDNÍ ŘÁD	TIMETABLE
METRO	SUBWAY/UNDERGROUND
NÁDRAŽÍ	TRAIN STATION
NÁSTUPIŠTĚ	PLATFORM NO
ODBAVENÍ	CHECK-IN COUNTER
ODJEZDY	DEPARTURES
PODEJ ZAVAZADEL	BAGGAGE COUNTER
POKLADNA	TICKET OFFICE
PŘÍCHOD ...	THIS WAY TO ...
PŘÍJEZDY	ARRIVALS
PŘISTÌHOVALECTVÍ	IMMIGRATION
REGISTRACE	REGISTRATION
STANICE	STATION (TRAIN OR BUS)
VÝCHOD/VCHOD	WAY OUT/WAY IN
VÝDEJ ZAVAZADEL	BAGGAGE COLLECTION

Booking Tickets

Excuse me, where's the ticket office?
pro-seem *gdeh*-yeh
po-klah-dnah? — *Prosím, kde je pokladna?*

Where can I buy a ticket?
gdeh-seh *pro*-daa-vah-yee
yeez-dehn-ki? — *Kde se prodávají jízdenky?*

I want to go to ...
khtsi yeht *do* ... — *Chci jet do ...*

Do I need to book?
po-trzheh-bu-yi
mees-tehn-ku? — *Potřebuji místenku?*

I'd like to book a seat to ...
pro-sil/*pro*-si-lah bikh
mees-tehn-kudo ... — *Prosil/Prosila bych místenku do ... (m/f)*

Is it completely full?
jeh pl-nyeh *o*-psah-zeh-no? — *Je plně obsazeno?*

CZECH

I'd like ...	raad/*raa*-dah bikh ...	*Rád/Ráda bych ... (m/f)*
a one-way ticket	*yeh*-dno-smyehr-noh yeez-dehn-ku	*jednosměrnou jízdenku*
a return ticket	*spaa*-teh-chnyee yeez-dehn-ku	*zpáteční jízdenku*
two tickets	dvyeh yee-zdehn-ki	*dvě jízdenky*
tickets for all of us	yeez-dehn-ki pro vshehkh-ni	*jízdenky pro všechny*
a student's fare	*stu*-dehnts-koh yeez-dehn-ku	*studentskou jízdenku*
a child's fare	dyets-koh yeez-dehn-ku	*dětskou jízdenku*
1st class	pr-vnyee trzhee-du	*první třídu*
2nd class	dru-hoh trzhee-du	*druhou třídu*

CZECH

Air

Is there a flight to ...?
  yeh *leh*-teh-tskair
  spo-yeh-nyee *do* ...?
  Je letecké spojení do ...?

When's the next flight to ...?
  gdi-yeh *przhee*-shtyee leht *do* ... ? *Kdy je příští let do ...?*
How long does the flight take?
  yahk *dloh*-ho *tr-vaa* leht? *Jak dlouho trvá let?*
What's the flight number?
  yah-kair yeh *chee*-slo *Jaké je číslo letu?*
  leh-tu?

airport tax	*leh*-tyish-tnyee	*letištní*
	po-plah-tehk	*poplatek*
boarding pass	*pah*-lub-nyee	*palubní*
	fstu-pehn-kah	*vstupenka*

Bus

Where's the bus/tram stop?
  gdeh-yeh *stah*-nyi-tseh *Kde je stanice autobusů/*
  ow-to-bu-soo/*trahm*-vah-yee? *tramvají?*
Which bus goes to ...?
  kteh-ree ow-to-bus yeh-deh *do* ...? *Který autobus jede do ...?*
Does this bus go to ...?
  yeh-deh *tehn*-hleh ow-to-bus *do* ...? *Jede tenhle autobus do ...?*
How often do buses pass by?
  yahk *chahs*-to *tu*-di *Jak často tudy*
  yehz-dyee ow-to-bus? *jezdí autobus?*
Could you let me know when
we get to ...?
  mohl/*mohl*-lah *bi*-steh-mi *Mohl/Mohla byste mi*
  pro-seem *rzhee*-tsi, gdi *prosím říci, kdy přijedeme*
  przhi-yeh-deh-meh *do* ...? *do ...?* (m/f)
I want to get off!
  khtsi *vi*-stow-pit! *Chci vystoupit!*

What time's the	gdi yeh-deh ...	Kdy jede ...
... bus?	ow-to-bus?	autobus?
first	pr-vnyee	první
last	po-sleh-dnyee	poslední
next	przheesh-tyee	příští

Train & Metro

Which line takes me to ...?
kteh-raa trah-sah   Která trasa vede do ...?
veh-deh do ...?

What's the next station?
yahk-seh ymeh-nu-yeh   Jak se jmenuje příští stanice?
przhee-shtyee stah- nyi-tseh?

Is this the right platform for ...?
yeh-deh vlahk do ...   Jede vlak do ...
sto-ho-to naa-stu-pi-shtyeh?   z tohoto nástupiště?

Passengers travelling to (Prague)
must change trains at ...
tsehs-tu-yee-tsee do (phrah-hah)   Cestující do (Praha) musí
mu-see przheh-stoh-pit f ...   přestoupit v ...

The train leaves from platform ...
vlahk ot-yeezh-dyee   Vlak odjíždí z nástupiště ...
znaas-tu-pi-shtyeh ...

dining car	yee-dehl-nyee vooz	jídelní vůz
express	ri-khleek	rychlík
local	mees-tnyee	místní
sleeping car	spah-tsee vooz	spací vůz
1st/2nd class	prv-nyeeh/ druh-haa	1./2. třída
	trzhee-dah	

CZECH

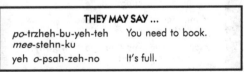

THEY MAY SAY ...	
po-trzheh-bu-yeh-teh mee-stehn-ku	You need to book.
yeh o-psah-zeh-no	It's full.

Taxi

Can you take me to ...?
moo-zheh-teh mnyeh
do-vairst *do* ...?   *Můžete mě*
                                              dovést do ...?

Please take me to ...
pro-seem, *od*-vehs-teh
mnyeh *do* ...?   *Prosím, odvezte mě do ...?*

How much does it cost to go to ...?
ko-lik sto-yee tsehs-tah do ...?   *Kolik stojí cesta do ...?*

Here's fine, thank you.
zahs-tahf-teh zdeh, *pro*-seem   *Zastavte zde, prosím.*

The next corner, please.
nah *przheesh*-tyeem *ro*-hu,
pro-seem   *Na příštím rohu,*
                                            prosím.

Continue!
po-krah-chuy-teh!   *Pokračujte!*

The next street to the left/right.
przhee-shtyee *u*-li-tsi   *Příští ulici vlevo/vpravo.*
vleh-vo/*fprah*-vo

Stop here!
zah-stahf-teh zdeh!   *Zastavte zde!*

Please slow down.
yehty-teh *po*-mah-leh-yi,
pro-seem   *Jeďtepomaleji,*
                                             prosím.

Please wait here.
poch-kehy-teh zdeh, *pro*-seem   *Počkejte zde, prosím.*

THEY MAY SAY ...

vlahk yeh *zru*-sheh-nee
   The train is cancelled.

vlahk maa   *spozh*-dyeh-nyee
   The train is delayed.

maa ... ho-dyi-no-vair *spozh*-dyeh-nyee
   There's a delay of ... hours.

CZECH

Useful Phrases

How long will it be delayed?
yah-kair maa *spozh*-dyeh-nyee?   *Jaké má zpoždění?*

Can I reserve a place?
mo-hu-si *reh*-zehr-vo-
vaht *mee*-stehn-ku?   *Mohu si reservovat
místenku?*

How long does the trip take?
yahk *dloh*-ho *trvaa tsehs*-tah?   *Jak dlouho trvá cesta?*

Is it a direct route?
yeh-to *przhee*-maa *tsehs*-tah?   *Je to přímá cesta?*

Is that seat taken?
yeh *to*-to *mees*-to *op*-sah-
zeh-no?   *Je toto místo obsazeno?*

I want to get off at ...
khtsi *vis*-toh-pit f ...   *Chci vystoupit v ...*

Excuse me.
zdo-vo-leh-nyeem   *S dovolením.*

Where can I hire a bicycle?
gdeh-si *mo*-hu *pooy*-chit *ko*-lo?   *Kde si mohu půjčit kolo?*

CZECH

Car

Where can I rent a car?
gdeh-si *mo*-hu *pro*-nahy-
moht *ow*-to?   *Kde si mohu pronajmout
auto?*

How much is it daily/weekly?
ko-lik *sto*-yee *deh*-nyeh/
tee-dnyeh?   *Kolik stojí denně/týdně?*

Does that include
(insurance/mileage)?
yeh *zah*-hr-nu-tah *ftseh*-
nyeh *po*-yist-kah/*po*-plah-
tehk zah *nah*-yeh-tair
ki-lo-meh-tri)?   *Je zahrnuta v ceně (pojistka/
poplatek za najeté
kilometry)?*

CZECH

What make is it?
  yah-kee yeh-to *mo*-dehl?   *Jaký je to model?*

Where's the next petrol station?
  gdeh-yeh *przheesh*-tyee   *Kde je příští benzínová*
  behn-zee-no-vaa *pum*-pah?   *pumpa?*

Please fill the tank.
  pl-noh *naa*-drzh, *pro*-seem   *Plnou nádrž, prosím.*

I want ... litres of petrol (gas).
  po-trzheh-*bu*-yi ... *li*-troo   *Potřebuji ... litrů benzínu.*
  behn-zee-nu

Please check the oil and water.
  pro-seem-vaas *skon*-tro-   *Prosím vás zkontrolujte*
  luy-teh *o*-lehy ah *vo*-du   *olej a vodu.*

How long can I park here?
  yahk *dloh*-ho zdeh   *Jak dlouho zde mohu*
  mo-hu *pahr*-ko-vaht?   *parkovat?*

Does this road lead to ...?
  veh-deh *tah*-to *tsehs*-tah *do* ...? *Vede tato cesta do ...?*

I need a mechanic.
  po-trzheh-*bu*-yi   *Potřebuji automechanika.*
  ow-to-meh-khah-ni-kah

The battery's flat.
  bah-tair-ri-eh yeh   *Baterie je vybitá.*
  vi-bi-taa

The radiator's leaking.
  khlah-dyich *teh*-cheh   *Chladič teče.*

I have a flat tyre.
  maam *pee*-khloh   *Mám píchlou pneumatiku.*
  pneh-u-mah-ti-ku

It's overheating.
  mo-tor-seh   *Motor se přehřívá.*
  przheh-hrzhee-vaa

It's not working.
  neh-fun-gu-yeh-to   *Nefunguje to.*

air (for tyres)	vzdukh	*vzduch*
battery	*bah*-teh-ri-yeh	*baterie*
brakes	*brz*-di	*brzdy*
clutch	*spoy*-kah	*spojka*
driver's licence	*rzhi*-dyich-skee	*řidičský*
	proo-kahz	*průkaz*
engine	*mo*-tor	*motor*
lights	*svyeh*-tlah	*světla*
oil	*o*-lehy	*olej*
petrol	*behn*-zee-nu	*benzínu*
puncture	*pee*-khlaa	*píchlá*
	pneh-u-mah-ti-kah	*pneumatika*
radiator	*khlah*-dyich	*chladič*
road map	*ow*-to-mah-pah	*automapa*
tyres	*pneh*-u-mah-ti-ki	*pneumatiky*
windscreen	*przheh*-dnyee sklo	*přední sklo*

CZECH

SIGNS

AUTOMECHANIK	MECHANIC
AUTOOPRAVNA	REPAIRS
BENZÍNOVÁ PUMPA	GARAGE
DÁLNICE	FREEWAY
DEJ PŘEDNOST V JÍZDĚ	GIVE WAY
JEDNOSMĚRNÝ PROVOZ	ONE WAY
OBJÍŽĎKA	DETOUR
PRO INVALIDY	DISABLED
SAMOOBSLUHA	SELF SERVICE
STANDART	UNLEADED
SUPER	SUPER
ZÁKAZ PARKOVÁNÍ NO	NO PARKING
ZÁKAZ VJEZDU	NO ENTRY
ZASTAVTE/STOP	STOP

ACCOMMODATION

I'm looking for ...	*hleh*-daam ...	*Hledám ...*
Where's a ... hotel?	*gdeh*-yeh ... *ho*-tehl?	*Kde je ... hotel?*
cheap	*leh*-vnee	*levný*
clean	*chis*-tee	*čistý*
good	*do*-bree	*dobrý*
nearby	*bleez*-kee	*blízký*

What's the address?
yah-kaa yeh *zdehy*-shee
ah-dreh-sah? — *Jaká je zdejší adresa?*

Could you write the address, please?
moo-zheh-teh mi *nah*-psaht *ah*-dreh-su, *pro*-seem? — *Můžete mi napsat adresu, prosím?*

At the Hotel

Do you have any rooms available?
maa-teh *vol*-nair po-ko-yeh? — *Máte volné pokoje?*

I'd like a ...	*przhaal/przhaa*-lah *bikh*-si ...	*Přál/Přála bych si ... (m/f)*
single room	*yeh*-dno-loozh-ko-vee *po*-koy	*jednolůžkový pokoj*
double room	*dvoh*-loozh-ko-vee *po*-koy	*dvoulůžkový pokoj*
I want a room with a ...	*mo*-hu meet *po*-koy ...	*Mohu mít pokoj ...*
bathroom	*skoh*-pehl-noh	*s koupelnou*
shower	*seh*-spr-khoh	*se sprchou*
television	*steh*-leh-vi-zee	*s televizí*
window	*so*-knehm	*s oknem*
I'm going to stay for ...	*zoo*-stah-nu ...	*Zůstanu ...*
one day	*yeh*-dehn dehn	*jeden den*
two days	*dvah* dni	*dva dny*
one week	*yeh*-dehn *tee*-dehn	*jeden týden*

How much is it per night?
   ko-lik *sto*-yee
   yeh-dnah *nots*?   *Kolik stojí jedna noc?*

How much is it per person?
   ko-lik to *sto*-yee *zah*
   o-so-bu?   *Kolik to stojí za osobu?*

Can I see it?
   mo-hu-seh *nah*-nyey
   po-dyee-vaht?   *Mohu se na něj podívat?*

Are there any others?
   neh-maa-teh *yi*-nee
   po-koj?   *Nemáte jiný pokoj?*

Are there any cheaper rooms?
   neh-maa-teh *leh*-
   vnyeh-shee *po*-ko-yeh?   *Nemáte levnější pokoje?*

Can I see the bathroom?
   mo-hu-seh *po*-dyee-vaht
   nah *koh*-pehl-nu?   *Mohu se podívat na*
                         koupelnu?

Is there a reduction for students/
children?
   maa-teh *sleh*-vu pro
   stu-dehn-ti/*dyeh*-tyi?   *Máte slevu pro studenty/*
                         děti?

Does it include breakfast?
   yeh ftom *zah*-hr-nu-tah
   snyee-dah-nyeh?   *Je v tom zahrnuta snídaně?*

It's fine, I'll take it.
   to-yeh *fpo*-rzhaat-ku,
   yaa toh *vehz*-mu   *To je v pořádku, já to*
                         vezmu.

I'm not sure how long I'm staying.
   nehy-sehm-si yist yahk
   dloh-ho zdeh *zoos*-tah-nu   *Nejsem si jist jak dlouho*
                         zde zůstanu.

Is there a lift?
   yeh tu *vee*-tah?   *Je tu výtah?*

Is there hot water all day?
   maa-teh-tu *hor*-koh
   vo-du *tseh*-lee *dehn*?   *Máte tu horkou vodu*
                         celý den?

CZECH

CZECH

I'm/We're leaving ... *od*-yeezh-dyeem/ *Odjíždím/*
                od-yeezh-dyee-meh ... *Odjíždíme ...*
  now/tomorrow *tehdy/zee-trah* *teď/zítra*

I'd like to pay the bill.
  raad bikh *zah*-plah-tyil *Rád bych zaplatil účet.* (m)
  oo-cheht
  raa-dah bikh *zah*-plah-t *Ráda bych zaplatila účet.* (f)
  tyi-lah oo-cheht

Requests & Complaints

Do you have a safe where I can
leave my valuables?
  maa-teh-tu *treh*-zor *Máte tu trezor kde si mohu*
  gde-si mo-hu *u*-lo-zhit *uložit cennosti?*
  tseh-no-styi?

Is there somewhere to wash clothes?
  gdeh-si mo-hu *vi*-praht *Kde si mohu vyprat*
  o-bleh-cheh-nyee? *oblečení?*

Can I use the kitchen?
  mo-hu-si *u*-vah-rzhit *Mohu si uvařit v kuchyni?*
  fku-khi-nyi?

Can I use the telephone?
  mo-hu-si *zah*-teh-leh- *Mohu si zatelefonovat?*
  fo-no-vaht?

Please wake me up at ...
  pro-seem, vzbudy-teh- *Prosím, vzbuďte mě v ...*
  mnyeh v ...

The room needs to be cleaned.
  mooy po-koy *Můj pokoj potřebuje*
  po-trzheh-bu-yeh *u*-kli-dyit *uklidit.*

Please change the sheets.
  pro-seem *Prosím, převlékněte mi*
  przheh-vlair-knyeh-teh- *ložní prádlo.*
  mi lo-zhnyee *praa*-dlo

I can't open/close the window.
   neh-mo-hu *o*-teh-vrzheet/   *Nemohu otevřít/*
   zah-vrzheet *o*-kno   *zavřít okno.*

I've locked myself out of my room.
   zah-klahp-nul/   *Zaklapnul/Zaklapnula*
   zah-klahp-nu-lah   *jsem si klíče v mém pokoji.*
   ysehm-si *klee*-cheh   (m/f)
   fmairm *po*-ko-yi

The toilet won't flush.
   zaa-khod *neh*-splah-   *Záchod nesplachuje.*
   khu-yeh

I don't like this room.
   po-koy seh mi *neh*-lee-bee   *Pokoj se mi nelíbí.*

It's too small.
   yeh *przhee*-lish *mah*-lee   *Je příliš malý.*

It's noisy.
   po-koy yeh *hlu*-chnee   *koj je hlučný.*

It's too dark.
   yeh *przhee*-lish *tmah*-vee   *Je příliš tmavý.*

It's expensive.
   yeh *przhee*-lish *drah*-hee   *Je příliš drahý.*

CZECH

SIGNS

MLÁDEŽNICKÁ /	YOUTH HOSTEL
TURISTICKÁ UBYTOVNA	
PENZIÓN	GUEST HOUSE
STANOVÝ TÁBOR/AUTOKEMP	CAMPING GROUND
STUDENTSKÁ NOCLEHÁRNA	STUDENT HOSTEL
ZIMMER FREI	VACANCY
ZIMMER PRIVÁT	PRIVATE
	ACCOMMODATION

CZECH

air-conditioned	*kli*-mah-ti-zah-tseh	*klimatizace*
balcony	*bahl*-kawn	*balkón*
bed	*loozh*-ko	*lůžko*
blanket	*po*-kreef-kah	*pokrývka*
candle	*sveech*-kah	*svíčka*
chair	*zhi*-dleh	*židle*
clean	*chis*-tee	*čistý*
cupboard	*kreh*-dehnts	*kredenc*
dirty	*shpi*-nah-vee	*špinavý*
double bed	*dvoh*-loozh-ko-vaa	*dvoulůžková*
	po-stehl	*postel*
electricity	*eh*-lehk-trzhi-nah	*elektřina*
excluded	*neh*-nyi *zahhr*-nu-tah	*není zahrnuta*
fan	*vyeh*-traak	*větrák*
included	*zah*-hr-nu-tair	*zahrnuté*
key	kleech	*klíč*
light bulb	*zhaa*-rof-kah	*žárovka*
a lock	*zaa*-mehk	*zámek*
mattress	*mah*-trah-tseh	*matrace*
mirror	*zr*-tsah-dlo	*zrcadlo*
padlock	*vi*-sah-tsee *zaa*-mehk	*visací zámek*
pillow	*pol*-shtaarzh	*polštář*
quiet	*tyi*-kho	*ticho*
room number	*chee*-slo *po*-ko-yeh	*číslo pokoje*
sheet	*pro*-styeh-rah-dlo	*prostěradlo*
soap	*mee*-dlo	*mýdlo*
suitcase	*ku*-fr	*kufr*
swimming pool	*bah*-zairn	*bazén*
table	stool	*stůl*
toilet	*zaa*-khod/*vair*-tsair	*záchod/WC*
toilet paper	*toah*-leh-tynyee *pah*-peer	*toaletní papír*
towel	*ru*-chnyeek	*ručník*
(cold/hot)	(*stu*-deh-naa/	(*studená/*
water	*teh*-plaa) *vo*-dah	*teplá) voda*

CZECH

> **THEY MAY SAY ...**
>
> *maa*-teh pahs/*o*-so-bnyee *proo*-kahz?
>   Do you have a passport/identification?
> *maa*-teh *chlehn*-skoh *leh*-gi-ti-ma-tsi *pro*-seem
>   Your membership card, please.
> *pro*-miny-teh neh-*maa*-meh *vol*-nair po-ko-yeh
>   Sorry, we're full.
> *yah*-kaa *bu*-deh *dairl*-kah vah-sheh-ho po-bi-tu?
>   How long will you be staying?
> *ko*-lik *no*-tsee?
>   How many nights?
> *sto*-yee-to ... *dehn*-nyeh/*zah* o-so-bu
>   It's ... per day/per person.

AROUND TOWN

I'm looking for a/the ...	*hleh*-daam ...	*Hledám* ...
art gallery	*u*-myeh-lehts-koh *gah*-lair-ri-i	uměleckou galérii
bank	*bahn*-ku	banku
church	*ko*-stehl	kostel
city (centre)	strzhehd *myehs*-tah (*tsehn*-trum)	střed města (centrum)
... embassy	*vehl*-vi-slah-nehts-vee ...	velvyslanectví ...
... hotel	... *ho*-tehl	... hotel
market	*tr*-zhi-shtyeh	tržiště
museum	*mu*-seh-um	museum
police	*po*-li-tsi-yi	policii
post office	*posh*-tu	poštu
public toilet	*veh*-rzhehy-nair *zaa*-kho-di	veřejné záchody
telephone centre	*teh*-leh-fo-nyee *oo*-strzheh-dnu	telefonní ústřednu
tourist information office	*in*-for-mah-chnyee *kahn*-tse-laarzh pro *tu*-ri-sti	informační kancelář pro turisty

What time does it open/close?
   fko-lik ho-dyin
   o-teh-vee-rah-yee/
   zah-vee-rah-yee?

*V kolik hodin otevírají/
zavírají?*

What ... is this?	yahk-seh ymeh-nu-yeh *tah*-hleh ...?	*Jak se jmenuje tahle ...?*
street	*u*-li-tseh	*ulice*
suburb	chtvrty	*čtvrť*

For directions, see the Getting Around section, page 31.

CZECH

At the Post Office

I'd like some stamps.
   raad/raa-dah bikh
   nyeh-yah-kair znaam-ki

*Rád/Ráda bych nějaké
námky. (m/f)*

How much is the postage?
   ko-lik *sto*-yee *posh*-to-vnair?

Kolik stojí poštovné?

I'd like to send a/an ...	khtyehl/*khtyeh*-lah bikh *pos*-laht ...	*Chtěl/Chtěla bych poslat ... (m/f)*
aerogram	*ah*-eh-ro-grahm	*aerogram*
letter	*do*-pis	*dopis*
postcard	*po*-hlehd	*pohled*
telegram	*teh*-leh-grahm	*telegram*

air mail	*leh*-teh-tski	*letecky*
envelope	*o*-baal-kah	*obálka*
mail box	*po*-shto-vnyee *skhraan*-kah	*poštovní schránka*
parcel	*bah*-leek	*balík*
registered mail	*do*-po-ru-cheh-nyeh	*doporučeně*
surface mail	*o*-bi-chehy-noh *posh*-toh	*obyčejnou poštou*

Telephone

I want to ring ...
> raad *bikh*-si
> zah-teh-leh-fo-no-vahl ...
> *raa*-dah *bikh*-si
> zah-teh-leh-fo-no-vah-lah ...

*Rád bych si
zatelefonoval ...* (m)
*Ráda bych si
zatelefonovala ...* (f)

The number is ...
> chees-lo yeh ...

Číslo je ...

I want to speak for three minutes.
> raad bikh *mlu*-vil
> trzhi *mi*-nu-ti
> *raa*-dah bikh *mlu*-vi-lah
> trzhi *mi*-nu-ti

*Rád bych mluvil tři
minuty.* (m)
*Ráda bych mluvila tři
minuty.* (f)

How much does a three-minute
call cost?
> *ko*-lik *sto*-yee trzhee-
> *mi*-nu-to-vee ho-vor?

*Kolik stojí tříminutový
hovor?*

How much does each extra
minute cost?
> *ko*-lik *sto*-yee *kazh*-daa
> *dahl*-shee *mi*-nu-tah?

*Kolik stojí každá další
minuta?*

I'd like to speak to Mr Perez.
> khtyehl bikh *mlu*-vit
> spah-nehm *Peh*-rehz
> *khtyeh*-lah bikh *mlu*-vit
> spah-nehm *Peh*-rehz

*Chtěl bych mluvit s panem
Perez.* (m)
*Chtěla bych mluvit
s panem Perez.* (f)

I want to make a reverse-charges call.
> raad bikh *zah*-vo-lal nah
> oo-cheht *vo*-lah-nair-ho
> *raa*-dah bikh *zah*-vo-la-lah
> nah oo-cheht *vo*-lah-nair-ho

*Rád bych zavolal
na účet volaného.* (m)
*Ráda bych zavolala
na účet volaného.* (f)

It's engaged.
> yeh *op*-sah-zeh-no

Je obsazeno.

I've been cut off.
> bil ysehm *przheh*-ru- shehn
> *bi*-lah ysehm *przheh*-ru-
> sheh-nah

Byl jsem přerušen. (m)
Byla jsem přerušena. (f)

CZECH

Internet

Where can I get Internet access?
gdeh yeh zdeh
kdis-poh-zih-tsi *inter*-net?

*Kde je zde
k dispozici internet?*

How much is it per hour?
koh-lick toh stoh-yee
nah *hoh*-dyi-nuh?

*Kolik to
stojí na hodinu?*

I want to check my email.
khtyehl/ *khtyeh*-lah bikh sih
zkon-troh-loh-vat *e*-mail

*Chtěl/Chtěla bych si
zkontrolovat e-mail.* (m/f)

At the Bank

I want to exchange some
(money/travellers cheques).
khtyehl/ *khtyeh*-lah bikh
vi-mnyeh-nyit *(peh*-nyee-zeh/
tsehs-tov-nyee *sheh*-ki)

*Chtěl/Chtěla bych
vyměnit (peníze/
cestovní šeky).* (m/f)

What's the exchange rate?
yah-kee yeh *vee*-mnyeh-
nee *kurs?*

Jaký je výměnný kurs?

How many crowns per US dollar?
ko-lik *ko*-run *do*-stah-nu
zah *yeh*-dehn *ah*-meh-
ri-tskee *do*-lahr?

*Kolik korun dostanu za
jeden americký dolar?*

Can I have money transferred
here from my bank?
mo-hoh mair peh-
nyee-zeh beet *zdeh* przheh-
veh-deh-ni *smair bahn*-ki?

*Mohou mé peníze být
zde převedeny z mé
banky?*

How long will it take to arrive?
yahk *dloh*-ho *bu*-deh *tr*-
vaht nehzh *zdeh bu*-doh?

*Jak dlouho bude
trvat než zde budou?*

Has my money arrived yet?
przhi-shli-mi mo-yeh
peh-nyee-zeh?

Přišly mi moje peníze?

bankdraft	*bahn*-ko-vnyee *smnyehn*-kah	*bankovní směnka*
banknotes	*bahn*-kof-ki	*bankovky*
cashier	po-*klah*-dnyeek	*pokladník*
coins	*min*-tseh	*mince*
credit card	oo-vyeh-ro-vaa *kahr*-tah	*úvěrová karta*
exchange	*smyeh*-naar-nah	*směnárna*
signature	*pot*-pis	*podpis*

CZECH

INTERESTS & ENTERTAINMENT
Sightseeing

Do you have a guidebook/local map?
maa-teh *proo*-vot-tseh/ *mah*-pu o-ko-lee? — *Máte průvodce/ mapu okolí?*

What are the main attractions?
yah-kair ysoh *zdehy*-shee po-zo-ru-ho-dno-styi? — *Jaké jsou zdejší pozoruhodnosti?*

What's that?
tso-yeh to? — *Co je to?*

How old is it?
yahk-yeh to *stah*-rair? — *Jak je to staré?*

Can I take photographs?
yeh zdeh po-vo-leh-no fo-to-grah-fo-vaht? — *Je zde povoleno fotografovat?*

What time does it open/close?
fko-lik ho-dyin o-teh-vee-rah-yee/za-vee-rah-yee? — *V kolik hodin otevírají/ zavírají?*

CZECH

ancient	*stah*-ro-vyeh-kee	starověký
archaeological	*ahr*-kheh-o-lo-gits-kair	archeologické
beach	plaazh	pláž
castle	hrahd/*zaa*-mehk	hrad/zámek
cathedral	*kah*-teh-draa-lah	katedrála
church	ko-stehl	kostel
concert hall	*kon*-tsehrt-nyee seeny	koncertní síň
library	*knyi*-ho-vnah	knihovna
main square	*hla*-vnyee *naa*- myeh-styee	hlavní náměstí
market	trh	trh
monastery	*klaash*-tehr	klášter
monument	*pah*-maa-tyneek/	památník/
	po-mnyeek	pomník
old city	*stah*-rair *myehs*-to	staré město
palace	*pah*-laats	palác
opera house	o-peh-rah	opera
ruins	zrzhee-tseh-nyi-ni	zříceniny
stadium	*stah*-di-awn	stadión
statues	so-khi	sochy
temple	khraam	chrám
university	*u*-ni-vehr-si-tah	universita

Going Out

What's there to do in the evenings?

| *kahm*-seh-tu daa *veh*-chehr yeet? | Kam se tu dá večer jít? |

Are there any nightclubs?

| ysoh zdeh *dis*-ko-tair-ki? | Jsou zde diskotéky? |

Are there places where you can hear local folk music?

| *hrah*-yee *nyeh*-gdeh *li*-do-voh *hud*-bu? | Hrají někde lidovou hudbu? |

cinema	*ki*-no	kino
concert	*kon*-tsehrt	koncert
nightclub	*dis*-ko-tair-kah	diskotéka
theatre	*dyi*-vah-dlo	divadlo

Sports & Interests

What sports do you play?
   yakeeh **spohrt** *dyieh*-laah-the?   *Jaký sport děláte?*
What are your interests?
   yakeh maateh *zaay*-mih?   *Jaké máte zájmy?*

art	*uh*-mnyeh-nyeeh	*umění*
basketball	*bas*-ket-bahl	*basketbal*
chess	*shah*-khih	*šachy*
collecting things	*zbyeh*-rah-tel-stveeh	*sběratelství*
dancing	*tah*-netz	*tanec*
food	*yeed*-loh	*jídlo*
football	*fot*-bahl/ *koh*-pah-no	*fotbal/kopanou*
hiking	*pyeh*-sheeh *tuh*-ris-tickuh	*pěší turistiku*
martial arts	*boh*-yo-vaah	*bojová*
	uh-myeh-nyeeh	*umění*
movies	*phil*-mih	*filmy*
music	*hood*-buh	*hudbu*
nightclubs	*bah*-rih/ *notch*-nyeeh	*bary/noční*
	pod-nyi-kih	*podniky*
photography	*phoh-toh*-graph-yee	*fotografii*
reading	*chteh*-nyeeh	*čtení*
shopping	*nah*-kuh-poh-vaa-nyeeh	*nakupování*
skiing	*lih*-zho-vaa-nyeeh	*lyžování*
swimming	*plah*-vaa-nyeeh	*plavání*
tennis	tennis	*tenis*
travelling	*tses*-toh-vaa-nyeeh	*cestování*
TV/videos	*teh*-leh-vih-zee/ *vih*-deh-ah	*televizi/videa*
visiting friends	*nah*-fshtyeh-voh-vaa-nyeeh przhaa-tell	*navštěvování přátel*
walking	*proh*-khaaz-kih	*procházky*

CZECH

Festivals & Public Holidays

1 January	New Year's Day	*Nový rok*
	Easter Friday	*Velikonoční pátek*
	Easter Monday	*Velikonoční pondělí*
1 May	Labour Day	*Svátek práce*
8 May	Liberation Day (1945)	*Den osvobození*
5 July	Cyril & Methodius	*od fašizmu*
	Memorial Day	*Cyril a Metoděj*
6 July	Jan Hus Memorial Day	*Mistr Jan Hus*
28 October	Czechoslovak	*Den vzniku*
	Independence Day (1918)	*Československa*
24 December	Christmas Eve	*Štědrý den*
25 December	Christmas Day	*1. svátek Vánoční*
26 December	Boxing Day	*2. svátek Vánoční*

CZECH

IN THE COUNTRY
Weather

What's the weather like?
  yah-kair yeh *po*-chah-see?   *Jaké je počasí?*

Will it be ...	*bu*-deh	*Bude*
tomorrow?	*zee*-trah ...?	*zítra ...?*
cloudy	*zah*-tah-zheh-no	*zataženo*
cold	*khlah*-dno	*chladno*
foggy	*ml*-hah-vo	*mlhavo*
frosty	mraaz	*mráz*
hot	*hor*-ko	*horko*
sunny	*slu*-neh-chno	*slunečno*
windy	vyeh-tr-no	*větrno*
It's raining.	*pr*-shee	*Prší.*
It's snowing.	*snyeh*-zhee	*Sněží.*

Camping

Am I allowed to camp here?
   mo-hu zdeh *stah*-no-vaht?   *Mohu zde stanovat?*
Is there a campsite nearby?
   yeh *fo*-ko-lee *taa*-bo-rzhi-shtyeh?   *Je v okolí tábořiště?*

backpack	*bah*-tyoh	*batoh*
can opener	o-tvee-rahch *kon*-zehrf	*otvírač konzerv*
compass	*kom*-pahs	*kompas*
crampons	*mah*-chki	*mačky*
firewood	*drzheh*-vo	*dřevo*
gas cartridge	*pli*-no-vaa *bom*-bi-chkah	*plynová bombička*
hammock	*ha*-mahk	*hamak*
ice axe	*tseh*-peen	*cepín*
mattress	*mah*-trah-tseh	*matrace*
penknife	*kah*-peh-snyee noozh	*kapesní nůž*
rope	*pro*-vahz	*provaz*
tent	stahn	*stan*
tent pegs	*stah*-no-vair ko-lee-kih	*stanové kolíky*
torch (flashlight)	*bah*-tehr-kah	*baterka*
sleeping bag	*spah*-tsee *pi*-tehl	*spací pytel*
stove	*vah*-rzhich	*vařič*
water bottle	*pol*-nyee *laa*-hehf	*polní láhev*

CZECH

FOOD

Czechs are big lovers of food and take great pride in the culinary experience that their country has to offer. Nowadays, typical Czech dishes may not be well known outside the Czech regions of Bohemia and Moravia, although not long ago Czech chefs were in high demand in the city of Vienna. Excellent smoked goods, beer and desserts are all worth experiencing as is the traditional fare of dumplings.

breakfast	*snyee*-dah-nyeh	*snídaně*
lunch	o-byehd	*oběd*
dinner	*veh*-cheh-rzheh	*večeře*

Table for ..., please.
    stool pro ..., pro-seem   *Stůl pro ..., prosím.*
Can I have the menu, please?
    yee-**dehl**-nyee *lee-stehk* **pro**-seem   *Jídelní lístek, prosím.*
What's today's special?
    yah-**kaa yeh** *speh*-tsi-ah-li-tah *dneh?*   *Jaká je specialita dne?*
I'd like ....
    mo-**hu**-si *o*-byeh-dnaht ...   *Mohu si objednat ...*
Is service included in the bill?
    yeh to *fcheh*-tnyeh *op*-slu-hi?   *Je to včetně obsluhy?*
Not too spicy.
    neh *przhee*-lish ko-rzheh-nyeh-nair   *Ne příliš kořeněné.*

Bon appetit!	*do*-broh khuty!	*Dobrou chuť*
Cheers!	*nah*-zdrah-vee!	*Na zdraví!*
ashtray	*po*-pehl-nyeek	*popelník*
bill	*oo*-cheht	*účet*
cup	*shaa*-lehk	*šálek*
dessert	*moh*-chnyeek	*moučník*
drink	*pi*-tyee	*pití*
fork	*vi*-dli-chkah	*vidlička*
fresh	*chehr*-stvee	*čerstvý*
glass	*skleh*-nyi-tseh	*sklenice*
knife	noozh	*nůž*
off/spoiled	*skah*-zheh-nee	*zkažený*
plate	*tah*-leerzh	*talíř*
spicy	*ko*-rzheh-nyeh-nee	*kořeněný*
spoon	*lzhee*-tseh	*lžíce*
stale	*o*-ko-rah-lee	*okoralý*
sweet	*slaht*-kee	*sladký*
teaspoon	*lzhi*-chkah	*lžička*
toothpick	*paa*-raat-ko	*párátko*

Vegetarian Meals
Vegetarian dishes aren't all that common on Czech menus, so
vegetarians may have some problems ordering certain dishes.

I'm a vegetarian.
ysehm *veh*-geh-tah-ri- aan		*Jsem vegetarián/*
veh-geh-tah-ri-aan-kah		*vegetariánka.* (m/f)

I don't eat meat.
neh-yeem *mah*-so   *Nejím maso.*

I don't eat chicken/fish/ham.
neh-yeem *ku*-rzheh/*ri*-bu/*shun*-ku   *Nejím kuře/rybu/šunku.*

Breakfast
bacon and eggs	*vei*-tseh seh *sla*-nyih-no	vejcese slaninou
ham and eggs	*vei*-tseh seh *shun*-kough	vejce se šunkou
omelette	*oh*-meh-leh-tah	omeleta
soft/hard-	*vei*-tseh nah	vejce na
boiled eggs	mnyeh-koh/tvr-doh	měkko/tvrdo
jam	jam/*mar*-meh-laa-dah	džem/marmeláda
type of croissant	*low*-paah-check	loupáček
... eggs	... *vei*-tseh	... vejce
boiled	*vah*-rzheh-naah	vařená
fried	*sma*-zheh-naah	smažená
scrambled	*mee*-kha-naah	míchaná

Soup
beef	*hoh*-vyeh-zee	hovězí
beef chunks	*guh*-laah-sho-vaah	gulášová
with spices		
broth with egg	*buh*-yohn	bujón
mushroom	*ho*-boh-vaah	houbová
pea	*hrah*-khoh-vaah	hrachová
potato	*bram*-boh-roh-vaah	bramborová
tomato with	*rai*-skaah	rajská
a little rice		
vegetable	*zeh*-leh-nyih-noh-vaah	zeleninová

CZECH

MENU DECODER

Starters & Buffet Meals

klobásy	*kloh*-baa-sih	sausages – can be mild or spicy
langoše	*lan*-goh-sheh	a snack made of fried pastry coated in garlic, cheese, butter or jam
obložené chlebíčky	*ob*-loh-zheh-neh *khleh*-beach-kih	open sandwiches
párky	*paar*-kih	frankfurt or wiener-type sausages
uherský salám s okurkou	*ooh*-her-skeeh *sah*-laam s *oh*-khur-kough	Hungarian salami with gherkin
sýrový nářez	*see*-roh-veeh *naah*-rzhez	a serve of two or three cheeses
tlačenka s octem a cibulí	*tlah*-chen-kah s *ots*-tem ah *tzih*-buh-leeh	seasoned jellied meat loaf with vinegar and fresh onion
zavináče	*zah*-vih-naa-tcheh	rollmops – herring fillets rolled around onion and/or gherkin, and pickled
houskové/ bramborové knedlíky	*hough*-skoh-veh/ *bram*-boh-roh-veh *kned*-lee-kih	potato/bread dumplings

Main Meals

dušená roštěnka	*duh*-shehnaa *rosh*-tyien-kah	braised slices of beef in sauce
hovězí guláš	*hoh*-vyeh-zee *guh*-laash	beef chunks in a brown sauce
hovězí karbanátky	*hoh*-vyeh-zee *kar*-bah-naat-kih	a type of beef burger with breadcrumbs, egg and onion

pečená ...	*peh*-tcheh-naah ...	roasted ...
husa	*hooh*-sah	goose
kachna	*kakh*-nah	duck
kuře	*kuh*-rzheh	chicken
plněné	*pl*-nyeh-neh	capsicum stuffed with a
papriky	*pah*-prickih	mixture of minced meat and rice, served with to mato sauce
řízek ...	*rzhee*-zeck ...	... schnitzel
telecí	*teh*-le-tseeh	veal
vepřový	*vep*-rzhoh-veeh	pork
segedínský	*seh*-geh-dean-skih	a goulash with three
guláš	*guh*-laash	types of meat, and sauer kraut
svíčková	*sveetch*-koh-vaah	roast beef served with a sour cream sauce and spices
vepřová	*vep*-rzhoh-vaah	roast pork with caraway
pečeně	*peh*-cheh-nyeh	seed
zajíc na	*zah*-yeets nah	hare in a cream sauce
smetaně	*smeh*-tah-nyeh	
znojemská	*znoh*-yem-skaah	slices of roast beef in a
pečeně	*peh*-cheh-nyeh	gherkin sauce
Desserts		
meruňkové	*meh*-runyi-koh-veh	apricots wrapped in pastry
knedlíky	*kned*-lee-kih	and topped with cottage cheese, melted butter and sugar
švestkové	*shvest*-koh-veh	plums wrapped in pastry
knedlíky	*kned*-lee-kih	and topped with crushed poppy seeds, melted butter and sugar

CZECH

CZECH

Desserts

apple strudel	*yah*-bl-koh-veeh *zaah*-vin	jablkový závin
preserved and canned fruit	*kohm*-pot	kompot
poppy-seed cake	*mah*-koh-veeh *koh*-laach	makový koláč
fruit slices	*oh*-vots-neh *koh*-laacheh	ovocné koláče
pancakes	*pah*-lah-chin-kih	palačinky
meringue with whipped cream	*rah*-qvich-kih	rakvičky
ice cream	zmrz-lih-nah	zmrzlina

Non-Alcoholic Drinks

... coffee	*kaah*-vah	káva
black	*chair*-naah	černá
white	*bee*-laah	bílá
espresso	*es*-press-soh	espreso
hot chocolate	*kah*-kah-oh	kakao
Vienna coffee	*vee*-dyen-skaah *kaah*-vah	vídeňská káva
tea	*cha*i	čaj
with sugar	s *tsuk*-rehm	s cukrem
with milk	s *mleh*-kehm	s mlékem
fruit juice	*oh*-vots-naah *sh*-tyaah-vah	ovocná šťáva
ice	led	led
mineral water	*mih*-neh-raal-kah	minerálka
milk	*mleh*-koh	mléko
soft drink	*lih*-moh-naah-dah	limonáda

Alcoholic Drinks

beer	*pih*-voh	pivo
spirits	*lih*-hoh-vih-nih	lihoviny
whiskey	*viskih*	whisky
(red/white) wine	(*cher*-veh-nair/ *bee*-lair) *vee*-noh	(červené/bílé) víno

At the Market

How much is it?
  ko-lik-to *sto*-yee?   *Kolik to stojí?*
Could you lower the price?
  neh-moo-zheh-teh-
  mi *nyeh*-tso *sleh*-vit?   *Nemůžete mi něco slevit?*
I don't have much money.
  neh-maam mots *peh*-nyehs   *Nemám moc peněz.*
I'd like ... grams/kilos.
  proh-sil/*proh*-si-lah bikh   *Prosil/prosila bych*
  ... *grah*-moo/*kih*-loh   *... gramů/kilo.* (m/f)

Staple Foods & Condiments

bread	khleehb	*chléb*
bread roll	*roh*-hleeck	*rohlík*
butter	*maas*-loh	*máslo*
cereal	*oh-bil*-nyih-noh-vee	*obilninové*
	kah-sheh	*kaše*
cheese	seer	*sýr*
chillies	*paa*-lih-vair *pap*-rich-kih	*pálivé papričky*
chips	*hrah*-nol-kih	*hranolky*
chocolate	*choh*-koh-laa-duh	*čokoládu*
eggs	*vei*-tseh	*vejce*
flour	*mow*-kuh	*mouku*
ginger	*zaaz*-vor	*zázvor*
honey	med	*med*
horseradish	krzhehn	*křen*
margarine	*mar*-gah-reen	*margarín*
marmalade	jam/*mar*-meh-laa-duh	*džem/marmeládu*
milk	*mleh*-koh	*mléko*
mustard	*horzh*-chi-tseh	*hořčice*
(olive) oil	(*oh*-lih-vo-vee) *oh*-ley	*(olivový) olej*
pasta	*tyes*-toh-vih-nih	*těstoviny*
pastry	*peh*-tchi-voh	*pečivo*
pepper	pep-rzh	*pepř*

CZECH

pickled cabbage/ vegetables	*steh*-rih-lih-zoh-vah-neh *zeh*-lee/*zeh*-leh-nyih-nah	*sterilizované zelí/zelenina*
rice	*reeh*-zheh	*rýže*
salt	sool	*sůl*
sugar	*tsuh*-kr	*cukr*
vinegar	*oh*-tset	*ocet*
yogurt	*yog*-oort	*jogurt*

Meat & Fish

beef	*hoh*-vyeh-zee *mah*-soh	*hovězí maso*
chicken	*kuh*-rzheh	*kuře*
ham	*shoon*-kah	*šunka*
hamburger	*hahm*-buhr-gr/ *kahr*-bah-naa-teck	*hamburger/ karbanátek*
kidneys	*led*-vin-kih	*ledvinky*
lamb	*yeh*-hnyeh-chee *mah*-soh	*jehněčí maso*
liver	*yaah*-trah	*játra*
lobster	*mohrzh*-skee rahk	*mořský rak*
mussels	*muhsh*-leh	*mušle*
oysters	*ooh*-strzhi-tseh	*ústřice*
pork	*veh*-przhoh-vee *mah*-soh	*vepřové maso*
sausage	*kloh*-baa-sah/ *uh*-zen-kah	*klobása/uzenka*
shrimp (prawns)	*kreh*-veh-tah/ *gar*-naaht	*kreveta/garnát*
turkey	*kroh*-tsan	*krocan*
veal	*teh*-leh-tsee *mah*-soh	*telecí maso*

Vegetables

beans	*fah*-zol-kih	*fazolky*
beetroot	*cher*-veh-naa *rzheh*-pah	*červená řepa*
broad beans	*fah*-zoh-leh (boh-bih	*fazole (boby)*
cabbage	*zeh*-lee	*zelí*
chick peas	*tick*-vich-kih	*cizrna*
capsicum	*pah*-prih-kah	*paprika*
carrot	*mrh*-kev	*mrkev*
cauliflower	*kvyeh*-taak	*květák*
celery	*tseh*-lehr	*celer*

cucumber	*oh*-kuhr-kah	*okurka*
eggplant (aubergine)	*bah*-klah-zhaan/*lih*-leck	*baklažán/lilek*
garlic	*ches*-neck	*česnek*
kidney beans	*vlash*-skair *fah*-zoh-leh	*vlašské fazole*
lentils	*choch*-kah	*čočka*
lettuce	*hlaav*-koh-vee *sah*-laat	*hlávkový salát*
mushrooms	*hough*-bih	*houby*
onion	*tsih*-buh-leh	*cibule*
peas	*hraa*-sheck	*hrášek*
potatoes	*bram*-boh-rih	*brambory*
spinach	*shpeh*-naat	*špenát*
tomato	*rai*-cheh	*rajče*

CZECH

Fruit

apple	*yah*-bl-koh	*jablko*
apricots	*meh*-roony-kih	*meruňky*
banana	*bah*-naan	*banán*
blueberries	*boh*-roove-kih	*borůvky*
cherries	trsheh-shnyeh	*třešně*
grapes	*vih*-nair *hroz*-nih	*vinné hrozny*
kiwi fruit	kih-vih	*kivi*
lemon	*tsit*-rawn	*citrón*
orange	*poh*-meh-ranch	*pomeranč*
peach	*bros*-kev	*broskev*
pears	hrooh-shkih	*hrušky*
pineapple	*ah*-nah-nas	*ananas*
plums	*shvest*-kih	*švestky*
raspberries	*mah*-lih-nih	*maliny*
sour cherries	vish-nyeh	*višně*
strawberries	*yah*-hoh-dih	*jahody*

CZECH

AT THE MARKET

Basics

bread	khleehb	chléb
butter	*maas*-loh	máslo
cereal	*oh-bil*-nyih-noh-vee	obilninové
	kah-sheh	kaše
cheese	seer	sýr
chocolate	*choh*-koh-laa-duh	čokoládu
eggs	*vei*-tseh	vejce
flour	*mow*-kuh	mouku
honey	med	med
margarine	*mar*-gah-reen	margarín
marmalade	jam/*mar*-meh-laa-duh	džem/marmeládu
milk	*mleh*-koh	mléko
(olive) oil	(*oh*-lih-vo-vee) *oh*-ley	(olivový) olej
pasta	*tyes*-toh-vih-nih	těstoviny
pepper	pep-rzh	pepř
rice	*reeh*-zheh	rýže
salt	sool	sůl
sugar	*tsuh*-kr	cukr
yogurt	*yog*-oort	jogurt

Meat & Poultry

beef	*hoh*-vyeh-zee *mah*-soh	hovězí maso
chicken	*kuh*-rzheh	kuře
ham	*shoon*-kah	šunka
hamburger	*hahm*-buhr-gr/	hamburger/
	kahr-bah-naa-teck	karbanátek
kidneys	*led*-vin-kih	ledvinky
lamb	*yeh*-hnyeh-chee *mah*-soh	jehněčí maso
pork	*veh*-przhoh-vee *mah*-soh	vepřové maso
sausage	*kloh*-baa-sah/*uh*-zen-kah	klobása/uzenka
turkey	*kroh*-tsan	krocan
veal	*teh*-leh-tsee *mah*-soh	telecí maso

Seafood

lobster	*mohrzh*-skee rahk	mořský rak
mussels	*muhsh*-leh	mušle
oysters	*ooh*-strzhi-tseh	ústřice
shrimp (prawns)	*kreh*-veh-tah/*gar*-naaht	kreveta/garnát

AT THE MARKET

Vegetables

beans	*fah*-zol-kih	fazolky
beetroot	*cher*-veh-naa *rzheh*-pah	červená řepa
cabbage	*zeh*-lee	zelí
capsicum	*pah*-prih-kah	paprika
carrot	*mrh*-kev	mrkev
cauliflower	*kvyeh*-taak	květák
celery	*tseh*-lehr	celer
cucumber	*oh*-kuhr-kah	okurka
eggplant (aubergine)	*bah*-klah-zhaan/*lih*-leck	baklažán/lilek
lettuce	*hlaav*-koh-vee *sah*-laat	hlávkový salát
mushrooms	*hough*-bih	houby
onion	*tsih*-buh-leh	cibule
peas	*hraa*-sheck	hrášek
potatoes	*bram*-boh-rih	brambory
spinach	*shpeh*-naat	špenát
tomato	*rai*-cheh	rajče

Fruit

apple	*yah*-bl-koh	jablko
apricots	*meh*-roony-kih	meruňky
banana	*bah*-naan	banán
grapes	*vihn*-nair *hroz*-nih	vinné hrozny
kiwi fruit	kih-vih	kivi
lemon	*tsit*-rawn	citrón
orange	*poh*-meh-ranch	pomeranč
peach	*bros*-kev	broskev
pears	hrooh-shkih	hrušky
plums	*shvest*-kih	švestky
strawberries	*yah*-hoh-dih	jahody

Spices & Condiments

chillies	*paa*-lih-vair *pap*-rich-kih	pálivé papričky
garlic	*ches*-neck	česnek
ginger	*zaaz*-vor	zázvor
mustard	*horzh*-chi-tseh	hořčice

CZECH

SHOPPING

How much is it?	*ko*-lik-to *sto*-yee?	*Kolik to stojí?*

Where's the nearest ...?	*nei*-blizh-shee ...?	*Kde je zde nejbližší ...?*
bookshop	*knyih*-ku-pets-tvee	*knihkupectví*
camera shop	*fo*-to po-trzheh-bi	*foto potřeby*
chemist (pharmacy)	*lair*-kaar-nah	*lékárna*
clothing store	o-*dyeh*-vi	*oděvy*
delicatessen	*lah*-hoot-ki	*lahůdky*
general store	*smee*-sheh-nair *zbo*-zhee/ po-*trah*-vi-ni; o-*pkhod*	*smíšené zboží/ potraviny; obchod*
greengrocer	*zeh*-leh-nyi-nah ah *oh*-vo-tseh	*zelenina a ovoce*
laundry	*praa*-dehl-nah	*prádelna*
market	trh	*trh*
newsagency	*no*-vi-no-vee *staa*-nehk/ *tah*-baak	*novinový stánek/tabák*
shoeshop	*oh*-buv	*obuv*
souvenir shop	su-*veh*-nee-ri	*suvenýry*
stationers	*pah*-peer-nyits-tvee	*papírnictví*
supermarket	*sah*-mo-op-slu-hah	*samoobsluha*

I'd like to buy ...
raad *bikh*-si ko-*pil* ...	*Rád bych si koupil ...* (m)
raa-dah *bikh*-si ko-pi- lah ...	*Ráda bych si koupila ...* (f)

Do you have other ...?
maa-teh *yi*-neh ...?	*Máte jiné ...?*

I don't like it.
to-seh mi *neh*-lee-bee	*To se mi nelíbí.*

Can I look at it?
mo-hu-seh *nah*-to po-*dyee*-vaht?	*Mohu se na to podívat?*

Can you write down the price?
moo-zheh-teh-mi *nah*-psaht *tseh*-nu	*Můžete mi napsat cenu*

I'm just looking.
yehn-seh *dyee*-vaam

Jen se dívám.

That's too much. (cost)
Toh stoh-yee przhee-lish
mnoh-hoh.

*To stojí příliš
mnoho.*

Do you accept credit cards?
przhi-yee-maa-teh
oo-vyeh-ro-vair *kahr*-ti?

Přijímáte úvěrové karty?

CZECH

Essential Groceries

I'd like ...	mohl/*moh*-lah bikh ... *doh*-staht?	*Mohl/Mohla bych ... dostat?* (m/f)
batteries	*bah*-ter-kih	*baterky*
bread	kh-lehb	*chléb*
butter	*maah*-sloh	*máslo*
cheese	seer	*sýr*
chocolate	*choh*-koh-laa-duh	*čokoládu*
eggs	*vei*-tseh	*vejce*
honey	med	*med*
margarine	*mar*-gah-reen	*margarín*
matches	*sir*-kih/*zaah*-pal-kih	*sirky/zápalky*
milk	*mleh*-koh	*mléko*
shampoo	*sham*-pohn	*šampon*
soap	*meed*-loh	*mýdlo*
toilet paper	*toah*-let-nyeeh *pah*-peer	*toaletní papír*
toothpaste	*zub*-nyeeh *pass*-tuh	*zubní pastu*
washing powder	*prah*-tseeh *praa*-shek	*prací prášek*

CZECH

Souvenirs

Glass and crystal, herb liqueurs and jewellery made with garnets are all popular souvenirs to be found in the Czech Republic.

earrings	*naah*-ooh-shnyi-tseh	*náušnice*
handicraft	*li*-do-vair *ooh*-myeh-nyee	*lidové umění*
necklace	*naa*-hr-dehl-nyeek	*náhrdelník*
pottery	*keh*-rah-mi-kah	*keramika*
ring	*pr*-stehn	*prsten*
rug	*ko*-beh-rehts	*koberec*

Clothing

clothing	*oh*-dyehv	*oděv*
coat	*kah*-baat	*kabát*
dress	*shah*-ti	*šaty*
jacket	*sah*-ko	*sako*
jumper (sweater)	*sveh*-tr	*svetr*
shirt	*ko*-shi-leh	*košile*
shoes	*bo*-tih	*boty*
skirt	*su*-knyeh	*sukně*
trousers	*kahl*-ho-tih	*kalhoty*
underwear	*spod*-nyee *praa*-dloh	*spodní prádlo*

It's too ...	ysoh mi mots ...	*Jsou mi moc ...*
big	*veh*-li-kair	*veliké*
small	*mah*-lair	*malé*
short	*kraat*-kair	*krátké*
long	*dloh*-hair	*dlouhé*
tight	*tyehs*-nair	*těsné*
loose	*vol*-nair	*volné*

Materials

brass	*mo*-sahz	*mosaz*
cotton	*bah*-vl-nah	*bavlna*
gold	*zlah*-to	*zlato*
handmade	*ru*-chnyeh *vi*-ro-beh-nair	*ručně vyrobené*
leather	*koo*-zheh	*kůže*
silk	*hehd*-vaa-bee	*hedvábí*
silver	*strzhree*-bro	*stříbro*
wool	*vl*-nah	*vlna*

Toiletries

comb	*hrzheh*-behn	*hřeben*
condoms	*preh*-zehr-vah-ti-vi	*prezervativy*
deodorant	*deh*-oh-do-rant	*deodorant*
hairbrush	*kahr*-taach *nah*-vlah-si	*kartáč na vlasy*
moisturising cream	*pleh*-tyo-vee krairm	*pletový krém*
razor	*brzhi*-tvah	*břitva*
shaving cream	*ho*-li-tsee krairm	*holící krém*
sunscreen	krairm nah	*krém na*
	oh-pah-lo-vaa-nyee	*opalování*
tampons	*tahm*-paw-ni	*tampóny*
tissues	*pah*-pee-ro-vair	*papírové*
	kah-pehs-nyee-ki	*kapesníky*
toothbrush	*kahr*-taa-check nah *zu*-bi	*kartáček na zuby*

CZECH

Colours

black	*chehr*-nee	*černý*
blue	*mo*-dree	*modrý*
brown	*hnyeh*-dee	*hnědý*
green	*zeh*-leh-nee	*zelený*
orange	*oh*-rahn-zho-vee	*oranžový*
pink	*roo*-zho-vee	*růžový*
red	*chehr*-veh-nee	*červený*
white	*bee*-lee	*bílý*
yellow	*zhloo*-tee	*žlutý*

Stationery & Publications

map	*mah*-pah	*mapa*
newspaper	*no*-vi-ni	*noviny*
paper	*pah*-peer	*papír*
pen (ballpoint)	*pro*-pi-so-vach-ka	*propisovačka*
scissors	*noozh*-ki	*nůžky*
English-language ...	... *v-ahn*-glich-tyi-nyeh	... *vangličtině*
newspaper	*no*-vi-ni	*noviny*
novels	*knyi*-hi	*knihy*

CZECH

Photography

How much is it to process this film?
    ko-lik *sto*-yee
    vi-vo-laa-nyee *fil*-mu?   *Kolik stojí vyvolání filmu?*
When will it be ready?
    gdi *bu*-deh *ho*-to-vee?   *Kdy bude hotový?*
I'd like a film for this camera.
    maa-teh film do *to*-ho-to   *Máte film do tohoto*
    fo-to-ah-pah-raa-tu   *fotoaparátu.*

B&W (film)	*chehr*-no-bee-lee	*černobílý*
camera	*fo*-to-ah-pah-raat	*fotoaparát*
colour (film)	*bah*-reh-vnee	*barevný*
film	film	*film*
flash	blehsk	*blesk*
lens	*ob*-yehk-tiv	*objektiv*
light meter	*ehks*-po-zi-meh-tr	*exposimetr*

Smoking

Do you smoke?
    khou-*rzheesh*? khou-*rzhee*-teh?
    Kouříš?/Kouříte? (inf/pol)
Please don't smoke.
    neh-kow-rzhit *proh*-seem
    Nekouřit prosím.
A packet of cigarettes, please.
    pro-sil/*pro*-si-lah bikh   *Prosil/Prosila bych*
    kra-*bich*-ku *tsi*-gah-reht   *krabičkucigaret.* (m/f)
Are these cigarettes strong/mild?
    ysoh-ti *tsi*-gah-reh-ti   *Jsou ty cigarety příliš silné/*
    przhee-lish *sil*-nair/*yehm*-nair?   *jemné?*
Do you have a light?
    maa-teh *zaa*-pahl-ki/   *Máte zápalky/zapalovač?*
    zah-pah-lo-vahch?

SIGNS

ZÁKAZ KOUŘENÍ
NO SMOKING

cigarette papers	*tsi*-gah-reh-to-vair	*cigaretové*
	pah-peer-ki	*papírky*
cigarettes	*tsi*-gah-reh-ti	*cigarety*
filtered	*sfil*-trehm	*sfiltrem*
lighter	*zah*-pah-lo-vahch	*zapalovač*
matches	*zaa*-pahl-ki/*sir*-ki	*zápalky/sirky*
menthol	*mehn*-tol-ki	*mentolky*
pipe	*deem*-kah	*dýmka*
tobacco (pipe)	*tah*-baak (pro *deem*-ku)	*tabák (pro dýmku)*

Sizes & Comparisons

small	*mah*-lair	*malé*
big	*veh*-li-kair	*veliké*
heavy	*tyezh*-kair	*těžké*
light	*leh*-kair	*lehké*
more	*vee*-tseh	*více*
less	*mair*-nyeh	*méně*
too much/ many	*przhee*-lish ho-dnyeh/*mno*-ho	*příliš hodně/ mnoho*

CZECH

THEY MAY SAY ...

tso-si *przheh*-yeh-teh?
  Can I help you?

bu-deh-to fsheh?
  Will that be all?

przheh-yeh-teh *si*-to *zah*-bah-lit?
  Would you like it wrapped?

pro-miny-teh *to*-hleh yeh *po*-sleh-dnyee kus
  Sorry, this is the only one.

ko-lik *ku*-soo si *przheh*-yeh-teh?
  How much/many do you want?

CZECH

HEALTH

Where's the ...?	gde-yeh ...?	Kde je ...?
chemist	*lair*-kaar-nah	lékárna
dentist	*zub*-nyee *lair*-kahrzh/	zubní lékař/
	zu-bahrzh	zubař
doctor	*dok*-tor	doktor
hospital	neh-mo-tsnyi-tseh	nemocnice

What's the matter?	Tso vaam yeh?	Co vám je?
Where does it hurt?	gdeh *vaas*-to bo-lee?	Kde vás to bolí?
It hurts here.	bo-lee-myeh zdeh	Bolí mě zde.

I'm sick.

ysehm neh-mo-tsnee	Jsem nemocný/
neh-mo-tsnaa	nemocná. (m/f)

Parts of the Body

My ... hurts.	bo-lee-myeh ...	Bolí mě ...
ankle	*kot*-nyeek	kotník
arm	*pah*-zheh	paže
back	*zaa*-dah	záda
chest	hroohdy/*hrood*-nyeek	hruď/hrudník
ear	*u*-kho	ucho
eye	*o*-ko	oko
finger	prst	prst
foot	*kho*-dyi-dlo	chodidlo
hand	*ru*-kah	ruka
head	*hlah*-vah	hlava
heart	*srd*-tse	srdce
leg	*no*-hah	noha
mouth	*foo*-stehkh	v ústech
nose	nos	nos
skin	koo-zheh	kůže
spine	*paa*-tehrzh	páteř
stomach	*zhah*-lu-dehk	žaludek
teeth	*zu*-bi	zuby
throat	*hr*-dlo	hrdlo

Ailments

I have (a/an) ...	maam ...	*Mám ...*
(low/high)	*(nyeez-kee/vi-so-kee)*	*(nízký/vysoký)*
blood pressure	*kreh-vnyee* tlak	*krevní tlak*
constipation	*zaats-pu*	*zácpu*
cough	*kah-shehl*	*kašel*
diarrhoea	*proo-yehm*	*průjem*
fever	*ho-rehch-ku*	*horečku*
hepatitis	*zhloh-tehn-ku*	*žloutenku*
infection	*in-fehk-tsi*	*infekci*
influenza	*khrzhip-ku*	*chřipku*
lice	fshi	*vši*
sprain	*pod-vr-tnu-tyee*	*podvrtnutí*
sunburn	*oo-zheh*	*úžeh*
venereal disease	*po-hlah-vnyee*	*pohlavní*
	neh-mots	*nemoc*
worms	*chehr-vi*	*červy*

I have ...	ysehm ...	*Jsem ...*
anaemia	*khu-do-kreh-vnee*	*chudokrevný*
a burn	*po-paa-leh-nee*	*popálený*
a cold	*nah-khlah-zeh-nee*	*nachlazený*

I have a ...	bo-lee-myeh ...	*Bolí mě ...*
headache	*hlah-vah*	*hlava*
sore throat	*fkr-ku*	*v krku*
stomachache	*brzhi-kho*	*břicho*

My friend is sick.
mooy *przhee-tehl* yeh
neh-mo-tsnee   *Můj přítel je nemocný.* (m)

mo-yeh *przhee-tehl-ki-*
nyeh yeh *neh-mots-naa*   *Moje přítelkyně je nemocná.* (f)

CZECH

Women's Health

Could I see a female doctor?
przhaa-la *bikh*-si
nahf-shtyee-vit *dok*-tor-ku?

*Přála bych
si navštívit doktorku?*

I'm pregnant.
ysehm *tyeh*-ho-tnaa

Jsem těhotná.

I'm on the Pill.
u-zhee-vaam *ahn*-ti-
kon-tsehp-chnyee *praash*-ki

*Užívám antikoncepční
prášky.*

I haven't had my period for
... months.
neh-mnyieh-lah ysehm
mehn- stru-ah-tsi
uzh ... *myeh*-see-tseh

*Neměla jsem menstruaci
už ... měsíců.*

Useful Phrases

I'm ...	maam ...	*Mám ...*
asthmatic	*ahst*-muh	*astmu*
diabetic	*tsu*-krof-ku	*cukrovku*
epileptic	*eh*-pi-leh-psi-i	*epilepsii*

I'm allergic to antibiotics/penicillin.
ysehm *ah*-lehr-gits-kee
nah *ahn*-ti-bio-ti-kah/
peh-ni-tsi-lean

*Jsem alergický
na antibiotika/
penicilín.*

I've been vaccinated.
bil ysehm *o*-chko-vah-nee
bi-lah ysehm *o*-chko-vah-naa

Byl jsem očkovaný. (m)
Byla jsem očkovaná. (f)

I have my own syringe.
maam *svough vlast*-nyee
i-nyeh-kchnyee *strzhee*-kahch-ku

*Mám svou vlastní
injekčnístříkačku.*

At the Chemist

I need medication for ...
po-trzheh-bu-yi *lair*-ki ... *Potřebuji léky ...*

I have a prescription.
maam *przhehd*-pis *Mám předpis.*

At the Dentist

I have a toothache.
bo-lee-myeh zub *Bolí mě zub.*

I've lost a filling.
vi-pah-dlah-mi *plom*-bah *Vypadla mi plomba.*

I've broken a tooth.
maam *zlo*-meh-nee zub *Mám zlomený zub.*

My gums hurt.
bo-lee-myeh *daa*-snyeh *Bolí mě dásně.*

I don't want it extracted.
neh-tr-hehy-teh-mi *Netrhejte mi tento zub.*
tehn-to zub

Please give me an anaesthetic.
pro-seem *umr*-tvyeh-teh *mi*-to *Prosím, umrtvěte mi to.*

HELICOPTER HALOS

Many people wonder why so many Czech statues
have golden-looking helicopter blades on their
heads – they're actually halos which indicate that
the statue is of a saint.

The one exception is the statue of St Jan Nepomucký,
who has no blades, but a circle of stars. No, he didn't
get hit on the head like in a cartoon – Jan Nepomucký
was thrown off Charles' Bridge in Prague and drowned.
According to legend, the stars appeared above the
water indicating where his body lay.

TIME & DATES

Telling the time in Czech is difficult to explain in the short space of this chapter. Ask for specific times to be written down.

What time is it?
    ko-lik-yeh *ho*-dyin?   *Kolik je hodin?*
Please write that down.
    nah-pi-shteh mi-to pro-seem.   *Napište mi to, prosím*
What date is it today?
    ko-li-kaa-tair-ho yeh dnehs?   *Kolikátého je dnes?*

in the morning	*raa*-no	*ráno*
in the afternoon	*ot*-po-leh-dneh	*odpoledne*
in the evening	*veh*-chehr	*večer*

Days

Monday	*pon*-dyeh-lee	*pondělí*
Tuesday	*oo*-teh-ree	*úterý*
Wednesday	*strzheh*-dah	*středa*
Thursday	*chtvr*-tehk	*čtvrtek*
Friday	*paa*-tehk	*pátek*
Saturday	*so*-bo-tah	*sobota*
Sunday	*neh*-dyeh-leh	*neděle*

Months

January	*leh*-dehn	*leden*
February	*oo*-nor	*únor*
March	*brzheh*-zehn	*březen*
April	*du*-behn	*duben*
May	*kvyeh*-tehn	*květen*
June	*chehr*-vehn	*červen*
July	*chehr*-veh-nehts	*červenec*
August	*sr*-pehn	*srpen*
September	*zaa*-rzhee	*září*
October	*rzhee*-yehn	*říjen*
November	*lis*-to-pahd	*listopad*
December	*pro*-si-nehtz	*prosinec*

CZECH

Seasons

summer	*lair*-to	*léto*
autumn	*pod*-zim	*podzim*
winter	*zi*-mah	*zima*
spring	*yah*-ro	*jaro*

Present

today	dnehs	*dnes*
this morning	dnehs *raa*-no	*dnes ráno*
tonight	dnehs *veh*-chehr/	*dnes večer/*
	dnehs *vno*-tsi	*dnes v noci*
this week	*tehm*-to *tee*-dehn	*tento týden*
this year	*leh*-tos/ *vleh*-	*letos/*
	tosh-nyeem *ro*-tseh	*v letošním roce*
now	teh-dyi	*ted'*

Past

yesterday	*fcheh*-rah	*včera*
day before yesterday	*przheh*-dehf-chee-rehm	*předevčírem*
last night	*fcheh*-rah *veh*-chehr	*včera večer*
last week/year	*mi*-nu-lee *tee*-dehn/ rok	*minulý týden/ rok*

Future

tomorrow	*zee*-trah	*zítra*
day after tomorrow	*po*-zee-trzhee	*pozítří*
tomorrow afternoon	*zee*-trah *ot*-po-leh-dneh/ *veh*-chehr	*zítra odpoledne/ večer*
next week	*przheesh*-tyee *tee*-dehn	*příští týden*
next year	*przheesh*-tyee rok	*příští rok*

During the Day

afternoon	ot-po-leh-dneh	odpoledne
dawn	svee-taa-nyee	svítání
day	dehn	den
early	br-zo	brzo
midday	po-leh-dneh	poledne
midnight	pool-nots	půlnoc
morning (9 am – midday)	raa-no/ do-po-leh-dneh	ráno/ dopoledne
night	nots	noc
sunrise	vee-khod slun-tseh	východ slunce
sunset	zaa-pahd slun-tseh	západ slunce

CZECH

NUMBERS & AMOUNTS

0	nu-lah	nula
1	yeh-dna	jedna
2	dvah	dva
3	trzhi	tři
4	chti-rzhi	čtyři
5	pyeht	pět
6	shehst	šest
7	seh-dum	sedm
8	o-sum	osm
9	deh-vyeht	devět
10	deh-seht	deset
11	yeh-deh-naatst	jedenáct
12	dvah-naatst	dvanáct
13	trzhi-naatst	třináct
14	chtr-naatst	čtrnáct
15	pah-tnaatst	patnáct
16	shehst-naatst	šestnáct
17	seh-dum-naatst	sedmnáct
18	o-sum-naatst	osmnáct
19	deh-vah-teh-naatst	devatenáct
20	dvah-tseht	dvacet

21	*dva*-tseht *yeh*-dnah/	*dvacet jedna*/
	yeh-dna-dvah-tseht	*jednadvacet*
30	*trzhi*-tseht	*třicet*
40	*chti*-rzhi-tseht	*čtyřicet*
50	*pah*-deh-saat	*padesát*
60	*sheh*-deh-saat	*šedesát*
70	*seh*-dum-deh-saat	*sedmdesát*
80	*o*-sum-deh-saat	*osmdesát*
90	*deh*-vah-deh-saat	*devadesát*
100	stoh	*sto*
1000	*tyi*-seets	*tisíc*
10 000	*deh*-seht *tyi*-seets	*deset tisíc*
100 000	stoh *tyi*-seets	*sto tisíc*
one million	*mi*-li-yawn	*milión*
1st	*pr*-vnyee	*první*
2nd	*dru*-hee	*druhý*
3rd	*trzheh*-tyee	*třetí*
1/4	*chtvr*-tyi-nah	*čtvrtina*
1/3	*trzheh*-tyi-nah	*třetina*
1/2	*po*-lo-vi-nah	*polovina*
3/4	*trzhi*-chtvr-tyi-nah	*třičtvrtina*

CZECH

CZECH

Useful Words

a little (amount)	*tro*-khu	*trochu*
double	*dvoh*-yi-tee	*dvojitý*
dozen	*tu*-tseht	*tucet*
Enough!	dost!	*Dost!*
few	*nyeh*-ko-lik	*několik*
less	*mair*-nyeh	*méně*
many	*mno*-ho	*mnoho*
more	*vee*-tseh	*více*
once	*yeh*-dnoh	*jednou*
pair	paar	*pár*
per cent	*pro*-tsehn-to	*procento*
some	*nyeh*-kteh-ree	*některý*
too much	*przhee*-lish *ho*-dnyeh	*příliš hodně*
twice	*dvah*-kraat	*dvakrát*

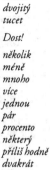

BEAUTIFUL BEER GUTS

The Czechs drink the largest volume of *pivo*, 'beer' per capita of any country in the world. Beer culture is centuries old, and is celebrated at hundreds of festivals, where competitions include speed drinking and the largest beer gut to name but a few.

A favourite Czech saying is:

Pivo dělá pěkná těkla.

'Beer makes beautiful bodies.'

ABBREVIATIONS

AMU	Academy of Performing Arts
ATS	Austrian schilling
cm/m/km	cm/m/km
č./čís.	number/s
ČAD	Czech Coachline
ČČK	Czech Red Cross
ČD	Czech Railway
ČEDOK	Czech Travel Agency
ČR	Czech Republic
ČSA	Czechoslovak Airlines
ČTK	Czech Press Agency
DEM	Deutschmark
EU	EU
atd.	etc.
FRF	French franc
GBP	British pound
h/hod	hour, or halíř (h), small unit of currency
hl. m.	capital city
JZD	State Farming Cooperative
Kč	Czech crown
KU or UK	Charles University in Prague
nám.	town square
OSN	United Nations
p./sl.	Mr/Miss
pí.	Mrs; Ms
SBČ	Czech State Bank
ul.	street
USD	American dollar

CZECH

EMERGENCIES

Help!
   po-mots!   *Pomoc!*

It's an emergency.
   to-yeh *nah*-lair-hah-vee   *To je naléhavý případ.*
   przhee-paht

There's been an accident.
   do-shlo kneh-ho-dyeh   *Došlo k nehodě.*

Call a doctor/ambulance/the police!
   zah-vo-lehy-teh *do*-kto-   *Zavolejte doktora/*
   rah/*sah*-nit-ku/*po*-li-tsi-yi!   *sanitku/policii!*

Where is the police station?
   gdeh-yeh *po*-li-tsehy-nyee   *Kde je policejní stanice?*
   stah-nyi-tseh?

I've been raped.
   bi-lah ysehm *znaa*-sil-   *Byla jsem znásilněna.*
   nyeh-nah

I've been robbed.
   bil ysehm *o*-krah-dehn   *Byl jsem okraden.* (m)
   bi-lah ysehm *o*-krah-deh-nah   *Byla jsem okradena.* (f)

Go away!
   dyih-teh prich!/*byezh*-teh   *Jděte pryč!/Běžte pryč!*
   prich!

I'll call the police.
   zah-vo-laam *po*-li-tsi-yi   *Zavolám policii.*

Thief!
   zlo-dyehy!   *Zloděj!*

I'm ill.
   ysehm *neh*-mo-tsnee/   *Jsem nemocný/*
   neh-mo-tsnaa   *nemocná.* (m/f)

I'm lost.
   zah-bloh-dyil-sem/   *Zabloudil/*
   zah-bloh-dyi-lah-sem   *Zabloudila jsem.* (m/f)

Where are the toilets?
   gdeh-ysoh *zaa*-kho-di?   *Kde jsou záchody?*

Could you help me, please?
  pro-seem *moo*-zheh-teh
  mi *po*-mo-tsi?

*Prosím, můžete mi
pomoci?*

Could I please use the telephone?
  do-vo-lee-teh, ah-bikh-si
  zah-teh-leh-fo-no-vahl/
  zah-teh-leh-fo-no-vah-lah?

*Dovolíte, abych si
zatelefonoval/
zatelefonovala?* (m/f)

I'm sorry. I apologise.
  pro-miny-teh.
  o-mloh-vaam-seh.

*Promiňte.
Omlouvám se.*

I didn't realise I was doing
anything wrong.
  neh-u-vyeh-do-mil
  ysehm-si zheh ysehm
  u-dyeh-lahl *nyeh*-tso
  shpaht-nair-ho

*Neuvědomil jsem si,
že jsem udělal něco
špatného.* (m)

  neh-u-vyeh-do-mi-lah
  ysehm-si zheh ysehm
  u-dyeh-lah-lah *nyeh*-tso
  shpaht-nair-ho

*Neuvědomila jsem si,
že jsem udělala něco
špatného.* (f)

I didn't do it.
  neh-u-dye-lahl/*neh*-u-dye-
  lahl-lah ysehm-to

*Neudělal/Neudělala
jsem to.* (m/f)

I wish to contact my
embassy/consulate.
  przheh-yi-si *mlu*-vit
  zmeem *vehl*-vi-slah-
  nehts-tveem/*kon*-zu-laa-tehm

*Přeji si mluvit s
mým velvyslanectvím/
konzulátem.*

I have medical insurance.
  maam *neh*-mo-tsehns-koh
  po-yist-ku

*Mám nemocenskou
pojistku.*

My possessions are insured.
  mo-yeh *zah*-vah-zah-dlah
  y-sow poh-yish-tyieh-nah

*Moje zavazadla
jsou pojištěna.*

My ... was stolen.	*u*-krah-dli mnyieh ...	*Ukradli mně ...*
I've lost my ...	*strah*-tyil/*strah*-tyi-lah ysehm ...	*Ztratil/Ztratila jsem ... (m/f)*
bags	*mo*-yeh *zah*-vah-zah-dlah	*moje zavazadla*
handbag	*mo*-yi *kah*-behl-kuh	*moji kabelku*
money	*mo*-yeh *peh*-nyee-zeh	*moje peníze*
passport	mooy pahs	*můj pas*
travellers cheques	*mo*-yeh *tsehs*-to-vnyee sheh-kih	*moje cestovní šeky*
wallet	*peh*-nyeh-zhen-*kah*	*peněženka*

CZECH

GERMAN

QUICK REFERENCE

Hello.	goo-ten taak	*Guten Tag.*
Goodbye.	owf *vee*-der-zeh-en	*Auf Wiedersehen.*
Yes./No.	yaa/nain	*Ja./Nein.*
Excuse me.	ent-*shul*-di-gung	*Entschuldigung.*
Sorry.	ent-*shul*-di-gung	*Entschuldigung.*
Please.	*bit*-te	*Bitte.*
Thank you.	*dahng*-ke	*Danke.*
You're welcome.	*bit*-te zair	*Bitte sehr.*
Where's ...?	vaw ist ...?	*Wo ist ...?*

I'd like a ... ticket.	ikh *merkh*-te ai-ne ...	*Ich möchte eine ...*
one-way	*ain*-fah-khe	*einfache*
return	*rük*-faar-kahr-teh	*Rückfahrkarte*

I (don't) understand.
ikh fer-shteh-e
(üü-ber-howpt *nikhts*)
Ich verstehe
(überhaupt nichts).

Do you speak English?
shpre-khen zee *eng*-lish?
Sprechen Sie Englisch?

Go straight ahead.
geh-en zee ge-raa-de-*ows*
Gehen Sie geradeaus.

Turn left/right.
bee-gen zee *lingks/rekhts*
Biegen Sie links/rechts.

Do you have any rooms available?
haa-ben zee nokh
tsim-mer frai?
Haben Sie noch
Zimmer frei?

I'm looking for a public toilet.
ikh *zoo*-kheh ai-neh
erf-fehnt-li-kheh
to-ah-*leht*-teh
Ich suche eine
öffentliche
Toilette.

1	ains	*eins*	6	zeks	*sechs*
2	tsvai	*zwei*	7	*zee*-ben	*sieben*
3	drai	*drei*	8	ahkht	*acht*
4	feer	*vier*	9	noyn	*neun*
5	fünf	*fünf*	10	tsehn	*zehn*

GERMAN

It might be a surprise to know that German is, in fact, a close relative of English. English, German and Dutch are all known as West Germanic languages. This means that you know quite a few German words already – *Arm*, *Finger*, *Gold* – and you'll be able to figure out many others – such as *Mutter*, 'mother', *trinken*, 'to drink', *gut*, 'good'.

A primary reason why English and German have grown apart is that the Normans, on invading England in 1066, brought with them a large number of non-Germanic words. This caused English to have lots of synonyms, with the more basic word being Germanic, and the more literary or specialised one coming from French. For instance, the Germanic 'start' and 'green' as opposed to the French 'commence' and 'verdant'.

German is spoken throughout Germany, Austria, Liechtenstein, Luxembourg and in most of Switzerland. Although you may hear

GENDER

Some German nouns can be either masculine or feminine. A feminine noun often looks like the masculine form, but with the suffix -*in* added to the end of the word. Where a word can be either masculine or feminine, in this chapter the feminine ending is separated with a slash.

secretary (m/f)   *Sekretär/in*

This indicates that the masculine form is *Sekretär* and the feminine form is *Sekretärin*.

In cases where the feminine is more complicated than adding -*in* to the masculine form, both forms of the word appear in full, masculine first:

nurse (m/f)   *Krankenpfleger/*
                              Krankenschwester

different dialects, there's a strong tradition of a prescribed official language – *Hochdeutsch*, 'High German'. High German is used in this book and will always be understood. In some areas, English is so widely spoken that you mightn't have a chance to use German, even if you want to. However, as soon as you move out of the larger cities, especially in what was East Germany, the situation is totally different. *Gute Reise!*

FORMALITIES

German has both polite and informal forms of the second person pronoun 'you' – Sie (pol) and du (inf). In this chapter, only the polite form, Sie, is given.

PRONUNCIATION

German pronunciation is relatively straightforward. Each letter or combination of letters is pronounced consistently, so you can almost always tell how a word is pronounced by the way it's spelt.

Vowels

German vowels can be long or short. Some letters or letter combinations in the German alphabet don't exist in English – these are the vowels with an umlaut (*ä, ö, ü*). Keep in mind that these vowels are pronounced differently.

Short Vowels

a	**ah**	as the 'u' in 'cut'
ä	**air**	as the 'ai' in 'air', but shorter;
	e	as the 'e' in 'bet'
äh	**air**	as the 'ai' in 'air'
e	**e**	as the 'e' in 'bet'
i	**i**	as in 'in'
o	**o**	as in 'hot'
ö	**er**	as the 'e' in 'her'
u	**u**	as the 'u' in 'pull'
ü, y	**ü**	as the 'i' in 'kiss', but with rounded lips

GERMAN

PRONOUNS

SG			PL		
I	ikh	*ich*	we	veer	*wir*
you (inf)	doo	*du*	you (inf)	eer	*ihr*
you (pol)	zee	*Sie*	you (pol)	zee	*Sie*
he	er	*er*	they	zee	*sie*
she	zee	*sie*			
it	es	*es*			

Long Vowels

A long vowel has the same sound quality as its short counterpart, but is pronounced longer. The spelling for long vowels is often indicated by an *h* after the vowel, or a doubling of the vowel, but not always. The vowel *i* is often lengthened by writing *ie*.

a, aa, ah	aa	as the 'a' in 'far'
e, ee, eh	eh	as the 'e' in 'egg', but longer
i, ie	ee	as the 'i' in 'marine'
o, oo, oh	aw	as the 'o' in 'for'
ö	er	as the 'e' in 'her'
u, uh	oo	as the 'oo' in 'zoo', pronounced with very rounded lips
ü, üh	üü	as the 'i' in 'kiss', but with rounded lips

Vowel Combinations

au	ow	as the 'ow' in 'cow'
äu	oy	as the 'oy' in 'toy'
ei	ai	as the 'ai' in 'aisle'
eu	oy	as the 'oy' in 'toy'

GERMAN

Consonants

Most German consonants are similar to their English counterparts. One important difference is that b, d and g sound like 'p', 't' and 'k' respectively at the end of a word or syllable.

Letters that may be unfamiliar include the ß (a sharp 's') that may also be written as ss and is pronounced as the 's' in 'sin'. There are also ch-sounds which may be pronounced in two ways depending on what letters come before and after. After a, o, u and au, the ch is a guttural sound like the 'ch' in Scottish 'loch'. Everywhere else, ch is pronounced like the 'h' in 'huge'.

Only consonants and double consonants that differ from English are given here.

b, bb	p	at the end of a word or syllable, as the 'p' in 'pet';
	b	elsewhere, as the 'b' in 'bliss'
c	ts	normally as the 'ts' in 'lets';
	k	in some foreign words, as the 'k' in 'king'
ch	kh	after a, o, u or au, as the 'ch' in Scottish 'loch'; elsewhere, as the 'h' in 'huge'
d, dd	t	at the end of a word or syllable, as the 't' in 'tang';
	d	elsewhere, as the 'd' in 'drink'
f, ff	f	as the 'f' in 'fun'
g, gg	g	as the 'g' in 'game'
g	k	at the end of a word or syllable, as the 'k' in 'king';
	kh	when part of the unit ig, as the 'h' in 'huge';
	zh	in some foreign words, as the 's' in 'pleasure'
h		silent following a vowel;
	h	elsewhere, as the 'h' in horse
j	y	as the 'y' in 'yes';
	zh	in some foreign words, as the 's' in 'treasure'
ng	ng	as the 'ng' in 'sing'
r, rr	r	slightly rolled at the back of the mouth
s	z	after a vowel, as the 'z' in 'zoo';
	s	elsewhere, as the 's' in 'sin'
ss, ß	s	as the 's' in 'sin'

v	f	mostly pronounced as the 'f' in 'fun';
	v	in words of Greek and Latin origin, as the 'v' in 'velvet'
w	v	as the 'v' in 'velvet'
z	ts	as the 'ts' in 'bets'

Letter Combinations

chs	ks	as the 'x' in 'fox'
ck	k	as the 'k' in 'king'
qu	kv	as the 'k' in 'king' + the 'v' in 'velvet'
sch	sh	as the 'sh' in 'ship'
sp/st	shp/sht	at the beginning of a word or syllable, the 's' is pronounced as the 'sh' in 'ship'
-tion	tsyawn	the 't' is pronounced as the 'ts' in 'bets'

Stress

Stress in German is very straightforward – the majority of German words are stressed on the first syllable. However, some prefixes aren't stressed, such as in the word *verstehen*, 'understand', which is stressed on *stehen*. Some foreign words, especially from Latin and Greek, are stressed on the last syllable (*Organisation*, *Appetit*).

GREETINGS & CIVILITIES
You Should Know

Hello.	goo-ten taak	*Guten Tag.*
Hi.	hah-*lo*	*Hallo.*
Goodbye.	owf *vee*-der-zeh-en	*Auf Wiedersehen.*
Bye.	tshüs	*Tschüss.*
Yes./No.	yaa/nain	*Ja./Nein.*
Excuse me.	ent-*shul*-di-gung	*Entschuldigung.*
May I?	dahrf ikh?	*Darf ich?*
Sorry. (excuse/ forgive me)	ent-*shul*-di-gung	*Entschuldigung.*
Please.	*bit*-te	*Bitte.*
Thank you.	*dahng*-ke	*Danke.*
Many thanks.	fee-len *dahngk*	*Vielen Dank.*
You're welcome.	*bit*-te zair	*Bitte sehr.*

GERMAN

Forms of Address

Frau (lit: Mrs) is regarded as a respectful form of address for women whether they're married or not. *Fräulein*, 'Miss', once used for young women, has become old-fashioned and is slowly disappearing from the spoken language.

companion/friend	froynt/*froyn*-din	*Freund/in*
Gentlemen!	mai-ne *her*-ren!	*Meine Herren!*
Ladies!	mai-ne *daa*-men!	*Meine Damen!*
Mr/Mrs	her/frow	*Herr/Frau*

Often when addressing a professional person or someone of status, the person's title is used.

Doctor ...	(frow) *dok*-tor ...	*(Frau) Doktor ...*
Professor ...	(frow) pro-*fes*-sor ...	*(Frau) Professor ...*

SMALL TALK
Meeting People

When Germans ask *Wie geht es Ihnen?*, 'How are you?', they expect a more or less honest answer, depending on the level of intimacy. Unlike English, 'How are you?' is never used on its own as a form of greeting.

Good day.	*goo*-ten taak	*Guten Tag.*
Good morning.	*goo*-ten *mor*-gen	*Guten Morgen.*
Good afternoon.	*goo*-ten taak	*Guten Tag.*
Good evening.	*goo*-ten *aa*-bent	*Guten Abend.*
Goodnight.	*goo*-te nahkht	*Gute Nacht.*
How are you?	vee *geht* es ee-nen?	*Wie geht es Ihnen?*
Well, thanks.	dahng-ke, goot	*Danke, gut.*
Not too bad.	es *geht*	*Es geht.*
Not so good.	nikht zaw *goot*	*Nicht so gut.*
And you?	unt *ee*-nen?	*Und Ihnen?*
What's your name?	vee hai-sen *zee*?	*Wie heißen Sie?*
My name's ...	ikh *hai*-se ...	*Ich heiße ...*

I'm pleased to meet you.

    ahn-ge-nehm; zair er-*froyt*   *Angenehm; Sehr erfreut.*

Nationalities

You'll find that many country names in German are similar in English. Remember, though, that even if a word looks like the English equivalent, it will have a German pronunciation, for instance, *Japan*, is pronounced *yaa*-pahn

Where are you from?
 vo-hair *kom*-men zee?   *Woher kommen Sie?*

I'm from ...	ikh *kom*-me ows ...	*Ich komme aus ...*
Australia	ows-*traa*-lyen	*Australien*
Canada	*ka*-na-da	*Kanada*
New Zealand	noy-*zeh*-lahnt	*Neuseeland*
the UK	dem fer-*ai*-nikh-ten	*dem Vereinigten*
	ker-nikh-raikh	*Königreich*
the US	den oo-es-*aa*	*den USA*

Occupations

What work do you do?
 ahls vahs *ahr*-bai-ten zee?   *Als was arbeiten Sie?*

I'm (a/an) ...	ikh bin ...	*Ich bin ...*
artist	*künst*-ler/in	*Künstler/in*
business	ge-*shefts*-mahn/	*Geschäftsmann/*
person	ge-*shefts*-frow	*Geschäftsfrau*
chef	kokh/*ker*-khin	*Koch/Köchin*
doctor	ahrtst/*erts*-tin	*Arzt/Ärztin*
engineer	in-zhen-*yerr*/in	*Ingenieur/in*
lawyer	*rekhts*-ahn-vahlt/	*Rechtsanwalt/*
	rekhts-ahn-vel-tin	*Rechtsanwältin*
nurse	*krahng*-ken-pfleh-ger/	*Krankenpfleger/*
	krahng-ken-shves-ter	*Krankenschwester*
office	bü-*raw-ahm*-ge-shtel-ter/	*Büroangestellter/*
worker	bü-*raw-ahm*-ge-shtel-te	*Büroangestellte*
retired	*rent*-ner/*rent*-ne-rin	*Rentner/in*
student	shtu-*dent*/shtu-*den*-tin	*Student/in*
teacher	*lair*-rer/*lair*-re-rin	*Lehrer/in*
unemployed	*ahr*-baits-laws	*arbeitslos*
waiter	*kel*-ner/*kel*-ne-rin	*Kellner/in*

Religion

What's your religion?

vahs ist ee-re re-li-*gyawn*?   *Was ist Ihre Religion?*

I'm not religious.

ikh bin nikht re-li-*gyers*   *Ich bin nicht religiös.*

I'm ...	ikh bin	Ich bin ...
atheist	**ah-te-*ist*/ ah-te-*is*-tin**	*Atheist/in*
Buddhist	**bu-*dist*/bu-*dis*-tin**	*Buddhist/in*
Catholic	**kah-*taw*-lish**	*Katholisch*
Christian	**krist/ *kris*-tin**	*Christ/in*
Hindu	**_hin_-doo**	*Hindu*
Jewish	**yoo-de/*yüü*-din**	*Jude/Jüdin*
Muslim	**_mos_-lem**	*Moslem*

Family

I'd like to	dahrf ikh ee-nen	Darf ich Ihnen ...
introduce my ...	... *for*-shtel-len?	vorstellen?
boyfriend	mai-nen *froynt*	meinen Freund
daughter	mai-ne *tokh*-ter	meine Tochter
girlfriend	mai-ne *froyn*-din	meine Freundin
grandchildren	mai-ne *eng*-kel	meine Enkel
grandparents	mai-ne *graws*-el-tern	meine Großeltern
husband	mai-nen *mahn*	meinen Mann
parents	mai-ne *el*-tern	meine Eltern
son	mai-nen *zawn*	meinen Sohn
wife	mai-ne *frow*	meine Frau

Feelings

How are you feeling?

vee *füü*-len zee zikh?   *Wie fühlen Sie sich?*

What's up?

vahs ist *laws*?   *Was ist los?*

I (don't) like ...

... ge-*felt* meer (nikht)   *... gefällt mir (nicht).*

I'm ...	ikh bin ...	Ich bin ...
angry	*ber-ze*	*böse*
grateful	*dahngk-baar*	*dankbar*
happy	*glük-likh*	*glücklich*
lonely	*ain-zaam*	*einsam*
sad	*trow-rikh*	*traurig*
sleepy	*shlairf-rikh*	*schläfrig*
tired	*müü-de*	*müde*

I'm ...		
right	ikh *haa-be rekht*	*Ich habe recht.*
hot/cold	meer ist *hais/kahlt*	*Mir ist heiß/kalt.*
in a hurry	ikh *haa-be* es *ai-likh*	*Ich habe es eilig.*
sorry	es toot meer *lait*	*Es tut mir leid.*
worried	ikh *mah-khe* meer *zor-gen*	*Ich mache mir Sorgen.*

GERMAN

Useful Phrases

Sure.	klaar!	*Klar!*
Just a minute.	ai-nen mo-*ment!*	*Einen Moment!*
It's (not) important.	es ist (nikht) *vikh-tikh*	*Es ist (nicht) wichtig.*
It's (not) possible.	es ist (nikht) *merk-likh*	*Es ist (nicht) möglich.*
Wait!	*vahr-ten* zee maal!	*Warten Sie mal!*
Good luck!	feel *glük!*	*Viel Glück!*

BREAKING THE LANGUAGE BARRIER

Do you speak English?
shpre-khen zee *eng*-lish?   *Sprechen Sie Englisch?*

Does anyone here speak English?
shprikht heer   *Spricht hier*
yeh-mahnt *eng*-lish?   *jemand Englisch?*

I don't speak ...
ikh shpre-khe kain ...   *Ich spreche kein ...*

Do you understand?
fer-*shteh*-en zee mikh?   *Verstehen Sie mich?*

I understand.
ikh fer-*shteh*-e   *Ich verstehe.*

I don't understand anything at all.
ikh fer-shteh-e   *Ich verstehe*
üü-ber-howpt *nikhts*   *überhaupt nichts.*

Could you translate
that for me, please?
kern-ten zee meer dahs   *Könnten Sie mir das*
bit-te üü-ber-*zet*-tsen?   *bitte übersetzen?*

Could you speak more
slowly please?
kern-ten zee bit-te   *Könnten Sie bitte*
lahng-zah-mer shpre-khen?   *langsamer sprechen?*

Could you please write that down?
kern-ten zee dahs bit-te   *Könnten Sie das bitte*
owf-shrai-ben?   *aufschreiben?*

How do you pronounce this word?
vee *shprikht* mahn   *Wie spricht man*
dee-zes vort *ows*?   *dieses Wort aus?*

Could you repeat that?
kern-ten zee dahs bit-te   *Könnten Sie das bitte*
vee-der-*haw*-len?   *wiederholen?*

How do you say ... in German?
vahs haist ... owf *doytsh*?   *Was heißt ... auf deutsch?*

What does ... mean?
vahs be-*doy*-tet ...?   *Was bedeutet ...?*

BODY LANGUAGE

Germans can be quite reserved, so don't always expect a hearty welcome. When meeting someone for the first time people normally shake hands, and if they know each other well enough, might exchange kisses. This is regarded as perfectly normal between women and between women and men. Men usually avoid it, giving each other a pat on the shoulder instead.

PAPERWORK

address	ah-*drehs*-seh	*Adresse*
age	*ahl*-tehr	*Alter*
birth certificate	geh-*burts*-oor-kun-deh	*Geburtsurkunde*
border	*grehn*-tseh	*Grenze*
customs	tsol	*Zoll*
date of birth	geh-*burts*-daa-tum	*Geburtsdatum*
drivers licence	*füü*-rehr-shain	*Führerschein*
identification	*ows*-vais-pah-pee-reh	*Ausweispapiere*
immigration	*ain*-vahn-deh-rung	*Einwanderung*
marital status	fah-*mee*-lyehn-shtahnt	*Familienstand*
name	*naa*-meh	*Name*
nationality	nah-tsyo-nah-li-*tairt*	*Nationalität*
passport	(*rai*-zeh-)pahs	*(Reise)pass*
passport number	*pahs*-num-mehr	*Passnummer*
place of birth	geh-*burts*-ort	*Geburtsort*
profession	beh-*roof*	*Beruf*
religion	reh-li-*gyawn*	*Religion*
sex	geh-*shlehkht*	*Geschlecht*
visa	*vee*-zum	*Visum*

GERMAN

SIGNS

AUSGANG	EXIT
AUSKUNFT	INFORMATION
DAMEN/FRAUEN	WOMEN
EINGANG	ENTRANCE
EINTRITT FREI	FREE ADMISSION
GEÖFFNET	OPEN
GESCHLOSSEN	CLOSED
HEISS	HOT
HERREN/MÄNNER	MEN
KALT	COLD
KEIN ZUTRITT	NO ENTRY
NOTAUSGANG	EMERGENCY EXIT
RESERVIERT	RESERVED
TOILETTEN	TOILETS
RAUCHEN VERBOTEN	NO SMOKING

GETTING AROUND

Trains are the most common form of transport for long distance. There are some long-distance buses, but mostly buses only ru within cities or connect rural areas with the nearest town. An alte native to trains are the special agencies called *Mitfahrzentralen* whic arrange lifts. You'll find them in all large cities.

Directions

Excuse me, can you help me please?

ent-*shul*-di-gen zee, kern-nen zee meer bit-te *hel*-fen?	*Entschuldigen Sie, können Sie mir bitte helfen?*

Where's ...?	vaw ist ...?	*Wo ist ...?*
How do I get to the ...?	vee *kom*-me ikh ...?	*Wie komme ich ...?*
city centre	tsum *shtaht*-tsen-trum	*zum Stadtzentrum*
metro (underground)	tsur *oo*-baan	*zur U-Bahn*
railway station	tsum *baan*-hawf	*zum Bahnhof*

GERMAN

Can you show me (on the map)?
    kern-nen zee es meer   *Können Sie es mir*
    (owf der kahr-te) tsai-gen?   *(auf der Karte) zeigen?*
Go straight ahead.
    geh-en zee ge-raa-de-ows   *Gehen Sie geradeaus.*
In that direction.
    in dee-zer rikh-tung   *In dieser Richtung.*

Turn left/right	bee-gen zee ...	*Biegen Sie ... links/*
at the ...	*links/rekhts* ahp	*rechts ab.*
bottom	*un-*ten	*unten*
end	ahm *en-*de	*am Ende*
next corner	bai der nairkhs-	*bei der nächsten*
	ten *ek-*ke	*Ecke*
top	*aw-*ben	*oben*
traffic lights	bai der *ahm-*pel	*bei der Ampel*

back	tsu-*rük*	*zurück*
behind	*hin-*ter	*hinter*
far	vait	*weit*
here	heer	*hier*
in front of	fawr	*vor*
near	*naa-*e	*nahe*
opposite	geh-gen-*üü*-ber	*gegenüber*

Booking Tickets
Where can I buy a ticket?
    vaw kahn ikh ai-ne   *Wo kann ich eine*
    *faar-*kahr-te kow-fen?   *Fahrkarte kaufen?*
I want to go to ...
    ikh merkh-te naakh   *Ich möchte nach*
    ... faa-ren   *... fahren.*

GERMAN

I'd like ...	ikh *merkh*-te ...	Ich möchte ...
a one-way ticket	ai-ne *ain*-fah-khe faar-kahr-te	eine einfache Fahrkarte
a return ticket	ai-ne *rük*-faar-kahr-teh	eine Rückfahrkarte
two tickets	tsvai *faar*-kahr-ten	zwei Fahrkarten

with ... concession	mit faar-prais-er-*mair*-si-gung füür ...	mit Fahrpreiser-mäßigung für ...
children's	*kin*-der	Kinder
pensioner	*rent*-ner	Rentner
student	shtu-*den*-ten	Studenten

| 1st class | *er*-ster klahs-se | erster Klasse |
| 2nd class | *tsvai*-ter klahs-se | zweiter Klasse |

Bus

Where do buses for ... stop?
vaw hahl-ten dee bus-se naakh ...?
Wo halten die Busse nach ...?

Which bus goes to ...?
vel-kher bus fairt naakh ...? *Welcher Bus fährt nach ...?*

Does this bus go to ...?
fairt *dee*-zer bus naakh ...? *Fährt dieser Bus nach ...?*

What time's the ... bus?	vahn fairt der ... bus?	Wann fährt der ... Bus?
first	*ers*-te	erste
last	*lets*-te	letzte
next	*nairkhs*-te	nächste

Could you let me know when we get to ...?
kern-ten zee meer bit-te be-*shait* zaa-gen, ven veer in ... *ahn*-kom-men?
Könnten Sie mir bitte Bescheid sagen, wenn wir in ... ankommen?

I want to get off!
ikh merkh-te *ows*-shtai-gen! *Ich möchte aussteigen!*

GERMAN

Metro

Where can I buy a ticket?
vaw kahn ikh ai-ne
faar-kahr-te kow-fen?

Wo kann ich eine
Fahrkarte kaufen?

Is there a ... ticket?   gipt es ai-ne ...
                          -faar-kahr-te?

Gibt es eine ...
-fahrkarte

daily   *taa*-ges   *Tages*
weekly   *vo*-khen   *Wochen*

Which line takes me to ...?
vel-khe leen-ye fairt naakh ...?   *Welche Linie fährt nach ...?*

Train

There are two extra-rapid trains
– the older IC (Inter City) and
the modern ICE (Inter City
Express). Both services only
stop in major cities and have
special fares. Normal speed
trains service the smaller cities.

> **THEY MAY SAY ...**
>
> er ist *ows*-ge-bukht
> It's full.

For the IC you have to pay a supplement in addition to the normal
ticket, for the ICE there are special tickets.

GERMAN

Is this the right platform
for the train to ...?
fairt der tsook naakh ...
owf *dee*-zem baan-shtaik ahp?

Fährt der Zug nach ...
auf diesem Bahnsteig ab?

Is this the train to ...?
ist *dahs* der tsook naakh ...?

Ist das der Zug nach ...?

Does this train stop at ...?
helt *dee*-zer tsook in ...?

Hält dieser Zug in ...?

Is the train from ... late?
haht der tsook ows ...
fer-*shpair*-tung?

Hat der Zug aus ...
Verspätung?

How long will it be delayed?
vee-feel fer-*shpair*-tung
virt air haa-ben?

Wieviel Verspätung
wird er haben?

Taxi

Are you free?
> **zint** zee *frai*?   *Sind Sie frei?*

How much is it to go to ...?
> **vahs** *kos*-tet es bis ...? *Was kostet es bis ...?*

Can you take me to the/this ...?	**kern**-nen zee mikh ... **bring**-en?	*Können Sie mich ... bringen?*
airport	tsum *flook*-haa-fen	*zum Flughafen*
city centre	tsum *shtaht*-tsen-trum	*zum Stadtzentrum*
hotel	tsoo dee-zem haw-*tel*	*zu diesem Hotel*
railway station	tsum baan-hawf	*zum Bahnhof*
street	tsoo *dee*-zer shtraa-se	*zu dieser Straße*

Continue!
> *vai*-ter!   *Weiter!*

Please slow down.
> faa-ren zee bit-te *lahng*-zah-mer *Fahren Sie bitte langsamer.*

The next street to the left/right.
> *bee*-gen zee ahn der *nairkhs*-ten *ek*-ke lingks/rekhts ahp *Biegen Sie an der nächsten Ecke links/rechts ab.*

Here's fine, thanks.
> *hahl*-ten zee bit-te *heer* *Halten Sie bitte hier.*

Please stop at the next corner.
> *hahl*-ten zee bit-te ahn der *nairkhs*-ten *ek*-ke *Halten Sie bitte an der nächsten Ecke.*

Stop here!
> *hahl*-ten zee *heer*! *Halten Sie hier!*

Please wait here.
> *bit*-te vaar-ten zee *heer* *Bitte warten Sie hier.*

GERMAN

Useful Phrases

What time does the ... leave?	vahn fairt ... ahp?	*Wann fährt ... ab?*
What time does the ... arrive?	vahn komt ... ahn?	*Wann kommt ... an?*
boat	dahs bawt	*das Boot*
bus	der bus	*der Bus*
train	der tsook	*der Zug*
tram	dee *shtraa-sen-baan*	*die Straßenbahn*
underground	dee *oo*-baan	*die U-Bahn*

Car

I'd like to hire a car.
ikh merkh-te ain *ow*-taw mee-ten
Ich möchte ein Auto mieten.

How much is it per day/week?
vee-feel *kos*-tet es praw taak/*vo*-khe?
Wieviel kostet es pro Tag/Woche?

Does that include ...?	ist ... *in*-be-grif-fen?	*Ist ... inbegriffen?*
insurance	dee fer-*zikh*-e-rung	*die Versicherung*
mileage	dahs ki-lo-*meh*-ter-gelt	*das Kilometergeld*

Where's the next petrol station?
vaw ist dee nairkhs-te *tahngk*-shtel-le?
Wo ist die nächste Tankstelle?

I want ... litres of petrol (gas).
geh-ben zee meer ... lee-ter ben-*tseen*
Geben Sie mir ... Liter Benzin.

I need a mechanic.
ikh brow-khe ai-nen me-*khaa*-ni-ker
Ich brauche einen Mechaniker.

I have a flat tyre.
ikh haa-be ai-ne *pahn*-ne
Ich habe eine Panne.

GERMAN

air	luft	*Luft*
battery	bah-te-*ree*	*Batterie*
brakes	*brem*-zen	*Bremsen*
diesel	*dee*-zel	*Diesel*
engine	maw-*tor*	*Motor*
gear	gahng	*Gang*
ignition	*tsün*-dung	*Zündung*
indicator	*bling*-ker	*Blinker*
jack	*vaa*-gen-heh-ber	*Wagenheber*
lights	*shain*-ver-fer	*Scheinwerfer*
oil	erl	*Öl*
... petrol (gas)	... ben-*tseen*	*... Benzin*
leaded	fer-*blai*-tes	*verbleites*
unleaded	blai-*frai*-es	*bleifreies*
radiator	*küü*-ler	*Kühler*
(spare) tyre	(re-zer-ve-)*rai*-fen	*(Reserve)reifen*
windscreen	*vint*-shuts-shai-be	*Windschutzscheibe*

ACCOMMODATION
At the Hotel

GERMAN

Do you have any
rooms available?
    haa-ben zee nokh
    tsim-mer frai?
    *Haben Sie noch
    Zimmer frei?*

SIGNS	
AUSGEBUCHT	NO VACANCIES
VOLL	FULL
ZIMMER	ROOMS
FREI	AVAILABLE

I'd/We'd like ...	ikh merkh-te/	*Ich möchte/*
	veer merkh-ten ain ...	*Wir möchten ein ...*
a single room	*ain*-tsel-tsim-mer	*Einzelzimmer*
a double room	*dop*-pel-tsim-mer	*Doppelzimmer*
to share a dorm	bet in ai-nem *shlaaf*-zaal	*Bett in einem Schlafsaal*
a room with a bathroom	tsim-mer mit *baat*	*Zimmer mit Bad*

How much is it per night/person?
    vee-feel *kos*-tet es praw   *Wieviel kostet es pro*
    nahkht/per-zawn?   *Nacht/Person?*

Can I see the room?
    kahn ikh dahs   *Kann ich das*
    tsim-mer *zeh*-en?   *Zimmer sehen?*

Where's the bathroom?
    vaw ist dahs *baat*?   *Wo ist das Bad?*

Do you have a safe where
I can leave my valuables?
    haa-ben zee ai-nen *sehf*,   *Haben Sie einen Safe,*
    in dehm ikh mai-ne   *in dem ich meine*
    ***vert*-zah-khen lahs-sen kahn?**   *Wertsachen lassen kann?*

I've locked myself out of my room.
    ikh haa-be mikh ows mai-   *Ich habe mich aus meinem*
    nem *tsim*-mer *ows*-ge-shpert   *Zimmer ausgesperrt.*

I'm/We are leaving now.
    ikh *rai*-ze/veer *rai*-zen yetst *ahp*   *Ich reise/Wir reisen jetzt ab.*

I'd like to pay the bill.
    kahn ikh bit-te dee   *Kann ich bitte die*
    ***rekh*-nung haa-ben?**   *Rechnung haben?*

(Also see Camping, page 110.)

AROUND TOWN
At the Post Office

I'd like to send a(n) ...	**ikh merkh-te ... zen-den**	*Ich möchte ... senden.*
aerogram	**ai-nen *luft*-post-laikht-breef**	*einen Luftpost-leichtbrief*
fax	**ain *fahks***	*ein Fax*
letter	**ai-nen *breef***	*einen Brief*
parcel	**ain pah-*keht***	*ein Paket*
postcard	**ai-ne *post*-kahr-te**	*eine Postkarte*
telegram	**ain te-le-*grahm***	*ein Telegramm*

How much is the postage?
   vee-feel kos-tet dahs *por*-to?   *Wieviel kostet das Porto?*
I'd like some stamps.
   ikh merkh-te   *Ich möchte*
   breef-mahr-ken kow-fen   *Briefmarken kaufen.*
I'd like to have my mail forwarded.
   ikh merkh-te mai-ne *post*   *Ich möchte meine Post*
   naakh-zen-den lahs-sen   *nachsenden lassen.*

airmail	*luft*-post	*Luftpost*
counter	*shahl*-ter	*Schalter*
destination	be-*shtim*-mungks-ort	*Bestimmungsort*
envelope	*um*-shlaak	*Umschlag*
mailbox	*breef*-kahs-ten	*Briefkasten*
parcel	pah-*keht*	*Paket*
post office box	*post*-fahkh	*Postfach*
poste restante	*post*-laa-gernt	*postlagernd*

Telephone

Where can I make a phone call?
   vaw kahn ikh   *Wo kann ich*
   teh-le-fo-*nee*-ren?   *telefonieren?*
I want to make a
long-distance call to ...
   bit-te ain *fern*-ge-   *Bitte ein*
   Shprairkh naakh ...   *Ferngespräch nach ...*
I want to make a
reverse-charges (collect) call.
   ikh *merkh*-te ain   *Ich möchte ein*
   er-ge-shprairkh   *R-Gespräch.*
The number is ...
   dee *num*-mer ist ...   *Die Nummer ist ...*
It's engaged.
   es ist be-*zetst*   *Es ist besetzt.*
I've been cut off.
   ikh bin *un*-ter-bro-khen   *Ich bin unterbrochen*
   vor-den   *worden.*

GERMAN

I'd like to speak to (Mrs Schmidt).

ikh merkh-te (frow *shmit*) shpre-khen	*Ich möchte (Frau Schmidt) sprechen.*

This is ...	**heer ist ...**	*Hier ist ...*

area code	**fawr-vaal**	*Vorwahl*
directory enquiries	**teh-le-*fawn*-ows-kunft**	*Telefonauskunft*
pay phone	**münts-teh-le-fawn**	*Münztelefon*
phone book	**teh-le-*fawn*-bookh**	*Telefonbuch*
phone box	**teh-le-*fawn*-tsel-le**	*Telefonzelle*
phonecard	**teh-le-*fawn*-*kahr*-te**	*Telefonkarte*
telephone	**teh-le-*fawn***	*Telefon*

Internet

Is there a local Internet cafe?

gibt ehs ain in-tehr-neht kah-fay in dehr *nair*-eh?	*Gibt es ein Internet Café in der Nähe?*

I want to connect to the Internet.

ikh merkh-teh dahs in-tehr-neht geh-*brow*-khehn	*Ich möchte das Internet gebrauchen.*

I'd like to send an email.

ikh mus ay-neh ee-mayl *ahb*-shi-kehn	*Ich muß eine E-mail abschicken.*

At the Bank

I'd like to change some travellers cheques.

ikh merkh-te *rai*-ze-sheks *ain*-ler-zen	*Ich möchte Reiseschecks einlösen.*

I'd like to exchange some money.

ikh merkh-te *gelt* um-tow-shen	*Ich möchte Geld umtauschen.*

What's the exchange rate?

vee ist der *vek*-sel-kurs?	*Wie ist der Wechselkurs?*

How much do I get for ...?

vee-feel be-*kom*-me ikh füür ...?	*Wieviel bekomme ich für ...?*

GERMAN

Can I have money transferred
here from my bank?
kahn ikh heer-hair *gelt*	*Kann ich hierher Geld*
fon mai-ner *bahngk*	*von meiner Bank*
ü-ber-*vai*-zen lahs-sen?	*überweisen lassen?*

amount	be-*traak*	*Betrag*
bank account	*bahngk*-kon-to	*Bankkonto*
cash	baar/*baar*-gelt	*bar/Bargeld*
cashier (m/f)	kahs-*see*-rer/	*Kassierer/in*
	kahs-*see*-re-rin	
cheque	*shek*-kahr-te	*Scheckkarte*
coin/s	*mün*-tse/n	*Münze/n*
commission	ge-*büür*	*Gebühr*
credit card	kre-*deet*-kahr-te	*Kreditkarte*
currency	*vair*-rung	*Währung*
Euro	*oy*-roh	*Euro*
exchange	*gelt*-vek-sel	*Geldwechsel*
receipt	*kvit*-tung	*Quittung*
signature	*un*-ter-shrift	*Unterschrift*
transfer	ü-ber-*vai*-zung	*Überweisung*

INTERESTS & ENTERTAINMENT
Sightseeing

Do you have a guidebook/street map?
haa-ben zee ai-nen	*Haben Sie einen*
***rai*-ze-füü-rer/*shtaht*-plaan?**	*Reiseführer/Stadtplan?*

What are the main attractions?
vahs zint dee *howpt*-zeh-	*Was sind die*
ens-vür-dikh-kai-ten?	*Hauptsehenswürdigkeiten?*

What's that?
vahs ist *dahs?*	*Was ist das?*

Can I take photographs?
dahrf ikh faw-to-grah-*fee*-ren?	*Darf ich fotografieren?*

What time does it open/close?
vahn mahkht es *owftsoo?*	*Wann macht es auf/zu?*

castle	shlos	*Schloss*
cathedral	dawm	*Dom*
church	*kir*-khe	*Kirche*
fountain	*brun*-nen	*Brunnen*
harbour	*haa*-fen	*Hafen*
main square	*howpt*-plahts	*Hauptplatz*
monument	*dengk*-maal	*Denkmal*
museum	mu-*zeh*-um	*Museum*
old part of the city	*ahlt*-shtaht	*Altstadt*
palace	pah-*lahst*	*Palast*
ruins	ru-*ee*-nen	*Ruinen*
stadium	shtaa-di-*on*	*Stadion*
statues	shtaa-*tu*-en	*Statuen*
tomb	graap	*Grab*
tower	turm	*Turm*
zoo	*teer*-gahr-ten	*Tiergarten*

Going Out

What's there to do in the evenings?

vahs kahn mahn aa-bents un-ter-*neh*-men? — *Was kann man abends unternehmen?*

Is there a concert on tonight?

gipt es hoy-te aa-bent ain kon-*tsert*? — *Gibt es heute abend ein Konzert?*

What band is playing tonight?

vahs füür ai-ne *bent* shpeelt hoy-te? — *Was für eine Band spielt heute?*

Would you like to do something ...?	hahst doo lust, ... vahs tsoo un-ter-*neh*-men?	*Hast du Lust, ... was zu unternehmen?*
tonight	hoy-te *aa*-bent	*heute abend*
tomorrow	*mor*-gen	*morgen*

cinema	*kee*-no	*Kino*
concert	kon-*tsert*	*Konzert*
dancing	*tahn*-tsen	*tanzen*
club	*dis*-ko	*Disco*

GERMAN

party	*paa*-ti	Party
performance	*owf*-füü-rung	Aufführung
pub	*knai*-pe	Kneipe
restaurant	re-sto-*rō*	Restaurant
theatre	teh-*aa*-ter	Theater

Sports & Interests

What are your favourite hobbies?
vahs zint dai-ne *ho*-bees? *Was sind deine Hobbys?*

Do you like ...?	mer-gen zee ...?	Mögen Sie ...?
arts	kunst	Kunst
literature	li-te-rah-*toor*	Literatur
music	mu-*zeek*	Musik
sports	shport	Sport
travel	*rai*-zen	Reisen

Do you play/go ...?	shpee-len zee ...?	Spielen Sie ...?
basketball	*baas*-ket-bahl	Basketball
cycling	*raat*-shport	Radsport
diving	*tow*-khen	Tauchen
fencing	*fekh*-ten	Fechten
figure skating	*ais*-kunst-lowf	Eiskunstlauf
hang-gliding	*drah*-khen-flee-gen	Drachenfliegen
ice hockey	*ais*-hok-ki	Eishockey
ice skating	*ais*-low-fen	Eislaufen
kayaking	*kaa*-yahk-faa-ren	Kajakfahren
paragliding	*glait*-shirm-flee-gen	Gleitschirmfliegen
parachuting	*fahl*-shirm-shpring-en	Fallschirmspringen
rafting	*raaf*-ting	Rafting
rowing	*roo*-dern	Rudern
sailing	*zeh*-geln	Segeln
shuttlecock	*feh*-der-bahl	Federball
speed skating	*ais*-shnel-lowf	Eisschnelllauf
table tennis	*tish*-ten-nis	Tischtennis
volleyball	*vol*-li-bahl	Volleyball

GERMAN

Festivals

Karneval (northwest Germany); *Fasching* (south Germany)
the carnival starts at 11 minutes past 11 o'clock on 11 November and lasts until Ash Wednesday, *Aschermittwoch*. The main celebrations are held during the last week.

Maibäume (Maypole)
the erection of a Maypole in spring, either of tall fir or birch, is a 400-year-old tradition. The Maypole is decorated with colourful ribbons, and in rural regions a dance around the Maypole is held on 1 May.

Oktoberfest
held in Munich at the end of September to early October, this is Germany's biggest festival. It starts with a procession of beer brewers and their traditional horses and carts. The opening's highlight is the tapping of the first beer barrel by the mayor of Munich, who then shouts *O'zapft is!* 'the barrel is tapped'.

CHEERS!

Cheers!
prawst!
ain *praw-zit* der
ge-müüt-likh-kait!
oahns, tsvoa, ksuf-fah!

Prost!
Ein Prosit der Gemütlichkeit!
(lit: cheers on the friendliness!)
Oans, zwoa, Gsuffa!
(lit: one, two, booze!)

GERMAN

Weihnachten (Christmas)
Germany's most important celebration. The main celebration is on Christmas Eve. After traditional dishes of stuffed goose, *Weihnachtsgans* or Christmas carp, *Weihnachtskarpfen,* many people go to midnight Mass.

Merry Christmas!   *frer*-li-khe   *Fröhliche*
                                 vai-nakh-ten!   *Weihnachten!*

IN THE COUNTRY
Weather

What's the weather like?

vee ist dahs *vet*-ter?		*Wie ist das Wetter?*

The weather's ... today.	dahs vet-ter ist hoy-te ...	*Das Wetter ist heute ...*
cloudy	*vol*-kikh	*wolkig*
cold	kahlt	*kalt*
fine	shern	*schön*
foggy	*neh*-blikh	*neblig*
frosty	*fros*-tikh	*frostig*
hot	hais	*heiß*
muggy	shvüül	*schwül*
stormy	*shtür*-mish	*stürmisch*
warm	vahrm	*warm*
windy	*vin*-dikh	*windig*

Camping

Am I/Are we allowed to camp here?

kahn ikh/kern-nen veer heer *tsel*-ten?	*Kann ich/Können wir hier zelten?*

Is there a campsite nearby?

gipt es in der nair-e ai-nen *kem*-ping-plahts?	*Gibt es in der Nähe einen Campingplatz?*

How much do you charge ...?	vee-feel be-*rekh*-nen zee ...?	*Wieviel berechnen Sie ...?*
per person	praw per-*zawn*	*pro Person*
for a tent	füür ain *tselt*	*für ein Zelt*

can opener	*daw*-zen-erf-ner	Dosenöffner
firewood	*bren*-holts	Brennholz
hammock	*heng*-e-maht-te	Hängematte
kettle	*kes*-sel	Kessel
matches	*shtraikh*-herl-tser	Streichhölzer
penknife	*tah*-shen-mes-ser	Taschenmesser
sleeping bag	*shlaaf*-zahk	Schlafsack
stove	hert	Herd
tent	tselt	Zelt
tent pegs	*tselt*-hair-ring-e	Zeltheringe
torch (flashlight)	*tah*-shen-lahm-pe	Taschenlampe

FOOD

breakfast	*früü*-shtük	Frühstück
lunch	*mit*-taak-es-sen	Mittagessen
dinner	*aa*-bent-es-sen	Abendessen

Vegetarian Meals

Do you serve vegetarian meals?

| haa-ben zee owkh ve-ge-*taa*-ri-she kost? | Haben Sie auch vegetarische Kost? |

I'm a vegetarian.

| ikh bin ve-ge-*taa*-ri-er/ ve-ge-*taa*-ri-er-in | Ich bin Vegetarier/in. (m/f) |

I'm a vegan.

| ikh bin maa-kro-bi-*aw*-ti-ker/in | Ich bin Makrobiotiker/in. (m/f) |

I don't eat ...	ikh *es*-se ...	Ich esse ...
chicken	kain *hüün*-khen	kein Hühnchen
fish	kai-nen fish	keinen Fisch
meat	kain flaish	kein Fleisch
pork	kain shvai-ne-flaish	kein Schweinefleisch

Staple Foods & Condiments

bread roll	*brert*-khen	*Brötchen*
cinnamon	tsimt	*Zimt*
cloves	*nel*-ken	*Nelken*
croissant	kro-ah-*sō*	*Croissant*
fish	fish	*Fisch*
fruit	*frükh*-te/awpst	*Früchte/Obst*
garlic	*knawp*-lowkh	*Knoblauch*
ham	*shing*-ken	*Schinken*
herbs	*kroy*-ter	*Kräuter*
meat	flaish	*Fleisch*
mustard	zenf	*Senf*
parsley	peh-ter-*zee*-lye	*Petersilie*
pepper	*pfef*-fer	*Pfeffer*
potatoes	kahr-*to*-feln	*Kartoffeln*
salt	zahlts	*Salz*
tomato sauce	to-maa-ten-*ket*-shahp	*Tomatenketchup*
vegetables	ge-*müü*-ze	*Gemüse*
vinegar	*es*-sikh	*Essig*

Breakfast Menu

cereal	tse-re-*aa*-li-en	*Zerealien*
honey	*haw*-nikh	*Honig*
jam	...-mahr-me-*laa*-de	...-*marmelade*
apricot	ah-pri-*kaw*-zen	*Aprikosen*
strawberry	*ert*-bair	*Erdbeer*
juice	*frukht*-zahft	*Fruchtsaft* ...
marmalade	o-rō-zhen-mahr-me-*laa*-de	*Orangenmarmelade*
muesli	*müüs*-li	*Müesli*
porridge	*haa*-fer-brai	*Haferbrei*
sausage	vurst	*Wurst*
boiled eggs	ge-*kokh*-te *ai*-er	*gekochte Eier*
fried eggs	*shpee*-gel-ai	*Spiegelei*
scrambled eggs	*rüür*-ai-er	*Rühreier*

GERMAN

MENU DECODER

Starters & Buffet Meals

Aufschnitt	*owf*-shnit	cold cuts
Bauernsuppe	*bow*-ern-zup-pe	'farmer's soup' (cabbage & sausage)
belegtes Brot	be-*lehk*-tes brawt	open sandwich
Brezel	*breh*-tsel	pretzel
Fleischbrühe	*flaish*-brüü-e	bouillon
Gemüsesuppe	ge-*müü*-ze-zup-pe	vegetable soup
geräucherte Forelle	ge-*roy*-kher-te fo-*rel*-le	smoked trout
geräucherter Lachs	ge-*roy*-kher-ter lahks	smoked salmon
geräucherter Schinken	ge-*roy*-kher-ter *shing*-ken	smoked ham
Linsensuppe	*lin*-zen-zup-pe	lentil soup
Pfannkuchen	*pfahn*-koo-khen	pancake
Rollmops	*rol*-mops	pickled herrings
Russische Eier	*rus*-si-she ai-er	eggs with mayonnaise
Zwiebelsuppe	*tsvee*-bel-zup-pe	onion soup
Wurst	vurst	sausage
Wurstplatte	*vurst*-plaht-te	cold cuts
Blutwurst	*bloot*-vurst	blood sausage
Bockwurst	*bok*-vurst	pork sausage
Bratwurst	*braat*-vurst	fried pork sausage
Leberwurst	*leh*-ber-vurst	liver sausage
Weißwurst	*vais*-vurst	veal sausage
Zwiebelwurst	*tsvee*-bel-vurst	liver-and-onion sausage

Main Dishes

Brathuhn	*braat*-hoon	roast chicken
Eintopf/Ragout	*ain*-topf/rah-*goo*	stew
Frikadelle	fri-kah-*del*-le	meatball
Hackbraten	*hahk*-braa-ten	meatloaf
Hasenpfeffer	*haa*-zen-pfef-fer	hare stew with mushroom and onion

GERMAN

GERMAN

Holsteiner Schnitzel	*hol*-shtai-ner *shnit*-tsel	veal schnitzel with fried egg, accompanied by seafood
Kohlroulade	kawl-ru-*laa*-de	cabbage leaves stuffed with minced meat
Königsberger Klopse	*ker*-nikhs-ber-ger *klop*-se	meatballs in a sour-cream-and-caper sauce
Labskaus	*lahps*-kows	thick meat-and-potato stew
Schlachtplatte	*shlahkht*-plaht-te	selection of pork and sausage
Schmorbraten	*shmawr*-braa-ten	beef pot roast
Schweinebraten	*shvai*-ne-braa-ten	roast pork
Wiener Schnitzel	*vee*-ner shnit-tsel	crumbed veal

Dessert & Pastries

Apfelstrudel	ahp-fel-*shtroo*-del	apple strudel
Cremespeise	*krehm*-shpai-ze	mousse
Gebäck	ge-*bek*	pastries
Kompott	kom-pot	stewed fruit
Königstorte	*ker*-nikhs-tor-te	rum-flavoured fruit cake
Kuchen	*koo*-khen	cake
Obstsalat	*awpst*-zah-laat	fruit salad
Schwarzwälder Kirschtorte	*shvahrts*-vel-der *kirsh*-tor-te	Black Forest cake (chocolate layer cake filled with cream and cherries)
Spekulatius	shpe-ku-*laa*-tsi-us	almond biscuits
Torte	*tor*-te	layer cake
Nürnberger Lebkuchen	*nürn*-ber-ger *lehp*-koo-khen	spicy biscuits with chocolate, nuts, fruit peel and honey

Non-Alcoholic Drinks

malt beer	*mahlts*-beer	*Malzbier*
mineral water	mi-ne-*raal*-vahs-ser	*Mineralwasser*
orange juice	o-*rö*-zhen-zahft	*Orangensaft*
water	*vahs*-ser	*Wasser*
coffee	*kahf*-feh	*Kaffee*
latte	*milkh*-kahf-feh	*Milchkaffee*
tea	teh	*Tee*
Vienna coffee (black, topped with whipped cream)	*kahf*-feh mit *zaa*-ne	*Kaffee mit Sahne*
with/without ...	mit/*aw*-ne ...	*mit/ohne ...*
cream	*zaa*-ne	*Sahne*
milk	milkh	*Milch*
sugar	*tsuk*-ker	*Zucker*

Alcoholic Drinks

apple brandy	*ahp*-fel-shnahps	*Apfelschnaps*
apple cider	*ahp*-fel-vain	*Apfelwein*
champagne	zekt/ shahm-*pahn*-yer	*Sekt/ Champagner*
spirit made from grain	shnahps	*Schnaps*
draught beer	beer fom *fahs*	*Bier vom Fass*
bitter	*ahlt*-beer	*Altbier*
dark beer	*bok*-beer	*Bockbier*
wheat-based beer	*vai*-tsen-beer	*Weizenbier*
strong beer	*shtahrk*-beer	*Starkbier*
... wine	... vain	*... wein*
dry	*trok*-ken	*trocken*
mulled	glüü	*Glüh*
red	rawt	*Rot*
sparkling	showm	*Schaum*
sweet	züüs	*süß*
white	vais	*Weiß*

GERMAN

GERMAN

AT THE MARKET

Basics

bread	brawt	Brot
butter	*but*-ter	Butter
cereal	tse-re-*aa*-li-en	Zerealien
cheese	*kair*-ze	Käse
chocolate	sho-ko-*laa*-de	Schokolade
croissant	kro-ah-*só*	Croissant
eggs	*ai*-er	Eier
flour	mayl	Mehl
margarine	mahr-gah-*ree*-ne	Margarine
marmalade	o-rö-zhen-mahr-me-*laa*-de	Orangenmarmelade
milk	milkh	Milch
mineral water	mi-ne-*raal*-vahs-ser	Mineralwasser
olive oil	o-*lee*-ven-erl/erl	Olivenöl/Öl
pasta	*pahs*-tah/*noo*-deln	Pasta/Nudeln
rice	rais	Reis
sugar	*tsuk*-kehr	Zucker
yogurt	*yaw*-gurt	Joghurt

Meat & Poultry

beef	*rint*-flaish	Rindfleisch
chicken	*hüün*-khen	Hühnchen
ham	*shing*-ken	Schinken
meat	flaish	Fleisch
pork	*shvai*-neh-flaish	Schweinefleisch
sausage	vurst	Wurst
turkey	*troot*-haan	Truthahn
veal	*kahlp*-flaish	Kalbfleisch

Seafood

fish	fish	Fisch
lobster	*hum*-mer	Hummer
mussels	*mu*-sheln	Muschel
oysters	*ows*-tern	Austern
shrimp	gahr-*neh*-le	Garnele

AT THE MARKET

Vegetables

beans	*baw*-ne	Bohnen
beetroot	*raw*-te *beh*-te	Rote Beete
cabbage	kawl	Kohl
carrot	kah-*rot*-te	Karotte
cauliflower	*bloo*-men-kawl	Blumenkohl
celery	*zel*-le-ree	Sellerie
cucumber	*gur*-ke	Gurke
lettuce	*kopf*-zah-laat	Kopfsalat
mushroom	pilts	Pilz
onion	*tsvee*-bel	Zwiebel
peas	*erp*-se	Erbse
potatoes	kahr-*to*-feln	Kartoffeln
pumpkin	*kür*-bis	Kürbis
spinach	shpi-*naat*	Spinat
tomato	to-*maa*-te	Tomate
vegetables	ge-*müü*-ze	Gemüse

Pulses

broad beans	*sow*-baw-ne	Saubohne
chickpeas	*keekh*-ehr-erb-se	Kichererbse
lentils	*leen*-se	Linse

Fruit

apple	*ahp*-fel	Apfel
apricot	ah-pri-*kaw*-ze	Aprikose
banana	bah-*naa*-ne	Banane
date	*daht*-tel	Dattel
fruit	*frükh*-te/awpst	Früchte/Obst
grapes	*vain*-trow-be	Weintraube
lemon	tsi-*traw*-ne	Zitrone
orange	ahp-fel-*zee*-ne	Apfelsine
peach	*pfir*-zikh	Pfirsich
pear	*bir*-ne	Birne
plum	*pflow*-me	Pflaume
strawberry	*ert*-bair-re	Erdbeere

GERMAN

SHOPPING

Do you accept credit cards?

neh-men zee kre-*deet*-kahr-ten?   *Nehmen Sie Kreditkarten?*

bakery	bek-ke-*rai*	*Bäckerei*
bookshop	*bookh*-hahn-dlung	*Buchhandlung*
chemist	ah-po-*teh*-ke	*Apotheke*
delicatessen	de-li-kah-*tes*-s en-ge-sheft	*Delikatessen- geschäft*
grocer	*leh*-bens-mit-tel-laa-den	*Lebensmittelladen*
hairdresser	fri-*zerr*	*Friseur*
laundry	ve-she-*rai*	*Wäscherei*
market	mahrkt	*Markt*
newsagent	*tsai*-tungks-hen-dler	*Zeitungshändler*
supermarket	*zoo*-per-mahrkt	*Supermarkt*

Essential Groceries

I'd like to buy ...	ikh *merkh*-te ...	*Ich möchte ...*
batteries	baht-te-*ree*-en	*Batterien*
bread	brawt	*Brot*
butter	*but*-ter	*Butter*
cheese	*kair*-ze	*Käse*
chocolate	sho-ko-*laa*-de	*Schokolade*
coffee	*kahf*-feh	*Kaffee*
ham	*shing*-ken	*Schinken*
matches	*shtraikh*-herl-tser	*Streichhölzer*
milk	milkh	*Milch*
mineral water	mi-ne-*raal*-vahs-ser	*Mineralwasser*
flour	mehl	*Mehl*
shampoo	shahm-*poo*	*Shampoo*
soap	*zai*-fe	*Seife*
sugar	*tsuk*-ker	*Zucker*
tea	teh	*Tee*
toilet paper	to-ah-*let*-ten-pah-peer	*Toilettenpapier*
toothpaste	*tsaan*-pahs-tah	*Zahnpasta*
washing powder	*ahsh*-pul-ver	*Waschpulver*
yogurt	*yaw*-gurt	*Joghurt*

Souvenirs

beer stein/mug	*beer*-krook	*Bierkrug*
cuckoo clock	kuk-*kuks*-oor	*Kuckucksuhr*
earrings	*awr*-ring-e	*Ohrringe*
embroidery	shtik-ke-*rai*	*Stickerei*
handicraft	*kunst*-hahnt-verk	*Kunsthandwerk*
necklace	*hahls*-ket-te	*Halskette*
porcelain	por-tsel-*laan*	*Porzellan*
ring	ring	*Ring*

Clothing

belt	*gür*-tel	*Gürtel*
bra	*büs*-ten-hahl-ter	*Büstenhalter*
button	knopf	*Knopf*
clothing	*klai*-dung	*Kleidung*
coat	*mahn*-tel	*Mantel*
dress	klait	*Kleid*
jacket	*yahk*-ke	*Jacke*
jumper (sweater)	*pul*-law-ver	*Pullover*
raincoat	*reh*-gen-mahn-tel	*Regenmantel*
panties	*shlüp*-fer; slip	*Schlüpfer*
scarf	*hahls*-tookh	*Halstuch*
shirt	hemt	*Hemd*
shoes	*shoo*-e	*Schuhe*
skirt	rok	*Rock*
trousers	*haw*-ze	*Hose*
T-shirt	*tee*-shert	*T-Shirt*

GERMAN

GERMAN

Materials

brass	*mes*-sing	*Messing*
cotton	*bowm*-vol-le	*Baumwolle*
gold	golt	*Gold*
leather	*leh*-der	*Leder*
linen	*lai*-nen	*Leinen*
silk	*zai*-de	*Seide*
silver	*zil*-ber	*Silber*
velvet	zahmt	*Samt*
wool	vol-le	*Wolle*

Colours

black	shvahrts	*schwarz*
blue	blow	*blau*
brown	brown	*braun*
green	grüün	*grün*
grey	grow	*grau*
orange	o-*rôzh*	*orange*
pink	*raw*-zah	*rosa*
purple	*lee*-lah	*lila*
red	rawt	*rot*
white	vais	*weiß*
yellow	gelp	*gelb*

Toiletries

comb	kahm	*Kamm*
condoms	kon-*daw*-me	*Kondome*
deodorant	de-o-do-*rahnt*	*Deodorant*
moisturiser	*foykh*-tikh-kaits-krehm	*Feuchtigkeitscreme*
razor	rah-*zee*-rer	*Rasierer*
razor blades	rah-*zeer*-kling-en	*Rasierklingen*
sanitary napkins	*daa*-men-bin-den	*Damenbinden*
shampoo	shahm-*poo*	*Shampoo*
shaving cream	rah-*zeer*-krehm	*Rasiercreme*
sunscreen	zon-nen-shuts-krehm	*Sonnenschutzcreme*
tampons	tahm-*pons*	*Tampons*
tissues	pah-*peer*-tüü-kher	*Papiertücher*
toothbrush	*tsaan*-bürs-te	*Zahnbürste*

Stationery & Publications

envelope	*breef*-um-shlaak	*Briefumschlag*
map	*kahr*-te	*Karte*
paper	pah-*peer*	*Papier*
pen	*koo*-gel-shrai-ber	*Kugelschreiber*
postcard	*pawst*-kahr-te	*Postkarte*
writing paper	*breef*-pah-peer	*Briefpapier*
English-language ...	... owf *eng*-lish	... *auf Englisch*
newspaper	*tsai*-tung	*Zeitung*
novels	ro-*maa*-ne	*Romane*

Photography

I'd like to have this film developed.
**bit-te ent-*vik*-keln
zee dee-zen *film*** — *Bitte entwickeln
Sie diesen Film.*

When will the photos be ready?
**vahn zint dee faw-tos
fer-tikh?** — *Wann sind die Fotos
fertig?*

I'd like a film for this camera.
**ikh *merkh*-te ai-nen *film*
füür dee-ze *kah*-me-rah** — *Ich möchte einen Film
für diese Kamera.*

B&W	*shvahrts*-vais	*schwarzweiß*
battery	baht-te-*ree*	*Batterie*
camera	*kah*-me-rah	*Kamera*
colour film	*fahrp*-film	*Farbfilm*
colour slide film	fahrp-*di*-ah-film	*Farbdiafilm*
film	film	*Film*
flash	blits	*Blitz*
lens	op-yek-*teef*	*Objektiv*
print	*ahp*-tsook	*Abzug*
slide	*di*-ah	*Dia*

Smoking

A packet of cigarettes, please.
ai-ne shahkh-tel	*Eine Schachtel*
tsi-gah-*ret*-ten, bit-te	*Zigaretten bitte.*

Do you have a light?
haa-ben zee *foy*-er?	*Haben Sie Feuer?*

cigarette papers	tsi-gah-*ret*-ten-pah-peer	*Zigarettenpapier*
cigarettes	tsi-gah-*ret*-ten	*Zigaretten*
filtered	mit *fil*-ter	*mit Filter*
lighter	*foy*-er-tsoyk	*Feuerzeug*
matches	*shtraikh*-herl-tser	*Streichhölzer*
menthol	men-*tawl*	*Menthol*
pipe	*pfai*-fe	*Pfeife*
tobacco (pipe)	tah-*bahk*	*Tabak*

Sizes & Comparisons

also	owkh	*auch*
big	graws	*groß*
enough	ge-*nookh*	*genug*
heavy	shvair	*schwer*
light	laikht	*leicht*
a little bit	ain *bis*-khen	*ein bisschen*
many	*fee*-le	*viele*
more	mair	*mehr*
less (not so much/ many)	nikht zaw feel/*fee*-le	*nicht so viel/viele*
small	klain	*klein*
too much/many	tsu feel/fee-le	*zu viel/viele*

HEALTH
Parts of the Body

ankle	*kner*-khel	*Knöchel*	head	kopf	*Kopf*
arm	ahrm	*Arm*	knee	knee	*Knie*
back	*rük*-ken	*Rücken*	leg	bain	*Bein*
chest	brust	*Brust*	nose	*naa*-ze	*Nase*
ear	awr	*Ohr*	skin	howt	*Haut*
eye	*ow*-ge	*Auge*	stomach	*maa*-gen	*Magen*
finger	*fing*-er	*Finger*	teeth	*tsair*-ne	*Zähne*
foot	foos	*Fuß*	throat	hahls	*Hals*
hand	hahnt	*Hand*			

Ailments

I'm sick.	meer ist *shlekht*	*Mir ist schlecht.*
My ... hurt/s.	meer toot ... veh	*Mir tut ... weh.*

I have (a/an) ...	ikh *haa*-be ...	*Ich habe ...*
allergy	ai-ne *ahl*-ler-*gee*	*eine Allergie*
constipation	fer-*shtop*-fung	*Verstopfung*
cough	*hoo*-sten	*Husten*
diarrhoea	*durkh*-fahl	*Durchfall*
fever	*fee*-ber	*Fieber*
infection	ai-ne in-fek-*tsyawn*	*eine Infektion*
influenza	dee *grip*-pe	*die Grippe*
nausea	*üü*-bel-kait	*Übelkeit*
pain	*shmer*-tsen	*Schmerzen*
sore throat	*hahls*-shmer-tsen	*Halsschmerzen*
sprain	ai-ne *mus*-kel-tser-rung	*eine Muskel zerrung*
venereal disease	ai-ne ge-*shlekhts*-krahngk-hait	*eine Geschlechts-krankheit*
worms	*vür*-mer	*Würmer*

Useful Words & Phrases

Where's a/the ...?	vaw ist ...?	Wo ist ...?
chemist	dee ah-po-*teh*-ke	*die Apotheke*
dentist	der *tsaan*-ahrtst	*der Zahnarzt*
doctor	ain ahrtst	*ein Arzt*
hospital	dahs *krahng*-ken-hows	*das Krankenhau*

I'm allergic to ...	ikh bin ahl-*ler*-gish geh-gen ...	Ich bin allergisch gegen ...
antibiotics	ahn-ti-bi-*aw*-ti-kah	*Antibiotika*
penicillin	pe-ni-tsi-*leen*	*Penizillin*

At the Chemist

Which chemist is open at night?
   vel-khe ah-po-*teh*-ke   *Welche Apotheke*
   haht *nahkht*-deenst   *hat Nachtdienst*
   ge-erf-net?   *geöffnet?*
I need medication for ...
   ikh *brow*-khe et-vahs   *Ich brauche etwas*
   geh-gen ...   *gegen ...*

antiseptic	ahn-ti-*zep*-ti-kum	*Antiseptikum*
bandage	fer-*bahnts*-mah-te-ri-aal	*Verbandsmaterial*
cough mixture	*hoo*-sten-zahft	*Hustensaft*
laxative	*ahp*-füür-mit-tel	*Abführmittel*
painkillers	*shmerts*-mit-tel	*Schmerzmittel*

At the Dentist

I have a toothache.
   ikh haa-be *tsaan*-shmer-tsen *Ich habe Zahnschmerzen.*
I've lost a filling.
   ikh haa-be ai-ne *fül*-lung   *Ich habe eine Füllung*
   fer-*law*-ren   *verloren.*
My gums hurt.
   dahs *tsaan*-flaish toot   *Das Zahnfleisch tut*
   meer veh   *mir weh.*

GERMAN

I don't want it extracted.
   ikh vil een nikht   *Ich will ihn nicht*
   *tsee-*en **lahs-sen**   *ziehen lassen.*
Can you fix it temporarily?
   kern-nen zee es pro-vi-   *Können Sie es provisorisch*
   *zaw-*rish **be-hahn-deln?**   *behandeln?*

abscess	**ahps-**tses	*Abszess*
anaesthetic	be-*toy-*bung	*Betäubung*
to extract	*tsee-*en	*ziehen*
infection	ent-*tsün-*dung	*Entzündung*
tooth	tsaan	*Zahn*
toothache	**tsaan-**shmer-tsen	*Zahnschmerzen*

TIME & DATES
Time

What time is it?	vee *spairt* ist es?	*Wie spät ist es?*

It's ...	es ist ...	*Es ist ...*
3 o'clock	*drai* oor	*drei Uhr*
3.15	feer-tel naakh *drai*	*Viertel nach drei*
3.30	hahlp *feer*	*halb vier*
3.45	feer-tel fawr *feer*	*Viertel vor vier*

Days

Monday	*mawn-*taak	*Montag*
Tuesday	*deens-*taak	*Dienstag*
Wednesday	mit-vokh	*Mittwoch*
Thursday	*don-*ners-taak	*Donnerstag*
Friday	*frai-*taak	*Freitag*
Saturday	*zahms-*taak/	*Samstag/*
	zon-*aa-*bent	*Sonnabend*
Sunday	zon-*taak*	*Sonntag*

GERMAN

GERMAN

Months

January	yahn-oo-*aar*	*Januar*
February	feh-broo-*aar*	*Februar*
March	mairts	*März*
April	ah-*pril*	*April*
May	mai	*Mai*
June	*yoo*-ni	*Juni*
July	*yoo*-li	*Juli*
August	ow-*gust*	*August*
September	zep-*tem*-ber	*September*
October	ok-*taw*-ber	*Oktober*
November	no-*vem*-ber	*November*
December	deh-*tsem*-ber	*Dezember*

Seasons

spring	*früü*-ling	*Frühling*
summer	*zom*-mer	*Sommer*
autumn	herpst	*Herbst*
winter	*vin*-ter	*Winter*

Present

now	yetst	*jetzt*
immediately	zo-*fort*/glaikh	*sofort/gleich*
today	*hoy*-te	*heute*
this morning	hoy-te *mor*-gen	*heute morgen*
this afternoon	hoy-te *naakh*-mit-taak	*heute nachmittag*
tonight	hoy-te *aa*-bent	*heute abend*
this week	dee-ze *vo*-khe	*diese Woche*
this month	dee-zen *maw*-naht	*diesen Monat*
this year	dee-zes *yaar*	*dieses Jahr*

Past

yesterday morning/ afternoon	*ges*-tern mor-*gen*/ *naakh*-mit-taak	*gestern Morgen/ Nachmittag*
last night	lets-te *nahkht*	*letzte Nacht*
day before yesterday	*foor*-ges-tern	*vorgestern*
last week	lets-te *vo*-khe	*letzte Woche*
last year	lets-tes *yaar*	*letztes Jahr*

Future

tomorrow ...	mor-gen ...	*morgen ...*
morning	*früü*	*früh*
afternoon	*naakh*-mit-taak	*nachmittag*
evening	*aa*-bent	*abend*
day after tomorrow	*üü*-ber-mor-gen	*übermorgen*
next week	nairkhs-te *vo*-khe	*nächste Woche*
next year	nairkhs-tes *yaar*	*nächstes Jahr*

During the Day

afternoon	*naakh*-mit-taak	*Nachmittag*
day	taak	*Tag*
early	früü	*früh*
midnight	*mit*-ter-nahkht	*Mitternacht*
morning	*mor*-gen	*Morgen*
night	nahkht	*Nacht*
noon	*mit*-taak	*Mittag*
sunrise	*zon*-nen-owf-gahng	*Sonnenaufgang*
sunset	*zon*-nen-un-ter-gahng	*Sonnenuntergang*

NUMBERS & AMOUNTS

0	nul	*null*
1	ains	*eins*
2	tsvai; (tsvaw)	*zwei; (zwo)*
3	drai	*drei*
4	feer	*vier*
5	fünf	*fünf*
6	zeks	*sechs*
7	*zee*-ben	*sieben*
8	ahkht	*acht*
9	noyn	*neun*
10	tsehn	*zehn*
11	elf	*elf*
12	tsverlf	*zwölf*

GERMAN

ZWEI – ZWO

Zwo is used instead of zwei when giving numbers over the phone. It's also used when giving someone your phone number.

GERMAN

13	*drai*-tsehn	dreizehn
14	*feer*-tsehn	vierzehn
15	*fünf*-tsehn	fünfzehn
16	*zekh*-tsehn	sechzehn
17	*zeep*-tsehn	siebzehn
18	*ahkht*-tsehn	achtzehn
19	*noyn*-tsehn	neunzehn
20	*tsvahn*-tsikh	zwanzig
21	*ain*-unt-tsvahn-tsikh	einundzwanzig
22	*tsvai*-unt-tsvahn-tsikh	zweiundzwanzig
30	*drai*-sikh	dreißig
40	*feer*-tsikh	vierzig
50	*fünf*-tsikh	fünfzig
60	*zekh*-tsikh	sechzig
70	*zeep*-tsikh	siebzig
80	*ahkht*-tsikh	achtzig
90	*noyn*-tsikh	neunzig
100	(ain-)*hun*-dert	(ein)hundert
1000	(ain-)*tow*-zent	(ein)tausend
one million	ai-ne mil-*yawn*	eine Million

ABBREVIATIONS

ADAC	AA (Automobile Association)	*Hbf.*	Main railway station
Ausw.	ID	*Hr./Fr.*	Mr/Mrs
Bhf.	Railway station	*KW*	Short Wave
BLZ	Bank code	*n. Chr./v. Chr.*	AD/BC
BRD	Federal Republic of Germany	*N/S*	Nth/Sth
		PLZ	Post code
DB	German Federal Railways	*Str.*	St/Rd/etc
		U(-Bahn)	Underground (Railway)
DJH	Youth Hostel		
DM	German Mark	*usw.*	etc
EG	EC	*vorm./nachm.*	am/pm
GB	UK	*z.B.*	eg

EMERGENCIES

Help!	*hil*-fe!	*Hilfe!*
Thief!	deep!	*Dieb!*
Fire!	*foy*-er!	*Feuer!*
Go away!	geh-en zee *vek*!	*Gehen Sie weg!*

Please call the police!
    roo-fen zee bit-te dee   *Rufen Sie bitte die*
    po-li-*tsai*!   *Polizei!*
Where's the nearest police station?
    vaw ist dahs nairkhs-te   *Wo ist das nächste*
    po-li-*tsai*-re-veer?   *Polizeirevier?*
Could you help me, please?
    kern-ten zee meer   *Könnten Sie mir*
    bit-te *hel*-fen?   *bitte helfen?*
Could I please use the telephone?
    kern-te ikh bit-te dahs   *Könnte ich bitte das*
    teh-le-*fawn* be-nut-tsen?   *Telefon benutzen?*
Call a doctor!
    haw-len zee ai-nen *ahrtst*!   *Holen Sie einen Arzt!*
Call an ambulance!
    roo-fen zee ai-nen   *Rufen Sie einen*
    krahng-ken-vaa-gen!   *Krankenwagen!*
I have medical insurance.
    ikh bin *krahng*-ken-   *Ich bin krankenversichert.*
    fer-*zi*-khert
I'm lost.
    ikh haa-be mikh fer-*irt*   *Ich habe mich verirrt.*

GERMAN

Dealing with the Police

I want to report	ikh merkh-te ai-nen	*Ich möchte einen*
a/an ...	... *ahm*-tsai-gen	*... anzeigen.*
accident	*un*-fahl	*Unfall*
attack	*üü*-ber-fahl	*Überfall*
loss	fer-*lust*	*Verlust*
theft	*deep*-shtaal	*Diebstahl*

I'm sorry. I apologise.
es toot meer *lait*. ent-*shul*-di-gen zee bit-te
Es tut mir leid. Entschuldigen Sie bitte.

Can I make a phone call?
kahn ikh maal teh-le-fo-*nee*-ren?
Kann ich mal telefonieren?

I want to see a lawyer.
ikh merkh-te ai-nen *ahn*-vahlt shpre-khen
Ich möchte einen Anwalt sprechen.

I want to contact my ...	**ikh *merkh*-te mikh mit ... in fer-*bin*-dung zet-tsen**	*Ich möchte mich mit ... in Verbindung setzen.*
consulate	**mai-nem kon-zu-*laat***	*meinem Konsulat*
embassy	**mai-ner *bawt*-shahft**	*meiner Botschaft*

HUNGARIAN

QUICK REFERENCE

Hello.	yoh nah-pot kee-vaa-nok si-ah	*Jó napot kívánok.* (pol) *Szia.* (inf)
Goodbye.	vi-sont-laa-taash-rah si-ah!	*Viszontlátásra.* (pol) *Szia!* (inf)
Yes./No.	i-ghen/nem	*Igen./Nem.*
Excuse me.	bo-chaa-naht	*Bocsánat.*
May I?	le-het?	*Lehet?*
Sorry.	bo-chaa-naht	*Bocsánat.*
Please.	keh-rem	*Kérem.*
Thank you.	ker-ser-nerm	*Köszönöm.*
You're welcome.	see-ve-shen	*Szívesen.*
What time is it?	haany oh-rah?	*Hány óra?*
Where's the ...?	hol vahn ah/ahz ...?	*Hol van a/az ...?*

Turn left/right.
for-dul-yon bahl-rah/ yobb-rah.   *Forduljon balra/ jobbra.*

Go straight ahead.
men-yen e-dje-ne-shen e-loere   *Menjen egyenesen előre*

I (don't) understand.
(nem) ehr-tem   *(Nem) értem.*

Do you speak English?
be-sehl ahn-gho-lul?   *Beszél angolul?*

Where are the toilets?
hol vahn ah veh-tseh?   *Hol van a WC?*

How much is it?
meny-nyi-be ke-rül?   *Mennyibe kerül?*

I'd like a ...	se-ret-nehk ...	*Szeretnék ...*
room	so-baat	*szobát*
ticket to ...	edj he-yet fogh-lahl-ni ...	*egy helyet foglalni ...*

| one-way | edj ye-djet chahk odah | *egy jegyet csak oda* |
| return | edj re-toor-ye-djet | *egy retúrjegyet* |

1	edj	*egy*	6	haht	*hat*
2	ket-toer	*kettő*	7	heht	*hét*
3	haa-rom	*három*	8	nyolts	*nyolc*
4	nehdj	*négy*	9	ki-lents	*kilenc*
5	ert	*öt*	10	teez	*tíz*

HUNGARIAN

HUNGARIAN

Hungarian, or Magyar as it is known to the Magyars (who constitute 95 per cent of the population in Hungary), is a unique language in Europe. The roots of this Finno-Ugric tongue and its people lie in the lands east of the Ural mountain chain, from where, in around 2000 BC, there was a major migration west. In the process, the group split, some moving north to Finland and Estonia, and the others, the Ugric people, moving through to Hungary. Their language was also split into two groups. While it picked up certain Persian, Turkish and Bulgar words along the way, it developed into modern Hungarian which is now only spoken in Hungary. Finnish is the nearest European relative, bearing some resemblances in form and structure, but the two languages are mutually incomprehensible.

There is a Hungarian-speaking population of 10.3 million in Hungary, and a sizable ethnic Hungarian-speaking community around the borders: nearly two million in Romania, mostly in Transylvania, some 600,000 in the Slovak Republic, half a million in Vojvodina and Croatia, and 200,000 in the Ukraine.

However daunting it may appear at first sight, there is a regularity and code to the language. Word formation is agglutinative, meaning that you start with a 'root' and build on it. There's a complicated set of rules governing prepositions, which in Hungarian are actually word endings. In order to simplify the language guide, we've generally omitted the wide variety of endings that could be used. Although this makes for some grammatically incorrect sentences, such as 'Which bus goes Buda?', there should be no problems in being understood. Just for your information, some of the common endings you may see or hear are: *-ba*, *-be*, *-ra*, *-re*, *-hoz*, *-hez*, *-höz*, *-nal*, *-nál* and *-nél*. The definite article ('the' in English) has two forms in Hungarian: *az* before a word starting with a vowel, and *a* before a consonant.

For beginners, good pronunciation will get you further than good grammar, and Hungarians are delighted to hear any of their tongue emerge from a non-Magyar.

PRONUNCIATION

The rules are simple, and the actual pronunciation just takes a little practice. There are no diphthongs (vowel combinations) – each vowel is pronounced.

Short Vowels

a	ah	between the 'o' in 'hot' and the 'a' in 'was'
e	e	as the 'e' in 'set'
i	i	as the 'i' in 'pit'
o	o	as the 'o' in 'solitude'
ö	er	as the 'o' in 'worse'
u	u	as the 'oo' in 'hoop'
ü	ü	as the 'ew' in 'few'

Long Vowels

Long vowels are indicated with an accent (*á, ó, ú*).

á	aa	as the 'a' in 'father'
é	eh	as the 'a' in 'make'
í	ee	as the 'ee' in 'flee'
ó	oh	as the 'o' in 'note'
ő	oer	as the 'o' in 'world'
ō	oer	as the 'o' in 'world'
ú	oo	as the 'u' in 'flute'
ű	üü	as the 'ew' in 'few'

QUESTION WORDS		
How?	hodj?	Hogy?
When?	mi-kor?	Mikor?
Where?	hol?	Hol?
Which?	me-yik?	Melyik?
Who?	ki?	Ki?
Why?	mi-ehrt?	Miért?

Consonants

Most double consonants should be lengthened to the point where you can just distinguish the two letters. Consonants not described here are pronounced as they are in English.

c	**ts**	as the 'ts' in 'hats'
cs	**ch**	as the 'ch' in 'church'
g	**gh**	as in 'ghost', slightly softer than the 'g' in 'got'
gy	**dj**	as the 'j' in 'jury'
j	**y**	as the 'y' in 'yellow'
ly	**y**	as the 'y' in 'yellow'
ny	**ny**	as in 'new'
r	**r**	as in 'red', but harder and sharper
s	**sh**	as the 'sh' in 'shower'
sz	**s**	as the 's' in 'sin'
ty	**ty**	a 'tch' sound, as the 'tu' in 'statue'
zs	**zh**	as the 's' in 'pleasure'

Stress

In the vast majority of words, there's a slight stress on the first syllable. Each syllable after the first is given equal weight, even in the longest words.

SUBJECT PRONOUNS		
SG		
I	ehn	*én*
you (inf)	te	*te*
you (pol)	ern-erk	*önök*
he/she/it	oer	*o*
PL		
we	mi	*mi*
you	ern-erk	*önök*
they	oerk	*ok*

HUNGARIAN

GREETINGS & CIVILITIES
Top Useful Phrases

Hello.
| yoh nah-pot kee-vaa-nok | *Jó napot kívánok.* (pol) |
| si-ah | *Szia.* (inf) |

Goodbye.
| vi-sont-laa-taash-rah | *Viszontlátásra.* (pol) |
| si-ah! | *Szia!* (inf) |

Yes./No.
| i-ghen/nem | *Igen./Nem.* |

Excuse me.
| bo-chaa-naht | *Bocsánat.* |

May I? Do you mind?
| le-het? | *Lehet?* |

Sorry. (excuse me, forgive me)
| bo-chaa-naht | *Bocsánat.* |

Please.
| keh-rem | *Kérem.* |

Thank you.
| ker-ser-nerm | *Köszönöm.* |

Many thanks.
| nah-djon ker-ser-nerm | *Nagyon köszönöm.* |

That's fine. You're welcome.
| rend-ben see-ve-shen | *Rendben. Szívesen.* |

Greetings

Good morning.
| yoh regh-ghelt | *Jó reggelt.* |

Good afternoon.
| yoh nah-pot | *Jó napot.* |

Good evening/night.
| yoh esh-teht/ehy-sah-kaat | *Jó estét/éjszakát.* |

How are you?
| hodj vahn/vahdj? | *Hogy van/vagy?* (pol/inf) |

Well, thanks.
| ker-ser-nerm, yohl | *Köszönöm, jól.* |

HUNGARIAN

Forms of Address

Madam/Mrs	herldj/as-sony	*Hölgy/Asszony*
Sir/Mr	oor	*Úr*
Miss	kish-as-sony	*Kisasszony*
companion	taarsh	*társ*
friend	bah-raat	*barát*

SMALL TALK
Meeting People

What's your name?
  hodj heev-yaak? *Hogy hívják?*
My name is ...
  ah ne-vem ... *A nevem ...*
I'd like to introduce you to ...
  se-ret-nehm ernt *Szeretném Önt*
  be-mu-taht-ni ... *bemutatni ...*
Pleased to meet you.
  er-rü-lerk hodj megh-ish- *Örülök, hogy*
  mer-he-tem *megismerhetem.*
How old are you?
  ern haany eh-vesh? *Ön hány éves?*
I'm ... years old.
  ... eh-vesh vah-djok *... éves vagyok.*

HUNGARIAN

Nationalities

Where are you from?

ern hon-nahn yertt?		*Ön honnan jött?*

I'm from ...	... **bohl yert-tem**	... *ból jöttem.*
Australia	**ah-ust-raa-li-ah**	*Ausztrália*
Canada	**kah-nah-dah**	*Kanada*
England	**ahn-ghli-ah**	*Anglia*
Ireland	**eer-or-saagh**	*Írország*
New Zealand	**ooy zeh-lahnd**	*Új-Zéland*
Scotland	**shkoh-tsi-ah**	*Skócia*
the USA	**ahz e-dje-shült**	*Az Egyesült*
	aal-lah-mok	*Államok*
Wales	**vels**	*Wales*

Occupations

What do you do?

mi ah fogh-lahl-ko-zaa-shah?	*Mi a foglalkozása?*

I'm unemployed.

mun-kah-nehl-kü-li vah-djok	*Munkanélküli vagyok.*

I'm a/an ...	... vah-djok	... vagyok
artist	müü-vehs	művész
businessperson	üz-let-em-ber	üzletember (m)
	üz-let-as-sony	üzletasszony (f)
computer	saa-mee-toh-ghehp	számítógép
programmer	progh-rah-mo-zoh	programozó
doctor	or-vosh	orvos
engineer	mehr-nerk	mérnök
farmer	ghahz-dah	gazda
journalist	ooy-shaagh-ee-roh	újságíró
lawyer	yo-ghaas	jogász
manual worker	fi-zi-kahi mun-kaash	fizikai munkás
mechanic	se-re-loer	szerelő
nurse	aa-po-loh	ápoló (m)
	aa-po-loh-noer	ápolónő (f)
office worker	iro-dah-i dol-gho-zoh	irodai dolgozó
scientist	tu-dohsh	tudós
student	di-aak	diák
teacher	tah-naar	tanár (m)
	tah-naar-noer	tanárnő (f)
waiter	pin-tsehr	pincér (m)
	pin-tsehr-noer	pincérnő (f)
writer	ee-roh	író

Religion

What's your religion?
mi-yen vahl-laa-shoo?   *Milyen vallású?*
I'm not religious.
nem vah-djok vahl-laa-shosh   *Nem vagyok vallásos.*

I'm ...	... vah-djok	... vagyok
Buddhist	bud-hish-tah	buddhista
Catholic	kah-to-li-kush	katolikus
Christian	ke-res-tehny	keresztény
Hindu	hin-du	hindu
Jewish	zhi-doh	zsidó
Muslim	mu-zul-maan	muzulmán

Family

Are you married?
noers?	*Nős?* (m)
fehry-nehl vahn?	*Férjnél van?* (f)

I'm single.
noert-len vah-djok	*Nőtlen vagyok.* (m)
hah-yah-don vah-djok	*Hajadon vagyok.* (f)

I'm married.
noersh vah-djok	*Nős vagyok.* (m)
fehry-nehl vah-djok	*Férjnél vagyok.* (f)

I'm widowed.
erz-vedj-ahs-sony vah-djok	*Özvegyasszony vagyok.* (m)
erz-vedj-em-ber vah-djok	*Özvegyember vagyok.* (f)

I'm divorced.
el-vaal-tahm	*Elváltam.*

I'm separated from my wife.
kü-lern-eh-lek ah fe-le-sheh-ghem-toerl	*Különélek a feleségemtől.*

I'm separated from my husband.
kü-lern-eh-lek ah fehr-yem-toerl	*Különélek a férjemtől.*

How many children do you have?
haany djer-me-ke vahn?	*Hány gyermeke van?*

I don't have any children.
ninch djer-me-kem	*Nincs gyermekem.*

I have a daughter/a son.
edj laa-nyom/fi-ahm vahn	*Egy lányom/fiam van.*

How many brothers/sisters
do you have?
haany baaty-ya/noer-veh-re vahn?	*Hány bátyja/nővére van?*

Is your husband/wife here?
itt vahn ah fehr-ye/fe-le-sheh-ghe?	*Itt van a férje/felesége?*

Do you have a boyfriend/girlfriend?
vahn bah-raat-yah/bah-raat-noer-ye?	*Van barátja/barátnője?*

brother	fioo-tesht-vehr	*fiútestvér*
children	dje-re-kek	*gyerekek*
daughter	laany	*lány*
family	chah-laad	*család*
father	ah-pah	*apa*
grandfather	nahdj-pah-pah	*nagypapa*
grandmother	nahdj-mah-mah	*nagymama*
husband	fehry	*férj*
mother	ah-nyah	*anya*
sister	le-aany-tesht-vehr	*leánytestvér*
son	fioo	*fiú*
wife	fe-le-shehgh	*feleség*

Kids' Talk

What's your name?
hodj heev-nahk? *Hogy hívnak?*

How old are you?
haany eh-vesh vahdj? *Hány éves vagy?*

What grade are you in?
mi-yen os-taay-bah yaars? *Milyen osztályba jársz?*

When's your birthday?
mi-kor vahn ah *Mikor van a*
sü-le-tehsh-nah-pod? *születésnapod?*

How many brothers and sisters
do you have?
haany tesht-veh-red vahn? *Hány testvéred van?*

Do you have your own room?
Vahn shah-yaat so-baad? *Van saját szobád?*

I share my room.
ninch shah-yaat so-baam. *Nincs saját szobám.*

I have my own room.
vahn shah-yaat so-baam. *Van saját szobám.*

What are your favourite
games/hobbies?
mi ah ked-vents *Mi a kedvenc*
yaa-teh-kohd/hob-bid? *játékod/hobbid?*

collecting things	djüüy-tehsh	*gyűjtés*
making things	bahr-kaa-cho-laash	*barkácsolás*
playing outside	yaa-tehk ah sah-bahd-bahn	*játék a szabadban*
sports	shport	*sport*
video games	videoh-yaa-teh-kok	*videójátékok*
watching TV	TV neh-zehsh	*TV nézés*

I have a ...	vahn edj ...	*Van egy ...*
bird	mah-dah-rahm	*madaram*
canary	kah-naa-rim	*kanárim*
cat	mahch-kaam	*macskám*
cow	te-he-nem	*tehenem*
dog	ku-tyaam	*kutyám*
donkey	sah-mah-rahm	*szamaram*
duck	kah-chaam	*kacsám*
frog	beh-kaam	*békám*
rabbit	nyúl	*nyool*

SIGNS

BEJÁRAT	ENTRANCE
ÉSZKIJÁRAT	EMERGENCY EXIT
FOGLALT	RESERVED
INFORMÁCIÓ	INFORMATION
KIJÁRAT	EXIT
MELEG/HIDEG	HOT/COLD
NYITVA/ZÁRVA	OPEN/CLOSED
SZABAD BELÉPÉS	FREE ADMISSION
TILOS BELÉPNI	NO ENTRY
TILOS A DOHÁNYZÁS	NO SMOKING
TILOS	PROHIBITED
TELEFON	TELEPHONE
WC/TOALETT	TOILETS

Feelings

I (don't) like ...
ne-kem (nem) tet-sik ...   *Nekem (nem) tetszik ...*

I'm sorry. (condolence)
shahy-naa-lom   *Sajnálom.*

I'm grateful.
haa-laash vah-djok   *Hálás vagyok.*

I'm ...

angry	mehr-ghesh vah-djok	*Mérges vagyok.*
cold	faa-zom	*Fázom.*
hot	me-le-ghem vahn	*Melegem van.*
happy	bol-dogh vah-djok	*Boldog vagyok.*
hungry	eh-hesh vah-djok	*Éhes vagyok.*
thirsty	som-yahsh vah-djok	*Szomjas vagyok.*
in a hurry	shi-e-tek	*Sietek.*
right	yohl vah-djok	*Jól vagyok.*
sad	so-mo-roo vah-djok	*Szomorú vagyok.*
sleepy	aal-mosh vah-djok	*Álmos vagyok.*
tired	faa-rahdt vah-djok	*Fáradt vagyok.*
well	yohl vah-djok	*Jól vagyok.*
worried	ahgh-ghoh-dom	*Aggódom.*

Useful Phrases

Sure!	per-se!	*Persze!*
Just a minute.	edj pil-lah-naht	*Egy pillanat.*
It's (not) important.	(nem) fon-tosh	*(Nem) Fontos.*
It's (not) possible.	(nem) le-het	*(Nem) Lehet.*
Wait!	vaar-yon!	*Várjon!*
Good luck!	shok se-ren-cheht!	*Sok szerencsét!*

BREAKING THE LANGUAGE BARRIER

Do you speak English?
be-sehl ahn-gho-lul? *Beszél angolul?*

Does anyone speak English?
be-sehl vah-lah-ki ahn-gho-lul? *Beszél valaki angolul?*

I speak a little ...
ehn be-seh-lek edj ki-chit *Én beszélek egy kicsit*
... ul/ül *... ul/ül.*

I don't speak ...
nem be-seh-lek ... ul/ül *Nem beszélek ... ul/ül.*

I (don't) understand.
(nem) ehr-tem *(Nem) értem.*

Could you speak more
slowly, please?
keh-rem tud-nah lahsh-shahb- *Kérem, tudna lassabban*
ban be-sehl-ni? *beszélni?*

Could you repeat that?
megh-ish-meh-tel-neh? *Megismételné?*

How do you say ...?
hodj kell mon-dah-ni ...? *Hogy kell mondani ...?*

What does ... mean?
mit ye-lent ...? *Mit jelent ...?*

BODY LANGUAGE

Waving the hands about, gesticulating wildly, nodding the head,
curious signals with fingers, rolling of the eyes – the Hungarians
don't do any of it. However, that's not to say that you shouldn't.
At the very least, it will get you noticed.

PAPERWORK

address	tseem	*cím*
age	kor	*kor*
birth certificate	sü-le-teh-shi	*születési*
	ah-nyah-kerny-vi	*anyakönyvi*
	ki-vo-naht	*kivonat*
border	hah-taar	*határ*
car owner's title	for-ghahl-mi	*forgalmi*
	en-ghe-dehy	*engedély*
car registration	ghehp-ko-chi	*gépkocsi*
	rend-saam	*rendszám*
customs	vaam	*vám*
date of birth	sü-le-teh-shi	*születési*
	daa-tum	*dátum*
driver's licence	yo-gho-sheet-vaany	*jogosítvány*
identification	se-mehy-ah-	*személya-*
	zo-nosh-shaagh	*zonosság*
immigration	be-vaan-dor-laash	*bevándorlás*
marital status	chah-laa-di	*családi*
	aal-lah-pot	*állapot*
name	nehv	*név*
nationality	nem-ze-ti-shehgh	*nemzetiség*
next of kin	ker-ze-li	*közeli*
	hoz-zaa-tahr-to-zoh	*hozzátartozó*
passport	oot-le-vehl	*útlevél*
passport number	oot-le-vehl-saam	*útlevélszám*
place of birth	sü-le-teh-shi hey	*születési hely*
profession	fogh-lahl-ko-zaa- shah	*foglalkozása*
reason for travel	ahz u-tah-zaash	*az utazás*
	tsehl-yah	*célja*
religion	vahl-laash	*vallás*
sex	nem	*nem*
tourist card	tu-rish-tah	*turista*
	kaar-tyah	*kártya*
visa	vee-zum	*vízum*

GETTING AROUND

What time does	mi-kor in-dul/	*Mikor indul/*
the ... leave/arrive?	ehr-ke-zik ah ...?	*érkezik a ...?*
aeroplane	re-pü-loer-ghehp	*repülőgép*
boat	hah-yoh	*hajó*
bus (city)	he-yi ah-u-toh-bus	*helyi autóbusz*
bus (intercity)	taa-vol-shaa-ghi	*távolsági*
	ah-u-toh-bus	*autóbusz*
train	vo-naht	*vonat*
tram	vil-lah-mosh	*villamos*

Directions

Where's ...?
hol vahn ah/ahz ...?   *Hol van a/az ...?*

How do I get to ...?
hodj yu-tok ah/ahz ...?   *Hogy jutok a/az ...?*

Is it far away?
mes-se vahn in-nen?   *Messze van innen?*

Is it near here?
ker-zel vahn ide?   *Közel van ide?*

Can I walk there?
me-he-tek odah djah-logh?   *Mehetek oda gyalog?*

Can you show me (on the map)?
megh tud-naa ne-kem   *Meg tudná nekem*
mu-taht-ni (ah tehr-keh-pen)?   *mutatni (a térképen)?*

GETTING AROUND

AUTÓBUSZ MEGÁLLÓ	**BUS STOP**
CSOMAG	**BAGGAGE COUNTER**
ÉRKEZÉS	**ARRIVALS**
HAJÓÁLLOMÁS	**DOCK**
INDULÁS	**DEPARTURES**
VÁMKEZELÉS	**CUSTOMS**
VASÚTÁLLOMÁS	**TRAIN STATION**

HUNGARIAN

Are there other means of
getting there?

maash-kehp-pen ish el   *Másképpen is el*
le-het odah yut-ni?   *lehet oda jutni?*

I want to go to ...

se-ret-nehk ... men-ni   *Szeretnék ... menni.*

Go straight ahead.

men-yen e-dje-ne-shen e-loere   *Menjen egyenesen előre.*

It's two blocks down.

keht shah-rok-rah vahn in-nen   *Két sarokra van innen.*

Turn left ...	**for-dul-yon bahl-rah ...**	*Forduljon balra ...*
Turn right ...	**for-dul-yon yobb-rah ...**	*Forduljon jobbra ...*
at the next corner	**ah ker-vet-ke-zoer shah-rok-naal**	*a következő saroknál*
at the traffic lights	**ah kerz-le-ke-deh-shi laam-paa-naal**	*a közlekedési lámpánál*

behind	**mer-ghertt**	*mögött*
in front of	**e-loertt**	*előtt*
far	**mes-se**	*messze*
near	**ker-zel**	*közel*
opposite	**sem-ben**	*szemben*

Booking Tickets

Excuse me, where is the ticket office?

el-neh-zehsht, hol vahn ah   *Elnézést, hol van a*
yedj-i-ro-dah?   *jegyiroda?*

Where can I buy a ticket?

hol ve-he-tem megh ah   *Hol vehetem meg a*
ye-djet?   *jegyet?*

I want to go to ...

se-ret-nehk ... men-ni   *Szeretnék ... menni.*

Do I need to book?

sük-sheh-ghesh he-yet   *Szükséges helyet*
fogh-lahl-nom?   *foglalnom?*

You need to book.
sük-sheh-ghesh he-yet fogh-lahl-ni-ah   *Szükséges helyet foglalnia.*

I'd like to book a seat to ...
se-ret-nehk edj he-yet fogh-lahl-ni ...   *Szeretnék egy helyet foglalni ...*

It's full.
te-le vahn   *Tele van.*

Is it completely full?
tel-ye-shen te-le vahn?   *Teljesen tele van?*

Can I get a stand-by ticket?
kahp-hah-tok edj stand-by ye-djet?   *Kaphatok egy stand-by jegyet?*

I'd like ...	se-ret-nehk ...	Szeretnék ...
a one-way ticket	edj ye-djet chahk odah	egy jegyet csak oda
a return ticket	edj re-toor-ye-djet	egy retúr-jegyet
two tickets	keht ye-djet	két jegyet
tickets for all of us	edj-edj ye-djet mind-ahny-nyi-unk-nahk	egy-egy jegyet mindannyi-unknak
a student's fare	edj di-aak-ye-djet	egy diákjegyet
a child's/ pensioner's fare	edj dje-rek-ye-djet/ ye-djet nyugh-dee-yash-el-shoer os-taay	egy gyerekjegyet/ nyugdíjasjegyet
1st class	el-shoer os-taay	első osztály
2nd class	maa-shod-os-taay	másodosztály

Air

Is there a flight to ...?
  vahn re-pü-loer-yaa-raht ...?   *Van repülőjárat ...?*
When's the next flight to ...?
  mi-kor vahn ah ker-vet-ke-zoer   *Mikor van a következő*
  re-pü-loer-yaa-raht ...?   *repülőjárat ...?*
How long does the flight take?
  meny-nyi i-de-igh tahrt   *Mennyi ideig tart*
  ah re-püloer-oot?   *a repülőút?*
What's the flight number?
  meny-nyi ah yaa-raht-saam?   *Mennyi a járatszám?*
You must check in at ...
  ah ... kell ye-lent-kez-ni-e   *A ... kell jelentkeznie*

AIR	
CSOMAG ÁTVÉTEL	BAGGAGE COLLECTION
REGISZTRÁCIÓ	REGISTRATION

airport tax   re-pü-loer-teh-ri ah-doh   *repülőtéri adó*
boarding pass   be-saal-loh-kaar-tyah   *beszállókártya*

Bus

Where's the bus/tram stop?
  hol vahn ahz ah-u-toh-bus/   *Hol van az autóbusz/*
  ah vil-lah-mosh megh-aal-loh?   *a villamos megálló?*
How often do buses pass by?
  mi-yen djahk-rahn yaar-   *Milyen gyakran járnak*
  nahk ahz ah-u-toh-busok   *az autóbuszok?*

BUS	
AUTÓBUSZ MEGÁLLÓ	BUS STOP
VILLAMOS MEGÁLLÓ	TRAM STOP

HUNGARIAN

Which bus goes to ...?
  me-yik ah-u-toh-bus medj ...?   *Melyik autóbusz megy ...?*
Does this bus go to ...?
  ez ahz ah-u-toh-bus medj ...?   *Ez az autóbusz megy ...?*
Could you let me know when
we get to ...?
  sohl-nah keh-rem ah-mi-kor   *Szólna kérem, amikor*
  megh-ehr-ke-zünk ...?   *megérkezünk ...?*
I want to get off!
  se-ret-nehk le-saall-ni!   *Szeretnék leszállni!*

What time's the	mi-kor in-dul ah/ahz	*Mikor indul a/az*
... bus?	... ah-u-toh-bus?	*... autóbusz?*
first	el-shoer	*első*
last	u-tol-shoh	*utolsó*
next	ker-vet-ke-zoer	*következő*

Train & Metro

Which line takes me to ...?
  me-yik vo-nahl medj...?   *Melyik vonal megy...?*
What's the next station?
  mi ah ker-vet-ke-zoer   *Mi a következő állomás?*
  aal-lo-maash?
Is this the right platform for ...?
  er-roerl ah vaa-ghaany-rohl   *Erről a vágányról*
  in-dul ah vo-naht ...?   *indul a vonat ...?*

dining car	eht-ke-zoer-ko-chi	*étkezőkocsi*
express	ex-press	*expressz*
local	he-yi	*helyi*
sleeping car	haa-loh-ko-chi	*hálókocsi*

TRAIN & METRO	
FÖLDALATTI	UNDERGROUND
KIJÁRAT	WAY OUT
VÁGÁNY	PLATFORM
VÁLTÁS	CHANGE (for coins)

THEY MAY SAY ...

ahz u-tah-shok-nahk aat kell saall-ni maa-shik	Passengers must change trains
ahz u-tah-shok-nahk vaa-ghaany-hoz kell men-ni	Passengers must change platforms
ah vo-naht ah saa-moo vaa-ghaany-rohl in-dul	The train leaves from platform ...
ah vo-naht keh-shik	The train is delayed.
ah vo-naht nem yaar	The train is cancelled.

Taxi

Can you take me to ...?
  el tud-nah vin-ni ...? — *El tudna vinni ...?*

Please take me to ...
  keh-rem vi-djen el ... — *Kérem, vigyen el ...?*

How much does it cost to go to ...?
  meny-nyi-be ke-rül ... igh? — *Mennyibe kerül ... ig?*

Here's fine, thank you.
  itt joh les, ker-ser-nerm — *Itt jó lesz, köszönöm.*

The next corner, please.
  ah ker-vet-ke-zoer shah-rok-naal, le-djen see-vesh — *A következő saroknál, legyen szíves.*

The next street to the left/right.
  ah ker-vet-ke-zoer ut-tsaa-naal bahl-rah/yobb-rah — *A következő utcánál balra/jobbra.*

Stop here!
  aall-yon megh itt! — *Álljon meg itt!*

Please slow down.
  keh-rem, lash-sheet-shon le — *Kérem, lassítson le.*

Please wait here.
  keh-rem, vaar-yon itt — *Kérem, várjon itt.*

HUNGARIAN

Useful Phrases

Can I reserve a place?
fogh-lahl-hah-tok edj he-yet? *Foglalhatok egy helyet?*

How long does the trip take?
meny-nyi i-de-igh tahrt ahz *Mennyi ideig tart az*
u-tah-zaash? *utazás?*

Is it a direct route?
ez edj kerz-vet-len *Ez egy közvetlen*
oot-vo-nahl? *útvonal?*

Is that seat taken?
fogh-lahlt ahz ah hey? *Foglalt az a hely?*

I want to get off at ...
se-ret-nehk le-saall-ni ... *Szeretnék leszállni ...*

Where can I hire a bicycle?
hol beh-rel-he-tek edj *Hol bérelhetek egy*
ke-rehk-paart? *kerékpárt?*

Car

Where can I rent a car?
hol beh-rel-he-tek *Hol bérelhetek egy autót?*
edj ah-u-toht?

How much is it daily/weekly?
meny-nyi-be ke-rül *Mennyibe kerül*
nah-pon-tah/he-ten-te? *naponta/hetente?*

Does that include insurance/mileage?
ahz aar tahr-tahl-mahz- *Az ár tartalmazza a*
zah ah biz-to-shee-taasht/ *biztosítást/kilómétert?*
ki-loh-meh-tert?

ON THE ROAD

AUTÓPÁLYA	**FREEWAY**
EGYIRÁNYÚ	**ONE WAY**
GARÁZS	**GARAGE**
JAVÍTÁSOK	**REPAIRS**
KERÜLŐÚT	**DETOUR**
NEM BEJÁRAT	**NO ENTRY**
NORMÁL	**NORMAL**
ÓLOMMENTES	**UNLEADED**
ÖNKISZOLGÁLÓ	**SELF SERVICE**
SZERELŐ	**MECHANIC**
SZUPER	**SUPER**
TILOS A PARKOLÁS	**NO PARKING**

Where's the next petrol station?
    **hol vahn ah legh-ker-ze-
    leb-bi ben-zin-koot?**
*Hol van a legközelebbi
benzinkút?*

Please fill the tank.
    **keh-rem terl-che megh ah
    ben-zin-tahr-taayt**
*Kérem töltse meg a
benzintartályt.*

I want ... litres of petrol (gas).
    keh-rek ... li-ter ben-zint
Kérek ... liter benzint.

Please check the oil and water.
    **keh-rem el-le-noer-riz-ze
    ahz o-lah-yaht ehsh ah vi-zet**
*Kérem, ellenőrizze
az olajat és a vizet.*

How long can I park here?
    med-digh pahr-kol-hah-tok itt
Meddig parkolhatok itt?

Does this road lead to...?
    ez ahz oot ve-zet ...?
Ez az út vezet ...?

I need a mechanic.
    **sük-sheh-ghem vahn edj
    se-re-loer-re**
*Szükségem van egy
szerelőre.*

What make is it?
    **mi-yen djaart-maa-nyoo
    ahz ah-u-toh?**
*Milyen gyártmányú az
autó?*

I have a flat tyre.
de-fek-tet kahp-tahm   *Defektet kaptam.*
The battery is flat.
le-me-rült ahz   *Lemerült az*
akku-mu-laa-tor   *akkumulátor.*
The radiator is leaking.
fo-yik ah hüü-toer   *Folyik a hűtű.*
It's overheating.
tool-füüt   *Túlfűt.*
It's not working.
nem müü-ker-dik   *Nem működik.*

air (for tyres)	le-ve-ghoer	*levegő*
battery	ahk-ku-mu-laa-tor	*akkumulátor*
brakes	fehk	*fék*
clutch	kup-lungh	*kuplung*
driver's licence	yo-gho-sheet-vaany	*jogosítvány*
engine	mo-tor	*motor*
lights	vi-laa-ghee-taash	*világítás*
oil	o-lahy	*olaj*
petrol	ben-zint	*benzint*
puncture	de-fekt	*defekt*
radiator	hüü-toer	*hűtő*
road map	ah-u-tohsh tehr-kehp	*autós térkép*
tyres	ke-rehk-ghu-mi	*kerékgumi*
windscreen	sehl-veh-doer	*szélvédő*

ACCOMMODATION

Where's a ...	hol vahn edj ...	*Hol van egy ...*
hotel?	saal-lo-dah?	*szálloda?*
cheap	ol-choh	*olcsó*
clean	tis-tah	*tiszta*
good	yoh	*jó*
nearby	ker-ze-li	*közeli*

What's the address?
mi ah tseem? *Mi a cím?*

Could you write the address, please?
le-eer-naa ah tsee-met keh-rem? *Leírná a címet kérem?*

At the Hotel

Do you have any rooms available?
vahn sah-bahd so-baa-yuk? *Van szabad szobájuk?*

I'd like ...	se-ret-nehk edj ...	*Szeretnék egy ...*
a single room	edj-aa-djahsh so-baat	*egyágyas szobát*
a double room	keht-aa-djahsh so-baat	*kétágyas szobát*
a room with a bathroom	für-doer-so-baash so-baat	*fürdőszobás szobát*
to share a dorm	aa-djaht edj haa-loh-te-rem-ben	*ágyat egy hálóteremben*
a bed	edj aa-djaht	*egy ágyat*

ACCOMMODATION

IFJÚSÁGI SZÁLLÓ	YOUTH HOSTEL
SZÁLLODA	HOTEL
VENDÉGHÁZ	GUESTHOUSE

HUNGARIAN

I want a room	se-ret-nehk edj	*Szeretnék egy*
with a ...	so-baat ...	*szobát...*
bathroom	für-doer-so-baa-vahl	*fürdőszobával*
shower	zu-hah-nyo-zoh-vahl	*zuhanyozóval*
window	ahb-lahk-kahl	*ablakkal*

I'm staying for ...	... mah-rah-dok	*... maradok*
one day	edj nah-pigh	*Egy napig*
two days	keht nah-pigh	*Két napig*
one week	edj heh-tigh	*Egy hétig*

I don't know how
long I'm staying.

	mehgh nem tu-dom	*Még nem tudom*
	pon-to-shahn hodj	*pontosan, hogy*
	med-digh mah-rah-dok	*meddig maradok.*

How much is it per night/per person?

	meny-nyi-be ke-rül	*Mennyibe kerül*
	ehy-sah-kaan-kehnt/	*éjszakánként/*
	se-meh-yen-kehnt?	*személyenként?*

THEY MAY SAY ...

van valamilyen a személyazonosságát igazoló papírja?	Do you have identification?
kérem a tagsági igazolványát.	Your membership card, please.
sajnálom, de tele vagyunk.	Sorry, we're full.
meddig marad?	How long will you be staying?
hány éjszakát marad?	How many nights?
... naponta/ személyenként.	It's ... per day/ per person.

HUNGARIAN

Can I see it?
   megh-neh-he-tem ah   *Megnézhetem a szobát?*
   so-baat?
Are there any others?
   vahn edj maa-shik so-bah?   *Van egy másik szoba?*
Are there any cheaper
rooms?
   vahn edj ol-chohbb   *Van egy olcsóbb szoba?*
   so-bah?

Can I see the bathroom?
   meg-nehz-he-tem ah   *Megnézhetem a*
   für-doer-so-baat?   *fürdőszobát?*
Is there hot water all day?
   e-ghehs nahp vahn   *Egész nap van meleg*
   me-legh veez?   *víz?*
Is there a reduction for
students/children?
   vahn ked-vez-mehny   *Van kedvezmény*
   di-aa-kok-nahk/   *diákoknak/*
   dje-re-kek-nek?   *gyerekeknek?*
Does it include breakfast?
   ahz aar tahr-tahl-   *Az ár tartalmazza a*
   mahz-zah ah regh-ghe-lit? *reggelit?*
It's fine, I'll take it.
   ez yoh les   *Ez jó lesz.*
I'm leaving now/tomorrow.
   mosht/hol-nahp   *Most/holnap megyek el.*
   me-djek el

HUNGARIAN

Requests & Complaints

Do you have a safe where I
can leave my valuables?
    vahn er-nerk-nehl sehf,   *Van önöknél széf, ahol az*
    ah-hol ahz ehr-teh-ke-   *értékeimet hagyhatom?*
    i-met-hahdj-hah-tom?

Is there somewhere to wash
clothes?
    vahn vah-lah-hol edj hey,   *Van valahol egy hely,*
    ah-hol mosh-hah-tok?   *ahol moshatok?*

Can I use the kitchen?
    hahs-naal-hah-tom ah   *Használhatom a konyhát?*

Can I use the telephone?
    hahs-naal-hah-tom ah   *Használhatom a telefont?*
    te-le-font?

Please wake me up at ...
    keh-rek ehb-res-tehsht ...   *Kérek ébresztést ... órakor.*
    oh-rah-kor

I've locked myself out of
my room.
    ki-zaar-tahm mah-ghahm   *Kizátam magam a*
    ah so-baam-bohl   *szobámból.*

The room needs to be cleaned.
    ah so-baat ki kell   *A szobát ki kell takarítani.*

HUNGARIAN

air-conditioned	lehgh-kon-di-tsi-o-naalt	*légkondicionált*
balcony	er-kehy	*erkély*
bathroom	für-doer-so-bah	*fürdőszoba*
bed	aadj	*ágy*
bill	saam-lah	*számla*
blanket	tah-kah-roh	*takaró*
candle	djer-tyah	*gyertya*
clean	tis-tah	*tiszta*
cupboard	sek-rehny	*szekrény*
dark	sher-teht	*sötét*
double bed	dup-lah aadj	*dupla ágy*
electricity	e-lekt-ro-mosh-shaagh	*elektromosság*
excluded	ki-veh-te-leh-vel	*kivételével*
included	be-le-ehrt-ve	*beleértve*
key	kulch	*kulcs*
lift (elevator)	lift	*lift*
a lock	zaar	*zár*
mattress	maht-rats	*matrac*
mirror	tü-kerr	*tükör*
padlock	lah-kaht	*lakat*
pillow	paar-nah	*párna*
quiet	chen-desh	*csendes*
room (in hotel)	so-bah	*szoba*
room number	so-bah-saam	*szobaszám*
sheet	le-pe-doer	*lepedő*
shower	zu-hah-nyo-zoh	*zuhanyozó*
soap	sahp-pahn	*szappan*
suitcase	boer-rernd	*bőrönd*
swimming pool	u-so-dah	*uszoda*
toilet	veh tseh	*WC*
towel	ter-rerl-ker-zoer	*törölköző*
(cold/hot) water	(hi-degh/me-legh) veez	*(hideg/meleg) víz*
window	ahb-lahk	*ablak*

AROUND TOWN

I'm looking for a/the ...	ke-re-shem ...	*Keresem ...*
art gallery	ah gah-leh-ri-aat	*a galériát*
bank	ah bahn-kot	*a bankot*
church	ah temp-lo-mot	*a templomot*
city centre	ah vaa-rosh-kerz-pon-tot	*a városköz-pontot*
... embassy	ah/ahz ... ker-vet-sheh-ghet	*a/az ... követ-séget*
hotel	ah saal-lo-daa-maht	*a szállodámat*
market	ah pi-ah-tsot	*a piacot*
museum	ah moo-ze-u-mot	*a múzeumot*
police	ah ren-doer-sheh-ghet	*a rendőrséget*
post office	ah posh-taat	*a postát*
public toilet	ah nyil-vaa-nosh veh tseht	*a nyilvános WCt*
telephone centre	ah te-le-fon-kerz-pon-tot	*a telefon-központot*
the tourist information office	ah tu-rish-tah in-for-maa-tsi-ohsh i-ro-daat	*a turista információs irodát*

What time does it open?
mi-kor nyit ki?　　　　*Mikor nyit ki?*

What time does it close?
mi-kor zaar be?　　　　*Mikor zár be?*

What street/suburb is this?
me-yik ut-tsah/ke-rü-let ez?　　　*Melyik utca/kerület ez?*

For directions, see the Getting Around section, page 146.

At the Post Office

I'd like some stamps.
beh-ye-ghet se-ret-nehk ven-ni   *Bélyeget szeretnék venni.*
How much is the postage?
meny-nyi-be ke-rül ah beh-yegh?   *Mennyibe kerül a bélyeg?*

I'd like to	se-ret-nehk	*Szeretnék*
send a/an ...	el-kül-de-ni ...	*elküldeni ...*
letter	edj le-ve-let	*egy levelet*
postcard	edj keh-pesh-lah-pot	*egy képeslapot*
parcel	edj cho-mah-ghot	*egy csomagot*
telegram	edj taa-vi-rah-tot	*egy táviratot*
air mail	leh-ghi-posh-tah	*légiposta*
envelope	bo-ree-tehk	*boríték*
mail box	posh-tah-laa-dah	*postaláda*
registered mail	ah-yaan-lott	*ajánlott*
	kül-de-mehny	*küldemény*
surface mail	shi-mah posh-tah	*síma posta*

Telephone

I want to ring ...
se-ret-nehm fel-heev-ni ...   *Szeretném felhívni ...*
The number's ...
ah saam ...   *A szám ...*
I want to speak for three minutes.
haa-rom per-tsigh   *Három percig*
se-ret-nehk be-sehl-ni   *szeretnék beszélni.*
How much does a three-minute
call cost?
meny-nyi-be ke-rül edj   *Mennyibe kerül egy*
haa-rom-per-tsesh hee-vaash?   *három perces hívás?*
I want to make a reverse-charges
phone call.
er be-sehl-ghe-tehsht se-ret-nehk   *R beszélgetést szeretnék.*
How much does each extra
minute cost?
meny-nyi-be ke-rül   *Mennyibe kerül minden*
min-den to-vaab-bi edj perts?   *további egy perc?*

I'd like to speak to (Mr Perez).
   (pe-rez oor-rahl)
   se-ret-nehk be-sehl-ni
It's engaged.
   fog-lahlt
I've been cut off.
   meg-sah-kahdt ah vo-nahl

(Perez úrral) szeretnék beszélni.

Foglalt.

Megszakadt a vonal.

Internet

Where can I get Internet access?
   hol hahs-naal-hah-tom ahz
   in-ter-ne-tet?
How much is it per hour?
   meny-nyibe ke-rül edj
   oh-raa-rah?
I want to check my email.
   se-ret-nehm meg-nehz-ni,
   hodj ehr-ke-zett-e i-meh-lem

Hol használhatom az Internetet?

Mennyibe kerül egy órára?

Szeretném megnézni, hogy érkezett-e emailem.

At the Bank

I want to exchange some
(money/travellers cheques).
   se-ret-nehk (pehnzt/utah-
   zaa-shi chek-ket) vaal-tah-ni
What's the exchange rate?
   meny-nyi ahz aar-fo-yahm?
How many forints per dollar?
   haany fo-rint edj dol-laar?
Can I have money transferred
here from my bank?
   aat-u-tahl-hah-tok pehnzt
   i-de ah bahn-kom-bohl?
How long will it take to arrive?
   meny-nyi idoer ah-lahtt
   ehr-ke-zik megh ah pehnz?

Szeretnék (pénzt/utazási csekket) váltani.

Mennyi az árfolyam?

Hány forint egy dollár?

Átutalhatok pénzt ide a bankomból?

Mennyi idő alatt érkezik meg a pénz?

HUNGARIAN

Has my money arrived yet?
   megh-ehr-ke-zett maar   *Megérkezett már*
   ah pehn-zem?   *a pénzem?*

bankdraft	bahnk-in-tehz-vehny	*bankintézvény*
banknotes	bahnk-ye-djek	*bankjegyek*
cashier	pehnz-taar	*pénztár*
coins	ehr-mehk	*érmék*
credit card	hi-tel-kaar-tyah	*hitelkártya*
exchange	vaal-taash	*váltás*
loose change	ahp-roh	*apró*
signature	ah-laa-ee-raash	*aláírás*

INTERESTS & ENTERTAINMENT
Sightseeing

Do you have a guidebook/local map?
   vahn ooti-kerny-vük/   *Van útikönyvük/*
   tehr-keh-pük?   *térképük?*
What are the main attractions?
   me-yek ah foerbb   *Melyek a főbb*
   laat-ni-vah-lohk?   *látnivalók?*
What's that?
   mi ahz?   *Mi az?*
How old is it?
   mi-yen reh-ghi?   *Milyen régi?*
Can I take photographs?
   fehny-keh-pez-he-tek?   *Fényképezhetek?*
What time does it open/close?
   mi-kor nyit ki/zaar be?   *Mikor nyit ki/zár be?*

HUNGARIAN

ancient	oer-shi	*ősi*
archaeological	reh-gheh-se-ti	*régészeti*
beach	shtrahnd	*strand*
building	eh-pü-let	*épület*
castle	vaar	*vár*
cathedral	seh-kesh-edj-haaz	*székesegyház*
church	temp-lom	*templom*
concert hall	hahngh-ver-sheny-te-rem	*hangversenyterem*
library	kernyv-taar	*könyvtár*
main square	foer tehr	*főtér*
market	pi-ahts	*piac*
monastery	ko-losh-tor	*kolostor*
monument	em-lehk-müü	*emlékmű*
mosque	me-chet	*mecset*
old city	reh-ghi vaa-rosh	*régi város*
palace	pah-lo-tah	*palota*
opera house	o-pe-rah-haaz	*operaház*
ruins	ro-mok	*romok*
stadium	shtah-di-on	*stadion*
statues	sob-rok	*szobrok*
synagogue	zhi-nah-ghoh-ghah	*zsinagóga*
temple	temp-lom	*templom*
university	e-dje-tem	*egyetem*

Going Out

What's there to do in the evenings?
    mit le-het chi-naal-ni   *Mit lehet csinálni*
    esh-tehn-kehnt?   *esténként?*

Are there any danceclubs?
    vahn-nahk dis-kohk?   *Vannak diszkók?*

Are there places where you can
hear local folk music?
    vah-nahk o-yahn he-yek,   *Vannak olyan helyek,*
    ah-hol he-yi nehp-ze-neht   *ahol helyi népzenét*
    le-het hahll-ghaht-ni?   *lehet hallgatni?*

How much does it cost to get in?
    meny-nyi-be ke-rül ah   *Mennyibe kerül a*
    be-leh-poer?   *belépő?*

HUNGARIAN

cinema	mo-zi	*mozi*
concert	kon-tsert	*koncert*
danceclub	dis-koh	*diszkó*
theatre	seen-haaz	*színház*

Sports & Interests

What sports do you play?
  Mit shpor-tol? *Mit sportol?*
What are your interests?
  Mi ehr-dek-li Ernt? *Mi érdekli Önt?*

art	müü-veh-set	*művészet*
basketball	ko-shaar-lahb-dah	*kosárlabda*
chess	shahk	*sakk*
collecting things	djüüy-tehsh	*gyűjtés*
dancing	taants	*tánc*
food	eh-tel	*étel*
football	lahb-dah-roo-ghaash	*labdarúgás*
hiking	djah-logh-too-raa-zaash	*gyalogtúrázás*
martial arts	hahr-tsi müü-veh-se-tek	*harci művészetek*
meeting friends	bah-raa-ti be-sehl-ghe-teh-shek	*baráti beszélgetések*
movies	fil-mek	*filmek*
music	ze-ne	*zene*
nightclubs	ehy-sah-kah-i klub-ok	*éjszakai klubok*
photography	fehny-keh-pe-zehsh	*fényképezés*
reading	ol-vah-shaash	*olvasás*
shopping	vaa-shaar-laash	*vásárlás*
skiing	shee-e-lehsh	*síelés*
swimming	oo-saash	*úszás*
tennis	te-ni-se-zehsh	*teniszezés*
travelling	u-tah-zaash	*utazás*
TV/videos	teh-veh-neh-zehsh/ vi-de-oh-zaash	*tévénézés/ videózás*
visiting friends	bah-raa-tok megh-laa-to-ghah-taa-shah	*barátok meglátogatása*
walking	sheh-taa-laash	*sétálás*

HUNGARIAN

Festivals

BudaFest Nyári Opera és Balett Fesztivál

BudaFest Summer Opera and Ballet Festival
staged in the Budapest Opera House to packed houses every
August, this festival attracts outstanding guest performers

Budapesti Őszszi Fesztivál

Budapest Autumn Festival
a festival of contemporary art held during the second half of
October

Budapesti Tavaszi Fesztivál (BTF)

Budapest Spring Festival
this festival of festivals covers a vast range of artistic fields and
attracts many international artists. It's held during the second
half of March.

Budapesti Nemzetközi Borfesztivál

Budapest International Wine Festival
everything about wine – Hungarian and international (early
September)

Soproni Ünnepi Hetek

Festive Weeks in Sopron
held June-July, this celebrates early music, street theatre, children's progammes and jazz

Gyulai Várszínház

Gyula Castle Theatre
held during July and August, this festival covers spectacular
historical dramas, opera, operetta, ballet, medieval music, jazz
and folk music

Pepsi Sziget

Pepsi Island
Hungary's very own weeklong pop festival on Shipyard Island
in Budapest is held in early August. Bring a tent and ear plugs.

Szegedi Szabadtéri Játékok

Summer Festival Szeged
popular theatrical productions, opera, folklore, musicals and
rock operas (July and August)

IN THE COUNTRY
Weather

What's the weather like?
mi-yen ahz i-doer?

Milyen az idő?

The weather's ...	ahz i-doer ...	*Az idő ...*
today.	mah	*ma.*
Will it be ...	... les	*... lesz*
tomorrow?	hol-nahp?	*holnap?*
cloudy	fel-hoersh	*felhős*
cold	hi-degh	*hideg*
foggy	ker-dersh	*ködös*
frosty	hüü-versh	*hűvös*
hot	me-legh	*meleg*
raining	e-shoer	*eső*
snowing	hah-vah-zaash	*havazás*
sunny	nah-posh	*napos*
windy	se-lesh	*szeles*

Camping

Am I allowed to camp here?
itt le-het kem-pin-ghez-ni?

Itt lehet kempingezni?

Is there a campsite nearby?
vahn itt vah-lah-hol ah
ker-zel-ben edj kem-pingh?

*Van itt valahol a
közelben egy kemping?*

backpack	haa-ti-zhaak	*hátizsák*
can opener	kon-zerv-nyi-toh	*konzervnyitó*
compass	i-raany-tüü	*iránytű*
crampons	yehgh-segh	*jégszeg*
firewood	tüü-zi-fah	*tűzifa*
gas cartridge	gaaz-paht-ron	*gázpatron*
hammock	fügh-ghoer-aadj	*függőágy*
ice axe	yehgh-chaa-kaany	*jégcsákány*
mattress	maht-rats	*matrac*
penknife	zheb-kehsh	*zsebkés*
rope	ker-tehl	*kötél*

tent	shaa-tor	*sátor*
tent pegs	shaa-tor tser-ler-perk	*sátor cölöpök*
torch (flashlight)	zheb-laam-pah	*zseblámpa*
sleeping bag	haa-loh-zhaak	*hálózsák*
stove	kem-pingh-foer-zoer	*kempingfőző*
water bottle	vi-zesh-pah-lahtsk	*vizespalack*

FOOD

As befits a country that has been at the crossroads of history for centuries, Hungarian cuisine is a special mixture of foods from many cultures, such as Balkan, Czech, German and Austrian. Add to this traditional regional specialities and the visitor won't be disappointed in the wide range of spicy, sweet, sour and smoky flavours.

Many dishes contain the famous Hungarian paprika, ranging from biting hot *csípős* to the sweet 'rose paprika'. Sour cream is also a favourite and accompanies a vast range of dishes. Pork is the most common meat, found in most establishments along with poultry dishes. Fish is often fresh and excellent, particularly around Lake Balaton, the Danube or the Tisza rivers; beef and lamb are not as common. Don't miss the game dishes if you find a restaurant specialising in these.

The main types of restaurants are:

Vendéglő **ven-dehgh-loer**
small with good food at reasonable prices

Étterem **eht-te-rem**
wide variety of dishes; wide variations in service

Csárda **chaar-dah**
country cooking; limited menu but usually good

Önkiszolgáló **ern-ki-sol-ghaa-loh**
self service, cheap and filling; no prizes for haute cuisine.

breakfast	regh-ghe-li	*reggeli*
lunch	e-behd	*ebéd*
dinner	vah-cho-rah	*vacsora*

Table for ..., please.
   se-ret-nehk edj   *Szeretnék egy asztalt ...*
   ahs-tahlt ... se-mehy-re   *személyre.*
Can I see the menu, please?
   megh-nehz-he-tem ahz   *Megnézhetem az*
   eht-lah-pot?   *étlapot?*
I'd like the set lunch.
   me-nüt keh-rek   *Menüt kérek.*
Not too spicy, please.
   nem tool füü-se-re-shen keh-rem   *Nem túl fűszeresen, kérem.*
What does it include?
   mi vahn ben-ne?   *Mi van benne?*
Is service included in the bill?
   ahz aar tahr-tahl-mahz-zah   *Az ár tartalmazza*
   ah fel-sol-ghaa-laasht?   *a felszolgálást?*

ashtray	hah-mu-tahr-toh	*hamutartó*
bill	ah saam-lah	*a számla*
cup	cheh-se	*csésze*
dessert	eh-desh-shehgh	*édesség.*
drink	i-tahl	*ital*
fork	vil-lah	*villa*
fresh	frish	*friss*
glass	po-haar	*pohár*
knife	kehsh	*kés*
plate	taa-nyehr	*tányér*
spicy	füü-se-resh	*fűszeres*
spoon	kah-naal	*kanál*
stale	nem frish	*nem friss*
sweet	eh-desh	*édes*
teaspoon	teaash-kah-naal	*teáskanál*
toothpick	fogh-pis-kaa-loh	*fogpiszkáló*

HUNGARIAN

MENU DECODER

Starters & Snacks

hortobágyi húsos palacsinta
    hor-to-baa-dji hoo-shosh pah-lah-chin-tah pancake stuffed with stewed and minced meat and herbs, covered with a sauce of gravy and sour cream

libamáj
    li-bah-maay goose liver; a particular delicacy in Hungary. May be cooked in several ways, either in a light meat stock, with onion and water, in milk, or fried. Often served cold with bread as a starter.

rántott gomba
    raan-tott ghom-bah fried mushrooms in breadcrumbs, generally served with rice and tartar sauce or mayonnaise

rántott sajt
    raan-tott shahyt fried cheese in breadcrumbs, served like *rántott gomba*

Soups

bableves
    bahb-le-vesh bean soup with turnip, carrot and sour cream

gombaleves
    ghom-bah-le-vesh a delicious mushroom soup with seasoning, onion, sour cream and parsley

gulyásleves
    ghu-yaash-le-vesh goulash soup, chopped meat fried in onions and paprika, and added to water or stock, with potatoes and a dash of white wine

halászlé
    hah-laas-leh a strong and rich broth of usually several kinds of fish (but always containing carp) in large pieces, with tomatoes, green paprika and red paprika. Beware, this soup has a bite to it! Usually brought to the table in a small cauldron called a *bogrács*, which is placed on a tripod.

hideg gyümölcsleves
    hi-degh djü-merlch-le-vesh cold fruit soup, often cherry, prepared with cream, lemon peel, cinnamon and red wine

káposzta leves
    kaa-pos-tah le-vesh cabbage soup; comes in several variations. A popular one is 'hangover' soup, *korhelyleves* (kor-hey-le-vesh), made with sauerkraut, smoked sausage, onion, paprika and sour cream.

újházy tyúkhúsleves
    ooy-haa-zi tyook-hoosh-le-vesh chicken-and-meat broth with root vegetables and vermicelli

Main Meals

lecsó
    le-choh a delicious thick stew of onions, tomatoes, green peppers and lard. Can be served either as a vegetarian dish with rice, or with smoked sausage.

pörkölt
    perr-kerlt beef *(marha)*, pork *(sertés)*, veal *(borjú)* and game *(vad)* stew cooked in lard with onions, bacon and paprika, plus the obligatory sour cream

töltött paprika
    terl-tertt pahp-ri-kah green peppers stuffed with a mixture of minced meat, bacon, egg, onion and rice, and baked in a sauce of sour cream

aprópecsenye
    ahp-roh-pe-che-nye braised cutlets of pork with paprika, onion and sour cream. Served with vinegar or lemon juice.

sült csülök
    shült chü-lerk knuckle of pork boiled then coated in flour and fried. Served with horseradish.

gombás fogas
    ghom-baash fo-ghahsh pike-perch, sometimes known as *süllő*, braised with mushrooms and a sauce of white wine, butter, lemon juice, eggs and bone stock

HUNGARIAN

rántott hal
  raan-tott hahl fish fried in breadcrumbs; may be carp (*ponty*) or catfish (*harcsa*)

becsinált csirke
  be-chi-naalt chir-ke chicken fricassee fried with cauliflower, kohlrabi, celery root, carrot, turnip and mushrooms then braised in stock with lemon juice. Flavoured with egg yolks.

pirított libamáj
  pi-ree-tott li-bah-maay fried goose liver, first boiled in milk and then fried without seasoning

fácán narancsos mártással
  faa-tsaan nah-rahn-chosh maar-taash-shahl pheasant in orange sauce, cooked with carrots, onions, mushrooms, lemon peel and smoked meat. Before serving, it is boiled in stock with sugar and orange peel.

nyúl vörös borban
  nyool ver-rersh bor-bahn hare braised in red wine, with butter, pork cubes and an onion

lángos
  laan-ghosh an institution in Hungary; light dough mixed with pureed potato, quick-fried in deep fat and served with cheese or sour cream. Also known as a 'heart attack special'.

túrós csusza
  too-rohsh chu-sah fine white noodles mixed with cottage cheese or curds, and lashings of sour cream. Can be savoury with bacon pieces, or sweet with powdered sugar.

Desserts

dobostorta
  do-bosh-tor-tah a sponge cake with layers of buttered cocoa, topped with a hard brown caramel coating

gesztenyepüré
  ghes-te-nye-pü-reh mashed sweet chestnuts cooked in milk with vanilla and served with cream and/or rum

rétes
  reh-tesh strudel filled with a variety of fruits such as sourcherry (*meggy*), apple (*alma*), walnut (*dió*), poppy seed (*mák*), or a particular Hungarian favourite, cottage cheese (*túró*)

HUNGARIAN

Vegetarian Meals

It's still not a great country for vegetarians who wish to eat out, although things are changing fast in the cities. In summer, vegetables and fruit are plentiful and cheap.

I'm a vegetarian.
  ve-ghe-taa-ri-aa-nush vah-djok *Vegetáriánus vagyok.*
I don't eat meat.
  nem e-sem hoosht *Nem eszem húst.*
I don't eat chicken, fish or ham.
  nem e-sem chir-keht, *Nem eszem csirkét,*
  hah-laht, shon-kaat *halat, sonkát.*

Staple Foods & Condiments

bread	ke-nye-ret	*kenyeret*
butter	vah-yaht	*vajat*
cereal	ghah-bonah-eh-te-lek	*gabonaételek*
	regh-ghe-li-re	*reggelire*
cheese	shahy-tot	*sajtot*
chocolate	cho-ko-laa-deht	*csokoládét*
eggs	to-yaasht	*tojást*
flour	lis-tet	*lisztet*
margarine	mahr-ghah-rint	*margarint*
marmalade	lek-vaart	*lekvárt*
milk	te-yet	*tejet*
olive oil	o-li-vah-o-lah-yaht	*olivaolajat*
pepper	bor-shot	*borsot*
rice	ri-zh	*rizs*
salt	shoht	*sót*
sugar	tsuk-rot	*cukrot*
yogurt	yogh-hur-tot	*joghurtot*

Breakfast Menu

On the whole, Hungarians aren't big breakfast eaters, preferring a cup of tea or coffee with an unadorned bread roll.

bread	ke-nye-ret	*kenyeret*
butter	vah-yaht	*vajat*
cereal	ghah-bonah-eh-te-lek	*gabonaételek*
	regh-ghe-li-re	*reggelire*
eggs	to-yaasht	*tojást*
fruit juice	djü-merlch-leh	*gyümölcslé*
margarine	mahr-ghah-rint	*margarint*
marmalade	lek-vaart	*lekvárt*
coffee	kaa-veh	*kávé*
tea	te-ah	*tea*
with milk	tey-yel	*tejjel*
with sugar	tsu-kor-rahl	*cukorral*

Alcoholic Drinks

brandy	paa-lin-kah	*pálinka*
champagne	pezh-ghoer	*pezsgő*
spirits	rer-vid i-tah-lok	*rövid italok*
spritzer	frertsch	*fröccs*
... beer	... sherr	*... sör*
bottled	ü-ve-ghesh	*üveges*
dark	bahr-nah	*barna*
draught	chah-polt	*csapolt*
lager	vi-laa-ghosh	*világos*
wine	bor	*bor*
dry	saa-rahz	*száraz*
red	ver-rersh	*vörös*
rosé	ro-zeh	*rozé*
semidry	fel-saa-rahz	*félszáraz*
semisweet	fe-leh-desh	*félédes*
sweet	eh-desh	*édes*
white	fe-hehr	*fehér*

HUNGARIAN

BOOZE BOX

Hungary has around 20 winegrowing areas, concentrated in Transdanubia, the Northern Upland and the Great Plain. Distinctive reds come from Villány and Szekszárd in Southern Transdanubia, while some of the best whites are from around Lake Balaton and the Mátra Hills.

When choosing wine, look for the words:
minőség bor   'quality wine'
These are the closest thing Hungary has to *appellation controlée*. The quality of a label can vary widely from bottle to bottle. On the label, the first word indicates where the wine comes from. The second word is the grape variety.

Non-Alcoholic Drinks

drinks	i-tah-lok	*italok*
fruit juice	djü-merlch-leh	*gyümölcslé*
ice	yehgh	*jég*
mineral water	aash-vaany-veez	*ásványvíz*
mineral water (carbonated)	krish-taay-veez	*kristályvíz*
soft drinks	ü-dee-toerk	*üdítők*
(boiled) water	(for-rahlt) veez	*(forralt) víz*
coffee	kaa-veh	*kávé*
tea	te-ah	*tea*
with milk	tey-yel	*tejjel*
with sugar	tsu-kor-rahl	*cukorral*

HUNGARIAN

AT THE MARKET

Basics

bread	ke-nye-ret	*kenyeret*
butter	vah-yaht	*vajat*
cereal	ghah-bonah-eh-te-lek	*gabonaételek*
	regh-ghe-li-re	*reggelire*
cheese	shahy-tot	*sajtot*
chocolate	cho-ko-laa-deht	*csokoládét*
eggs	to-yaasht	*tojást*
flour	lis-tet	*lisztet*
margarine	mahr-ghah-rint	*margarint*
marmalade	lek-vaart	*lekvárt*
milk	te-yet	*tejet*
olive oil	o-li-vah-o-lah-yaht	*olivaolajat*
pepper	bor-shot	*borsot*
rice	ri-zh	*rizs*
salt	shoht	*sót*
sugar	tsuk-rot	*cukrot*
yogurt	yogh-hur-tot	*joghurtot*

Meat & Poultry

ham	shon-kaat	*sonkát*
hamburger	hahm-bur-gher	*hamburger*
lamb	baa-raany	*bárány*
sausage	kol-baas	*kolbász*
turkey	puy-kahv	*pulyka*
veal	bor-yoo	*borjú*

Vegetables

beetroot	tsehk-lah	*cékla*
broad beans	bahb	*bab*
cabbage	kaa-pos-tah	*káposzta*
green beans	zerld-bahb	*zöldbab*
(red/green)	(pi-rosh/zerld)	*(piros/zöld)*
capsicum	pahp-ri-kah	*paprika*
cauliflower	kahr-fi-ol	*karfiol*
carrot	shaar-gha h-reh-pah	*sárgarépa*
celery	zel-ler	*zeller*

AT THE MARKET

chickpeas	chi-che-ri-bor-shoh	csicseriborsó
chillies	e-roersh pi-rosh pahp-ri-kah	erős piros paprika
cucumber	u-bor-kah	uborka
eggplant (aubergine)	pahd-li-zhaan	padlizsán
garlic	fok-hadj-mah	fokhagyma
gherkin	u-bor-kah	uborka
ginger	djerm-behr	gyömbér
kidney beans	shpah-nyol-bahb	spanyolbab
lentils	len-che	lencse
lettuce	fe-yesh shah-laa-tah	fejes saláta
onion	hahdj-mah	hagyma
peas	bor-shoh	borsó
potato	bur-gho-nyah/krump-li	burgonya/krumpli
spinach	pah-rahy/shpe-noht	paraj/spenót
tomato	pah-rah-di-chom	paradicsom
zucchini	tsuk-ki-ni	cukkini

Seafood

lobster	ho-maar	homár
mussels	kahdj-loh	kagyló
oysters	ost-ri-gha	hosztriga
shrimp	ahp-roh ten-ghe-ri raak	apró tengeri rák

Fruit

apricot	shaar-ghah-bah-ratsk	sárabarack
banana	bah-naan	banán
fig	fu-ghe	füge
grapes	soer-loer	szőlő
kiwifruit	ki-vi	kivi
lemon	tsit-rom	citrom
orange	nah-rahnch	narancs
peach	oersi-bah-rahtsk	őszibarack
pear	kerr-te	körte
plum	sil-vah	szilva
strawberry	ferl-di-e-per	földieper

HUNGARIAN

SHOPPING

How much is it?	meny-nyi-be ke-rül?	*Mennyibe kerül?*
Where's the	hol vahn ah	*Hol van a*
nearest ...?	leg-ker-ze-leb-bi ...?	*legközelebbi...?*
bookshop	kerny-vesh-bolt	*könyvesbolt*
camera shop	fo-toh-üz-let	*fotóüzlet*
clothing store	ru-haa-zah-ti bolt	*ruházati bolt*
delicatessen	de-li-kaat-üz-let	*delikátüzlet*
general store	aa-ru-haaz	*áruház*
laundry	pah-tyo-laht	*patyolat*
market	pi-ats	*piac*
newsagency	ooy-shaa-ghosh	*újságos*
stationer's	pah-peer-üz-let	*papírüzlet*
pharmacy/chemist	djohdj-ser-taar	*gyógyszertár*
shoeshop	tsi-poer-üz-let	*cipőüzlet*
souvenir shop	ah-yaan-dehk-bolt	*ajándékbolt*
supermarket	eh-lel-mi-ser-	*élelmiszer-*
	aa-ru-haaz	*áruház*
green grocer	zerld-sheh-ghesh	*zöldséges*

I'd like to buy ...
se-ret-nehk ... t ven-ni   *Szeretnék ...t venni.*

Do you have any others?
vahn vah-lah-mi maash?   *Van valami más?*

I don't like it.
ez nem tet-sik   *Ez nem tetszik.*

Can I look at it?
megh-nehz-he-tem ezt?   *Megnézhetem ezt?*

I'm just looking.
chahk neh-ze-loer-derm   *Csak nézelődöm.*

Can you write down the price?
le-eer-naa ahz aa-raat?   *Leírná az árát?*

Do you accept credit cards?
el-fo-ghahd-nahk   *Elfogadnak hitelkártyát?*
hi-tel-kaar-tyaat?

Essential Groceries

I'd like ...	keh-rek ...	*Kérek ...*
batteries	e-le-met	*elemet*
bread	ke-nye-ret	*kenyeret*
butter	vah-yaht	*vajat*
cheese	shahy-tot	*sajtot*
chocolate	cho-ko-laa-deht	*csokoládét*
eggs	to-yaasht	*tojást*
ham	shon-kaat	*sonkát*
honey	meh-zet	*mézet*
margarine	mahr-ghah-rint	*margarint*
marmalade	lek-vaart	*lekvárt*
matches	dju-faat	*gyufát*
milk	te-yet	*tejet*
shampoo	shahm-pont	*sampont*
soap	sahp-pahnt	*szappant*
toilet paper	veh tseh pah-peert	*WC papírt*
toothpaste	fogh-kreh-met	*fogkrémet*
washing powder	mo-shoh-port	*mosóport*

Clothing

clothing	ru-haa-zaht	*ruházat*
coat	kah-baat	*kabát*
dress	ru-hah	*ruha*
jacket	zah-koh	*zakó*
jumper (sweater)	pu-loh-ver	*pulóver*
shirt	ingh	*ing*
shoes	tsi-poer	*cipő*
skirt	sok-nyah	*szoknya*
trousers	nahd-raagh	*nadrág*
underwear	fe-hehr-ne-müü	*fehérnemű*

HUNGARIAN

It's too ...	ez tool ...	*Ez túl ...*
big	nadj	*nagy*
small	kichi	*kicsi*
short	rer-vid	*rövid*
long	hos-soo	*hosszú*
tight	so-rosh	*szoros*
loose	boer	*bő*

Materials

What's it made of?	mi-boerl keh-sült?	*Miből készült?*
brass	rehz	*réz*
cotton	pah-mut	*pamut*
gold	ah-rahny	*arany*
handmade	keh-zi-mun-kah	*kézimunka*
leather	boer	*bőr*
pure alpaca	tis-tah ahl-pah-kah	*tiszta alpaka*
silk	she-yem	*selyem*
silver	e-züsht	*ezüst*
wool	djahp-yoo	*gyapjú*

Colours

black	fe-ke-te	*fekete*
blue	kehk	*kék*
brown	bahr-nah	*barna*
green	zerld	*zöld*
orange	nah-rahnch-shaar-ghah	*narancssárga*
pink	roh-zhah-seen	*rózsaszín*
red	pi-rosh	*piros*
white	fe-hehr	*fehér*
yellow	shaar-ghah	*sárga*

Souvenirs

earrings	fül-be-vah-loh	*fülbevaló*
handicraft	keh-zi-mun-kah	*kézimunka*
necklace	nyahk-laants	*nyaklánc*
pottery	ah-djagh-aa-ru	*agyagáru*
ring	djüü-rüü	*gyűrű*
rug	ki-shebb soer-nyegh	*kisebb szőnyeg*

THEY MAY SAY ...

she-gheet-he-tek?	Can I help you?
ez min-den?	Will that be all?
be-cho-mah-ghol-yuk?	Would you like it wrapped?
shay-nosh chahk ez ahz edj vahn	Sorry, this is the only one.
meny-nyit/haany dah-rah-bot se-ret-ne?	How much/many do you want?

Toiletries

comb	feh-shüü	*fésű*
condoms	ko-ton	*koton*
deodorant	de-zo-dor	*dezodor*
hairbrush	hahy-ke-fe	*hajkefe*
moisturiser	krehm saa-rahz boer-re	*krém száraz bőrre*
razor	bo-rot-vah	*borotva*
sanitary napkins	e-ghehs-shehgh-üdji be-teht	*egészségügyi betét*
shampoo	shahm-pont	*sampont*
shaving cream	bo-rot-vaal-ko-zoh-krehm	*borotválkozó-krém*
soap	sahp-pahnt	*szappant*
sunscreen	nahp-o-lahy	*napolaj*
tampons	tahm-pon	*tampon*
tissues	pah-peer-zheb-ken-doer	*papírzsebkendő*
toothbrush	fogh-ke-fe	*fogkefe*

HUNGARIAN

Stationery & Publications

map	tehr-kehp	*térkép*
paper	pah-peer	*papír*
pen (ballpoint)	go-yohsh-toll	*golyóstoll*
scissors	ol-loh	*olló*
(English-language) ...	ahn-ghol nyel-vüü ...	*angol nyelvű ...*
newspaper	ooy-shaagh	*újság*
novels	re-gheh-nyek	*regények*

Photography

How much is it to process this film?
    meny-nyi-be ke-rül   *Mennyibe kerül*
    eloer-heev-ni ezt ah fil-met?   *előhívni ezt a filmet?*
When will it be ready?
    mi-kor les kehs?   *Mikor lesz kész?*
I'd like a film for this camera.
    edj fil-met se-ret-nehk eb-be   *Egy filmet szeretnék ebbe*
    ah fehny-keh-pe-zoer-ghehp-be   *a fényképezőgépbe.*

B&W (film)	fe-ke-te fe-hehr-film	*fekete-fehér film*
camera	fehny-keh-pe-zoer-ghehp	*fényképezőgép*
colour (film)	see-nesh-film	*színesfilm*
film	film	*film*
lash	vah-ku	*vaku*
lens	len-che	*lencse*
light meter	fehny-meh-roer	*fénymérő*

Smoking

A packet of cigarettes, please.
    edj cho-mahgh   *Egy csomag*
    tsi-ghah-ret-taat keh-rek   *cigarettát kérek.*
Are these cigarettes strong/mild?
    ez ah tsi-ghah-ret-tah   *Ez a cigaretta*
    e-roersh/djen-ghe?   *erős/gyenge?*
Do you have a light?
    vahn tü-ze?   *Van tüze?*
Do you smoke?
    ern do-haany-zik?   *Ön dohányzik?*
Please don't smoke.
    keh-rem ne do-haa-nyoz-zon!   *Kérem, ne dohányozzon!*

cigarette papers	tsi-ghah-ret-tah pah-peer	*cigaretta papír*
cigarettes	tsi-ghah-ret-tah	*cigaretta*
filtered	füsht-süü-roersh	*füstszűrős*
lighter	ern-djooy-toh	*öngyújtó*
matches	dju-fah	*gyufa*
menthol	men-to-losh	*mentolos*
pipe	pi-pah	*pipa*
tobacco (pipe)	pi-pah-do-haany	*pipadohány*

SIGNS

TILOS A DOHÁNYZÁS	NO SMOKING

Sizes & Comparisons

small	ki-chi	*kicsi*
big	nahdj	*nagy*
heavy	ne-hehz	*nehéz*
light	kerny-nyüü	*könnyű*
more	terbb	*több*
less	ke-ve-shebb	*kevesebb*
too much/many	tool shok	*túl sok*

HUNGARIAN

HEALTH

Where's the ...?	hol vahn ...?	*Hol van ...?*
chemist	ah djohdj-ser-taar	*a gyógyszertár*
dentist	ah fogh-or-vosh	*a fogorvos*
doctor	ahz or-vosh	*az orvos*
hospital	ah kohr-haaz	*a kórház*

I'm sick.
 ros-sul vah-djok   *Rosszul vagyok.*
My friend is sick.
 ah bah-raa-tom ros-sul vahn   *A barátom rosszul van.*
What's the matter?
 mi ah prob-leh-mah?   *Mi a probléma?*
Where does it hurt?
 hol faay?   *Hol fáj?*
It hurts here.
 itt faay   *Itt fáj.*

Parts of the Body

My ... hurts.	ah/ahz ... faay	*A/az ... fáj.*
ankle	bo-kaam	*bokám*
arm	kah-rom	*karom*
back	haa-tahm	*hátam*
chest	mell-kah-shom	*mellkasom*
ear	fü-lem	*fülem*
eye	se-mem	*szemem*
finger	uy-yahm	*ujjam*
foot	laab-fe-yem	*lábfejem*
hand	ke-zem	*kezem*
head	fe-yem	*fejem*
heart	see-vem	*szívem*
leg	laa-bahm	*lábam*
mouth	saam	*szám*
nose	or-rom	*orrom*
ribs	bor-daam	*bordám*
skin	boer-rerm	*bőröm*

spine	ghe-rin-tsem	*gerincem*
stomach	djom-rom	*gyomrom*
teeth	fo-ghahm	*fogam*
throat	tor-kom	*torkom*

Ailments

I have (a/an) ...

allergy	ahl-ler-ghi-aash vah-djok	*Allergiás vagyok.*
blister	hoh-yahgh vahn rahy-tahm	*Hólyag van rajtam.*
burn	megh-eh-ghet-tem mah-ghahm	*Megégettem magam.*
cold	megh-faaz-tahm	*Megfáztam.*
constipation	sehk-re-ke-deh-shem vahn	*Székrekedésem van.*
cough	ker-her-gherk	*Köhögök.*
diarrhoea	hahsh-me-neh-shem vahn	*Hasmenésem van.*
fever	laa-zahm vahn	*Lázam van.*
headache	faay ah fe-yem	*Fáj a fejem.*
hepatitis	maay-djul-lah-daa-shom-vahn	*Májgyulladá-somvan.*
influenza	in-flu-en-zaash va-djok	*Influenzás vagyok.*
(low/high) blood pressure	(ah-lah-chony/ mah-ghahsh) ah vehr-nyo-maa-shom	*(Alacsony/ Magas) a vérnyomásom.*
pain	faay-dahl-mahm vahn	*Fájdalmam van.*
sore throat	faay ah tor-kom	*Fáj a torkom.*
sprain	fi-tsah-mom vahn	*Ficamom van.*
stomachache	faay ah djom-rom	*Fáj a gyomrom.*
sunburn	le-ehgh-tem	*Leégtem.*
venereal disease	ne-mi be-tegh-sheh-ghem vahn	*Nemi betegségem van.*
worms	ghi-lis-taam vahn	*Gilisztám van.*

Women's Health

Could I see a female doctor?
   edj dok-tor-noert ke-re-shek?   *Egy doktornőt keresek?*
I'm pregnant.
   ter-hesh vah-djok   *Terhes vagyok.*
I'm on the Pill.
   fo-ghahm-zaash-ghaat-loh   *Fogamzásgátlótablettát*
   tab-let-taat se-dek   *szedek.*
I haven't had my period for ....
months.
   nem yertt meg ah mensht-   *Nem jött meg a mens-*
   ruaa-tsiohm ... hoh-nahp-yah   *truációm ... hónapja.*

Useful Words & Phrases

I'm ...
asthmatic	ahst-maash vah-djok	*Asztmás vagyok.*
diabetic	tsu-kor-be-tegh vah-djok	*Cukorbeteg vagyok.*
epileptic	e-pi-lep-si-aash vah-djok	*Epilepsziás vagyok.*

I'm allergic to antibiotics/penicillin.
   ahl-ler-ghi-aash vah-djok   *Allergiás vagyok*
   ahz ahn-ti-bi-o-ti-kum-rah/   *az antibiotikumra/*
   ah pe-ni-tsi-lin-re   *a penicillinre.*
I've been vaccinated.
   be vah-djok olt-vah   *Be vagyok oltva.*
I feel better/worse.
   yob-bahn/ros-sahb-bul   *Jobban/rosszabbul*
   vah-djok   *vagyok.*

accident	bah-le-shet	*baleset*
bite	hah-rah-paash	*harapás*
blood test	vehr-vizh-ghaa-laht	*vérvizsgálat*
injection	in-yek-tsi-oh	*injekció*
injury	sheh-rü-lehsh	*sérülés*
medicine	or-vosh-shaagh	*orvosság*
menstruation	mensht-ru-aa-tsioh	*menstruáció*
wound	sheb	*seb*

At the Chemist

I need medication for ...

    djohdj-ser-re vahn sük-   *Gyógyszerre van*
    sheh-ghem ...   *szükségem ...*

I have a prescription.

    vahn edj re-tsep-tem   *Van egy receptem.*

antibiotics	ahn-ti-bi-o-ti-kum	*antibiotikum*
antiseptic	fer-toer-zehsh-ghaat-loh	*fertőzésgátló*
aspirin	as-pi-rin	*aszpirin*
bandage	ker-tehsh	*kötés*
contraceptive	fo-ghahm-zaash-ghaat-loh	*fogamzásgátló*
vitamins	vi-tah-mi-nok	*vitaminok*

At the Dentist

I have a toothache.

    faay ah fo-ghahm   *Fáj a fogam.*

I've lost a filling.

    ki-e-shett ah ter-mehsh   *Kiesett a tömés.*

I've broken a tooth.

    el-tert edj fo-ghahm   *Eltört egy fogam.*

My gums hurt.

    faay ahz ee-nyem   *Fáj az ínyem.*

I don't want it extracted.

    nem ah-kah-rom ki-hoo-zaht-ni *Nem akarom kihúzatni.*

Please give me an anaesthetic.

    keh-rem ahd-yon   *Kérem adjon*
    ehr-zehsh-te-le-nee-toert   *érzéstelenítőt.*

HUNGARIAN

TIME & DATES

What time is it?
   haany oh-rah?   *Hány óra?*
What date is it today?
   haa-nyah-di-kah vahn mah?   *Hányadika van ma?*
It's ... o'clock.
   ... oh-rah vahn   *... óra van.*

in the morning	regh-ghel	*reggel*
in the afternoon	deh-lu-taan	*délután*
in the evening	esh-te	*este*

Days

Monday	heht-foer	*hétfő*
Tuesday	kedd	*kedd*
Wednesday	ser-dah	*szerda*
Thursday	chü-ter-terk	*csütörtök*
Friday	pehn-tek	*péntek*
Saturday	som-baht	*szombat*
Sunday	vah-shaar-nahp	*vasárnap*

Months

January	yah-nu-aar	*január*
February	feb-ru-aar	*február*
March	maar-tsi-ush	*március*
April	aap-ri-lish	*április*
May	maa-yush	*május*
June	yoo-ni-ush	*június*
July	yoo-li-ush	*július*
August	ah-u-ghus-tush	*augusztus*
September	sep-tem-ber	*szeptember*
October	ok-toh-ber	*október*
November	no-vem-ber	*november*
December	de-tsem-ber	*december*

HUNGARIAN

Seasons

summer	nyaar	*nyár*
autumn	oers	*ősz*
winter	tehl	*tél*
spring	tah-vahs	*tavasz*

Present

now	mosht	*most*
this morning	mah regh-ghel	*ma reggel*
today	mah	*ma*
tonight	mah esh-te	*ma este*
this week	e-zen ah heh-ten	*ezen a héten*
this year	eb-ben ahz ehv-ben	*ebben az évben*

Past

last night	tegh-nahp esh-te	*tegnap este*
yesterday	tegh-nahp	*tegnap*
day before yesterday	tegh-nahp-e-loertt	*tegnapelőtt*
last week/year	moolt heh-ten/ ehv-ben	*múlt héten/ évben*

Future

tomorrow	hol-nahp	*holnap*
tomorrow evening	hol-nahp esh-te	*holnap este*
day after tomorrow	hol-nahp-u-taan	*holnapután*
next week	yer-voer heh-ten	*jövő héten*
next year	yer-voer-re	*jövőre*

HUNGARIAN

During the Day

afternoon	deh-lu-taan	*délután*
dawn; very early morning	hahy-nahl	*hajnal*
day	nahp	*nap*
early	ko-raan	*korán*
midday	dehl	*dél*
midnight	ehy-fehl	*éjfél*
morning	regh-ghel	*reggel*
night	ehy-yel	*éjjel*
sunrise	nahp-fel-kel-te	*napfelkelte*
sunset	nahp-le-men-te	*naplemente*

NUMBERS & AMOUNTS

0	nul-lah	*nulla*
1	edj	*egy*
2	ket-toer	*kettő*
3	haa-rom	*három*
4	nehdj	*négy*
5	ert	*öt*
6	haht	*hat*
7	heht	*hét*
8	nyolts	*nyolc*
9	ki-lents	*kilenc*
10	teez	*tíz*
20	hoos	*húsz*
30	hahr-mints	*harminc*
40	nedj-ven	*negyven*
50	ert-ven	*ötven*
60	haht-vahn	*hatvan*
70	het-ven	*hetven*
80	nyolts-vahn	*nyolcvan*
90	ki-lents-ven	*kilencven*
100	saaz	*száz*
1000	e-zer	*ezer*
one million	edj mil-li-oh	*egy millió*

1st	el-shoer	*első (1.)*
2nd	maa-sho-dik	*második (2.)*
3rd	hahr-mah-dik	*harmadik (3.)*
last	u-tol-shoh	*utolsó*
1/4	edj-ne-djed	*egynegyed*
1/3	edj-hahr-mahd	*egyharmad*
1/2	fehl	*fél*
3/4	haa-rom-ne-djed	*háromnegyed*

Useful Words

Enough!	e-lehgh!	*Elég!*
a little (amount)	edj ke-vehsh	*egy kevés*
double	dup-lah	*dupla*
dozen	edj tu-tsaht	*egy tucat*
few	neh-haany	*néhány*
less	ke-ve-shebb	*kevesebb*
many	shok	*sok*
more	terbb	*több*
once	edj-ser	*egyszer*
pair	edj paar	*egy pár*
per cent	saa-zah-lehk	*százalék*
some	vah-lah-meny-nyi	*valamennyi*
too much	tool shok	*túl sok*
twice	keht-ser	*kétszer*

HUNGARIAN

ABBREVIATIONS

db	piece
de./du.	am/pm
É/D	Nth/Sth
EK	UK
EU	EU
ENSZ	UN
Ft/HUF	Hungarian Forint (currency)
gr/kg	gm/kg
id.	snr
ifj.	jnr
i.sz./i.e.	AD/BC

kb.	approx.
MALÉV	Hungarian Airlines
MÁV	Hungarian State Railways
n/f/hn	quarter past/half past/quarter to (time)
Oszt./Közp.	Dept/HQ
OTP	National Savings Bank
p/mp	minute/second
stb.	etc
u.i./ford.	ps/pto
u/ú/krt/k	St/Rd/Blvd/Lane
I.Vh/II.Vh	WWI/WWII

HUNGARIAN

EMERGENCIES

Help!	she-gheet-shehgh!	*Segítség!*
Go away!	men-yen el!	*Menjen el!*
Thief!	tol-vahy!	*Tolvaj!*
I'm ill.	be-tegh vah-djok	*Beteg vagyok.*
I'm lost.	el-teh-ved-tem	*Eltévedtem.*
I've been robbed!	ki-rah-bol-tahk!	*Kiraboltak!*
I'll call the police!	hee-vom ah ren-doert!	*Hívom a rendőrt!*
It's an emergency!	shüür-ghoersh!	*Sürgős!*
Call a doctor!	heev-yon edj or-vosht!	*Hívjon egy orvost!*
I've been raped.	megh-eroer-sah-kol-tahk	*Megerőszakoltak.*
My friend is ill.	ah bah-raa-tom be-tegh	*A barátom beteg.*

There's been an accident!
  bah-le-shet ter-tehnt!   *Baleset történt!*

Call an ambulance!
  heev-yah ah men-toer-ket!   *Hívja a mentőket!*

Call the police!
  heev-yah ah ren-doer-
  sheh-ghet!   *Hívja a rendőrséget!*

Where's the police station?
  hol ah ren-doer-shehgh?   *Hol a rendőrség?*

Where are the toilets?
  hol vahn ah veh-tseh?   *Hol van a WC?*

Could you help me, please?
  tud-nah she-ghee-te-ni
  keh-rem?   *Tudna segíteni kérem?*

Could I please use the
telephone?
  keh-rem hahs-naal-haht   *Kérem, használhatnám*
  naam ah te-le-font?   *a telefont?*

I'm sorry. I apologise.
  shahy-naa-lom.   *Sajnálom.*
  el-neh-zehsht keh-rek   *Elnézést kérek.*

I didn't do it.
  nem ehn chi-naal-tahm   *Nem én csináltam.*

I didn't realise I was doing anything wrong.

    nem tud-tahm hodj vah-lah-mi ros-saht tet-tem   *Nem tudtam, hogy valami rosszat tettem.*

I want to contact my embassy/consulate.

    se-ret-nehk ah ker-vet-shehgh-ghel/kon-zu-laa-tush-shahl be-sehl-ni   *Szeretnék a követséggel/ konzulátussal beszélni.*

I speak English.

    be-seh-lek (ahn-gho-lul)   *Beszélek (angolul).*

I have medical insurance.

    vahn be-tegh-biz-to-shee-taa-shom   *Van betegbiztosításom.*

My possessions are insured.

    vahn vah-djon-biz-to-shee-taa-shom   *Van vagyonbiztosításom.*

I've lost my ...	el-ves-tet-tem ...	*Elvesztettem ...*
My ... was stolen.	el-lop-taak ...	*Ellopták ...*
bags	ah taash-kaa-i-maht	*a táskáimat*
handbag	ah keh-zi-taash-kaa-maht	*a kézitáskámat*
money	ah pehn-ze-met	*a pénzemet*
travellers cheques	ahz u-tah-zaa-shi chekk-ye-i-met	*az utazási csekkjeimet*
passport	ahz oot-le-ve-le-met	*az útlevelemet*
wallet	pehnz-taar-tsah	*pénztárca*

POLISH

POLISH

QUICK REFERENCE

Hello.	djen *do*-bri	Dzień dobry.
Goodbye.	do vee-*dze*-nya	Do widzenia.
Yes./No.	tak/nye	Tak./Nie.
Excuse me.	pshe-*pra*-sham	Przepraszam.
May I?	chi *mo*-ge?	Czy mogę?
Sorry.	pshe-*pra*-sham	Przepraszam.
Please.	*pro*-she	Proszę.
Thank you.	djen-*koo*-ye	Dziękuję.
You're welcome.	*pro*-she	Proszę.
Where's the ...?	gdje yest ...?	Gdzie jest ...?
What time is it?	*ktoo*-ra (yest)	Która (jest)
	go-*djee*-na?	godzina?
I'd like a ...	po-*pro*-she ...	Poproszę ...
room	po-kooy	pokój
ticket to ...	*bee*-let do ...	bilet do ...
one-way ticket	*bee*-let *fyed*-nom	bilet w jedną
	stro-ne	stronę
return ticket	*bee*-let po-*vrot*-ni	bilet powrotny

I (don't) understand.
  (nye) ro-*zoo*-myem   (Nie) rozumiem.
Do you speak English? (m/f)
  chi pan/*pa*-nee *moo*-vee   Czy pan/pani mówi po
  po an-*gyel*-skoo?   angielsku?
Where are the toilets?
  gdje som to-a-*le*-ti?   Gdzie są toalety?
Turn left/right.
  pro-she *skren*-cheech   Proszę skręcić w
  fle-vo/*fpra*-vo   lewo/prawo.
Go straight ahead.
  pro-she ye-hach da-ley *pros*-to   Proszę jechać dalej prosto.
How much is it ?
  ee-le to kosh-*too*-ye?   Ile to kosztuje?

1	*ye*-den	jeden	6	sheshch	sześć
2	dva	dwa	7	*she*-dem	siedem
3	tshi	trzy	8	*o*-shem	osiem
4	*chte*-ri	cztery	9	*dje*-vyench	dziewięć
5	pyench	pięć	10	*dje*-shench	dziesięć

POLISH

Polish, along with Czech and Slovak, is a western variety of the group of Slavonic languages, which covers a dozen languages spoken in a number of Central and Eastern European countries, including Russia, the Ukraine, Bulgaria, Serbia, Croatia, and the Czech and Slovak republics. The group is a branch of the large Indo-European family of languages which includes English, Greek and Latin, and has its distant origins back in ancient Sanskrit.

Although Polish is a language with a long, if obscure, history, its written form didn't actually develop until the Middle Ages. In medieval Poland, Latin was the lingua franca and the language used by the Crown's state offices, administration and the Church. The oldest known text in Polish, the song *Bogurodzica*, *'Mother of God'*, was reputedly written in the 13th century and was the national anthem until the 18th century.

It wasn't until the Renaissance period that the Polish language came into wider use. The invention of printing contributed to the spread of books; the first printed text in Polish was published in 1475. During the course of the 16th century, Latin became largely dominated by Polish in both its spoken and written form. Polish literature began to develop at a remarkable pace and saw its first major achievements, with a range of Polish literature published.

The Latin alphabet was adapted to write the Polish language, but in order to represent the complex sounds of the tongue, a number of consonant clusters and diacritical marks were applied. In effect, the visual appearance of Polish is pretty fearsome for people from outside the Slavic circle, and undoubtedly it's not the world's easiest language to master. It has a complicated grammar, with word endings changing depending on case, number and gender, and its rules abound in exceptions. Yet, it's not the most difficult language either. Despite its bewildering appearance, Polish script is phonetic, largely consistent, and has a logical structure.

Today, Polish is the official language of Poland and is spoken by over 99 percent of the country's population of 39 million. It's also spoken by roughly up to 10 million Poles scattered all over the world, with the largest Polish emigre community living in the US.

POLISH

Save for a few tiny areas, Polish has no pronounced regional dialects or variations, and sounds pretty much the same the breadth and width of the country. Understandably, there are some minor regional differences in the language's sound and melody, which locals can distinguish but for outsiders won't be noticeable.

As for Western languages, English and German are the best known in Poland though by no means are they commonly spoken or understood. English is most often heard in larger urban centres among educated youth, while German is largely a heritage of pre-WWII territorial divisions and the war itself. German is mainly spoken by the older generation, particularly in regions which were once German. Taking this as a rough rule, you may have some English conversations in major cities, but when travelling in remote parts of Masuria or Silesia, German will be a better tool for communication than English.

This said, remember that most ordinary Poles don't speak any other language than Polish. This includes attendants of public services such as shops, post offices, banks, bus and train stations, restaurants and hotels (except for some top-end ones), and you may even encounter language problems at tourist offices. It's also true of phone emergency lines, including police, ambulance and the fire brigade.

Ideally, everyone who wants to travel in Poland should know some basic Polish – the more you know the easier your travel is likely to be and the more you'll get out of your time in the country. Enjoy your travels!

QUESTIONS

How?	yak?	Jak?
What?	tso?	Co?
When?	*kye*-di?	Kiedy?
Where?	gdje?	Gdzie?
Which?	*ktoo*-ri?	Który?
Who?	ktoo?	Kto?
Why?	dla-*che*-go?	Dlaczego?

POLISH

PRONUNCIATION

Unlike English, Polish is essentially a phonetic language, which means that there's a consistent relationship between pronunciation and spelling. In other words, a letter or a cluster of letters is always pronounced the same way. For example, Polish *a* has one pronunciation rather than the numerous pronunciations we find in English, such as the 'a' in 'cake', 'art' and 'all'.

Following are the transliterations used in this phrasebook to imitate their pronunciation. Consonants not mentioned here are pronounced as they are in English.

	POLISH ALPHABET				
a	a	ę	e	rz	zh/sh
ą	on/om	ę	en/em/e	s	s
b	b/p	g	g/k	sz	sh
c	ts	h	h	ś	sh
ć	ch	i	ee	u	oo
ch	h	j	y	w	v/f
cz	ch	ł	w	y	i
d	d/t	ń	n	z	z/s
dz	dz	o	o	ź	zh
dź	dj	ó	oo	ż	zh
dż	dj	r	r	szcz	shch

Transliterations

Vowels

Polish vowels are of roughly even length.

a	as the 'u' in 'cut'
e	as the 'e' in 'ten'
ee	similar to the 'i' in 'marine' but shorter
em	as the 'em' in 'emblem'
en	as the 'en' in 'engage'
i	as the 'i' in 'bit'
o	as the 'o' in 'not'
oo	as the 'u' in 'put'
om	as the 'om' in 'tomb'
on	as the 'on' in 'bond'

POLISH

Consonants

ch	as the 'ch' in 'church'
dj	as the 'j' in 'jam'
dz	as the 'ds' in 'adds up'
g	as the 'g' in 'get'
h	as the 'ch' in the Scottish 'loch'
n	as the 'ni' in 'onion'
r	always trilled
s	as the 's' in 'sin'
shch	as the 'shch' in 'fresh cheese'
ts	as the 'ts' in 'its'
w	as the 'w' in 'wine'
y	as the 'y' in 'yet'
zh	as the 's' in 'pleasure';
	as the 's' in 'pleasure', but softer

SUBJECT PRONOUNS		
SG		
I	ya	*ja*
you	ti	*ty*
he	on	*on*
she	ona	*ona*
it	ono	*ono*
PL		
we	mi	*my*
you	vi	*wy*
they (m; m+f)	oni	*oni*
they (f; m+f + neut)	one	*one*

Stress

As a rule, the stress falls on the second-last syllable of a word. In some words of foreign origin (mostly from Latin and Greek), stress falls on to the third-last syllable:

music	*moo*-zi-ka	*muzyka*
university	oo-nee-*ver*-si-tet	*uniwersytet*

GREETINGS & CIVILITIES

It's a good idea to use greetings whenever you approach someone. *Dzień dobry*, 'good morning/afternoon', is good in any situation, at any time of the day until evening. In more informal encounters with friends and the people you know well, and particularly with young people, *cześć*, 'hi', is commonly used as both a greeting or when saying goodbye.

POLISH

Top Useful Phrases

Hello.	djen *do*-bri	*Dzień dobry.*
Hi.	cheshch	*Cześć.*
Goodbye.	do vee-*dze*-nya	*Do widzenia.*
Bye.	cheshch	*Cześć.*
See you later.	do zo-ba-*che*-nya	*Do zobaczenia.*
Good evening.	*do*-bri *vye*-choor	*Dobry wieczór.*
Goodnight.	do-*bra*-nots	*Dobranoc.*
Yes./No.	tak/nye	*Tak./Nie*
Excuse me.	pshe-*pra*-sham	*Przepraszam.*
Please.	*pro*-she	*Proszę.*
Thank you (very much).	djen-*koo*-ye (*bar*-dzo)	*Dziękuję (bardzo).*
You're welcome.	*pro*-she	*Proszę.*
Excuse me; Sorry.	pshe-*pra*-sham	*Przepraszam.*
May I; Do you mind?	chi *mo*-ge?	*Czy mogę?*

Forms of Address

Poland is still very much a traditional territory where formal forms of address predominate, particularly among strangers. It's best (and safest) to use *pan*, 'Mr/Sir', and *pani*, 'Mrs/Madam', unless you're among friends or hanging around with younger people, where informality is the norm. Both terms can be written with an initial capital letter, depending on context.

The term *panna*, 'Miss', is old-fashioned and has largely been replaced by *pani*, 'Ms', which can be used for all women, regardless of age and marital status.

POLISH

Mr	pan/pa-*no*-vye	*Pan/Panowie* (sg/pl)
Mrs	*pa*-nee/*pa*-nye	*Pani/Panie* (sg/pl)
Miss	*pan*-na/*pan*-ni	*Panna/Panny* (sg/pl)
Mr & Mrs	*pan*-stfo	*Państwo*
ladies and gentlemen	*pan*-stfo	*Państwo*

PAN & PANI

Remember that the terms *pan* and *pani* are polite
ways of addressing a man or woman respectively.

To strike up a conversation with someone in a formal situation,
it's usual to start with *proszę pana* (lit: please, sir) or *proszę pani*
(lit: please, madam). To address a group of people, you can say
proszę państwa, 'ladies and gentlemen'.

If you want to politely attract a stranger's attention (such as
when asking for directions), begin with *przepraszam pana/pani*,
'excuse me, sir/madam'.

WHATS NEW?!

Polish has a number of expressions roughly equivalent
to the English 'how are you' or 'what's new'. The following list features some of the most common ones.
    They can be used interchangeably, and each is OK
in any informal situation. Except for the last one, they're
also suitable for most formal occasions. They don't
require any specific answer other than just *Dziękuję*,
dobrze, 'fine, thanks'.

tso *swi*-hach?	Co słychać?
tso no-*ve*-go?	Co nowego?
tso do-*bre*-go?	Co dobrego?
yak *zdro*-vye?	Jak zdrowie?
yak *ee*-dje?	Jak idzie?
yak *le*-chee?	Jak leci?

SMALL TALK
Meeting People

POLISH

How are you?
 yak she pan/*pa*-nee ma?   *Jak się pan/pani ma?* (pol)
 yak she mash?   *Jak się masz?* (inf)

Fine, thanks. And you?
 djen-*koo*-ye, *do*-bzhe   *Dziękuję, dobrze.*
 ee pan/*pa*-nee?   *I pan/pani?* (pol)
 djen-*koo*-ye, *do*-bzhe, ee ti? *Dziękuję, dobrze. I ty?* (inf)

My name's ...
 na-*zi*-vam she ...   *Nazywam się ...* + surname (pol)
 mam na *ee*-mye ...   *Mam na imię ...* + first name (inf)

I'm pleased to meet you.
 mee-wo mee *pa*-na/   *Miło mi pana/*
 pa-nyom *poz*-nach   *panią poznać.* (pol)
 mee-wo mee che *poz*-nach *Miło mi cię poznać.* (inf)

Do you live here?
 chi pan/*pa*-nee too   *Czy pan/pani tu*
 myesh-ka?   *mieszka?* (pol)
 chi too *myesh*-kash?   *Czy tu mieszkasz?* (inf)

How long are you here for?
 yak *dwoo*-go pan/*pa*-nee *Jak długo pan/pani*
 too *ben*-dje?   *tu będzie?* (pol)
 yak *dwoo*-go too *ben*-djesh? *Jak długo tu będziesz?* (inf)

I'm/We're here for ... weeks/days.
 ben-de/ben-*dje*-mi too ... *Będę/Będziemy tu ...*
 ti-*god*-nee/dnee   *tygodni/dni.*

Do you like it here?
 chi *pa*-noo/*pa*-nee she too *Czy panu/pani się tu*
 po-*do*-ba?   *podoba?* (pol)
 chi chee she too po-*do*-ba? *Czy ci się tu podoba?* (inf)

I/We like it here very much.
 po-*do*-ba mee/nam she too *Podoba mi/nam się tu*
 bar-dzo   *bardzo.*

It's very nice here.
 yest too *bar*-dzo *wad*-nye *Jest tu bardzo ładnie.*

POLISH

How do you do this in
your country?
    yak to she *ro*-bee *vva*-shim   *Jak to się robi w waszym*
    ***kra*-yoo?**   *kraju?*
Is this a local or national custom?
    chi to yest *zvi*-chay   *Czy to jest zwyczaj lokalny czy*
    lo-*kal*-ni chi na-ro-*do*-vi?   *narodowy?*
How old are you?
    ***ee*-le ma pan/*pa*-nee lat?**   *Ile ma pan/pani lat?* (pol)
    ***ee*-le mash lat?**   *Ile masz lat?* (inf)
How old is your son/daughter?
    ***ee*-le lat ma *pa*-na/*pa*-nee**   *Ile lat ma pana/pani*
    sin/*tsoor*-ka?   *syn/córka?*

I'm ... years old.   **mam ... lat**   *Mam ... lat.*

(See Numbers on page 268 for your age.)

Nationalities

Where are you from?
    skont pan/*pa*-nee   *Skąd pan/pani*
    po-*ho*-djee/yest?   *pochodzi/jest?* (pol)
    skont po-*ho*-djeesh/yes-tesh?   *Skąd pochodzisz/jesteś?* (inf)

I'm from ...	**yes-tem s ...**	*Jestem z ...*
Australia	**a-woos-*tra*-lyee**	*Australii*
Canada	**ka-*na*-di**	*Kanady*
England	**an-glee**	*Anglii*
Europe	**ew-*ro*-pi**	*Europy*
Ireland	**eer-*lan*-dyee**	*Irlandii*
Japan	**ya-*po*-nyee**	*Japonii*
the US	**sta-noof**	*Stanów*
	zye-dno-*cho*-nih	*Zjednoczonych*

I live in/by the ...	**myesh-kam ...**	*Mieszkam ...*
city	**vmyesh-che**	*w mieście*
countryside	**na fshee**	*na wsi*
mountains	**vgoo-rah**	*w górach*
seaside	**nat *mo*-zhem**	*nad morzem*

Occupations

Where do you work?
gdje pan/*pa*-nee pra-*tsoo*-ye? *Gdzie pan/pani pracuje?*
What's your occupation?
ya-kee yest *pa*-na/*pa*-nee *Jaki jest pana/pani*
za-voot? *zawód?*

POLISH

I'm a/an ...	*yes*-tem ...	*Jestem ...*
artist	ar-*tis*-tom	*artystą* (m)
	ar-*tist*-kom	*artystką* (f)
businessperson	biz-nes-*me*-nem	*biznesmenem* (m)
	biz-nes-*men*-kom	*biznesmenką* (f)
doctor	le-*ka*-zhem	*lekarzem* (m)
	le-*kar*-kom	*lekarką* (f)
engineer	een-zhi-*nye*-rem	*inżynierem*
farmer	rol-*nee*-kyem	*rolnikiem*
journalist	re-por-*te*-rem	*reporterem* (m)
	re-por-*ter*-kom	*reporterką* (f)
lawyer	prav-*nee*-kyem	*prawnikiem* (m)
	prav-*neech*-kom	*prawniczką* (f)
mechanic	me-ha-*nee*-kyem	*mechanikiem*
nurse	pye-leng-*nya*-zhem	*pielęgniarzem* (m)
	pye-leng-*nyar*-kom	*pielęgniarką* (f)
office worker	pra-tsov-*nee*-kyem	*pracownikiem*
	byoo-*ro*-vim;	*biurowym* (m)
	pra-tsov-*nee*-tsom	*pracownicą* (f)
	byoo-*ro*-vom	*biurową* (f)
scientist	na-oo-*kof*-tsem	*naukowcem*
student	stoo-*den*-tem	*studentem* (m)
	stoo-*dent*-kom	*studentką* (f)
teacher	na-oo-chi-*che*-lem	*nauczycielem* (m)
	na-oo-chi-*chel*-kom	*nauczycielką* (f)
waiter	kel-*ne*-rem	*kelnerem* (m)
	kel-*ner*-kom	*kelnerką* (f)
writer	pee-*sa*-zhem	*pisarzem* (m)
	pee-*sar*-kom	*pisarką* (f)

POLISH

I'm unemployed.
   yes-tem bez-ro-*bot*-ni/a   *Jestem bezrobotny/a.*

What are you studying?
   tso stoo-*dyoo*-yesh?   *Co studiujesz?* (inf)

I'm studying ...	stoo-*dyoo*-ye ...	*Studiuję ...*
art	*shtoo*-ke	*sztukę*
arts/humanities	na-*oo*-kee hoo-ma-nees-*tich*-ne	*nauki humanistyczne*
business	*biz*-nes	*biznes*
teaching	pe-da-go-*gee*-ke	*pedagogikę*
engineering	een-zhi-*nye*-rye	*inżynierię*
languages	yen-*zi*-kee	*języki*
law	*pra*-vo	*prawo*
medicine	me-di-*tsi*-ne	*medycynę*
Polish	yen-zik *pol*-skee	*język polski*

Religion

What's your religion?
   ya-*kye*-go yest pan/*pa*-nee   *Jakiego jest pan/pani*
   viz-*na*-nya?   *wyznania?* (pol)
   ya-*kye*-go *yes*-tesh   *Jakiego jesteś*
   viz-*na*-nya?   *wyznania?* (inf)

I'm ...	*yes*-tem ...	*Jestem ...*
Buddhist	bood-*dis*-tom	*buddystą* (m)
	bood-*dist*-kom	*buddystką* (f)
Catholic	ka-to-*lee*-kyem	*katolikiem* (m)
	ka-to-*leech*-kom	*katoliczką* (f)
Hindu	heen-doo-*ees*-tom	*hinduistą* (m)
	heen-doo-*eest*-kom	*hinduistką* (f)
Jewish	*zhi*-dem	*żydem* (m)
	zhi-*doof*-kom	*żydówką* (m)
Muslim	moo-zoow-ma-*nee*-nem	*muzułmaninem* (m)
	moo-zoow-*man*-kom	*muzułmanką* (f)

I'm not religious.
    yes-tem nye-vye-*zhon*-tsi/a   *Jestem niewierzący/a.*
I'm an atheist.
    yes-tem a-te-*ees*-tom/   *Jestem ateistą/ateistką.*
    a-te-*eest*-kom
I'm (Catholic), but not practising.
    yes-tem (ka-to-*lee*-kyem/   *Jestem (katolikiem/*
    ka-to-*leech*-kom) *a*-le nye   *katoliczką), ale nie*
    prak-ti-*koo*-ye   *praktykuję.*

POLISH

Family

Are you married?
    chi yest pan zho-*na*-ti?   *Czy jest pan żonaty?* (m)
    chi yest *pa*-nee za-*men*-zhna?   *Czy jest pani zamężna?* (f)
I'm single.
    yes-tem ka-va-*le*-rem   *Jestem kawalerem.* (m)
    yes-tem *pan*-nom   *Jestem panną.* (f)
I'm married.
    yes-tem zho-*na*-ti   *Jestem żonaty.* (m)
    yes-tem za-*men*-zhna   *Jestem zamężna.* (f)
How many children do you have?
    ee-le pan/*pa*-nee ma *dje*-chee?   *Ile pan/pani ma dzieci?* (pol)
    ee-le mash *dje*-chee?   *Ile masz dzieci?* (inf)
We don't have any children.
    nye *ma*-mi *dje*-chee   *Nie mamy dzieci.*
Do you have any brothers/sisters?
    chi ma pan/*pa*-nee   *Czy ma pan/pani*
    bra-chee/*shos*-tri?   *braci/siostry?* (pol)
    chi mash *bra*-chee/*shos*-tri?   *Czy masz braci/siostry?* (inf)
Do you live with your family?
    chi pan/*pa*-nee *myesh*-ka   *Czy pan/pani mieszka z*
    zro-*djee*-nom?   *rodziną?* (pol)
    chi *myesh*-kash zro-*djee*-nom?   *Czy mieszkasz z rodziną?* (inf)
Do you have a boyfriend?
    chi mash na-zhe-cho-*ne*-go?   *Czy masz narzeczonego?* (inf)
Do you have a girlfriend?
    chi mash na-zhe-*cho*-nom?   *Czy masz narzeczoną?* (inf)

POLISH

aunt	*chot*-ka	ciotka
boy	*hwo*-pyets	chłopiec
brother	brat	brat
child	*djets*-ko	dziecko
children	*dje*-chee	dzieci
cousin	*koo*-zin	kuzyn (m)
	koo-*zin*-ka	kuzynka (f)
dad	*ta*-ta	tata
daughter	*tsoor*-ka	córka
family	ro-*djee*-na	rodzina
father	*oy*-chets	ojciec
girl	djef-*chi*-na	dziewczyna
grandfather	*dja*-dek	dziadek
grandmother	*bap*-ka	babka
husband	monsh	mąż
man	men-*shchiz*-na	mężczyzna
mother	*mat*-ka	matka
mum	*ma*-ma	mama
parents	ro-*djee*-tse	rodzice
sister	*shos*-tra	siostra
son	sin	syn
uncle	*voo*-yek	wujek
wife	*zho*-na	żona
woman	ko-*bye*-ta	kobieta

Kids' Talk

What's your name?
  yak mash na *ee*-mye?   *Jak masz na imię?*
How old are you?
  ee-le mash lat?   *Ile masz lat?*
When's your birthday/saint's day?
  kye-di mash oo-ro-*djee*-ni/ *Kiedy masz urodziny/imieniny?*
  ee-mye-*nee*-ni?
Have you got brothers or sisters?
  chi mash *bra*-chee *al*-bo   *Czy masz braci albo siostry?*
  shos-tri?

Do you go to school/kinder?
chi *ho*-djeesh do *shko*-wi/
pshet-*shko*-la?

*Czy chodzisz do szkoły/
przedszkola?*

Do you like school?
chi *loo*-beesh *shko*-we?

Czy lubisz szkołę?

Do you play sport?
chi oo-*pra*-vyash sport?

Czy uprawiasz sport?

What sport do you play?
ya-kee sport oo-*pra*-vyash?

Jaki sport uprawiasz?

Do you learn English?
chi *oo*-chish she an-gyel-*skye*-go?

Czy uczysz się angielskiego?

I come from far away.
yes-tem zda-le-*kye*-go *kra*-yoo

Jestem z dalekiego kraju.

We speak a different language
in my country.
fmo-eem *kra*-yoo ros-ma-
vya-mi *feen*-nim yen-*zi*-koo

*W moim kraju rozmawiamy
w innym języku.*

I don't understand you very well.
nye bar-dzo che ro-*zoo*-myem

Nie bardzo cię rozumiem.

Do you want to play a game?
chi htsesh *za*-grach?

Czy chcesz zagrać?

What shall we play?
ftso za-*gra*-mi?

W co zagramy?

cat	kot	*kot*
dog	pyes	*pies*
rabbit	*kroo*-leek	*królik*

POLISH

Feelings

I'm sorry. (condolence)	pshi-kro mee	Przykro mi.
I'm sorry. (regret)	zha-woo-ye	Żałuję.
I'm afraid.	o-ba-vyam she	Obawiam się.
I'm cold/hot.	yest mee zheem-no/ go-ron-tso	Jest mi zimno/ gorąco.
I'm in a hurry.	spye-she she	Spieszę się.
I'm right.	mam ra-tsye	Mam rację.
I'm well.	choo-ye she do-bzhe	Czuję się dobrze.

I'm ...	yes-tem ...	Jestem ...
angry	zwi/a	zły/a
grateful	vdjench-ni/a	wdzięczny/a
happy	shchen-shlee-vi/a	szczęśliwy/a
hungry	gwod-ni/a	głodny/a
sad	smoot-ni/a	smutny/a
sleepy	shpyon-tsi/a	śpiący/a
thirsty	spra-gnyo-ni/a	spragniony/a
tired	zmen-cho-ni/a	zmęczony/a
worried	za-nye-po-ko-yo-ni/a	zaniepokojony/a

Useful Phrases

Sure.	o-chi-veesh-che	Oczywiście.
It's OK.	do-bzhe	Dobrze.
Really?	na-prav-de?	Naprawdę?
It's true.	to prav-da	To prawda.
Just a minute.	hfee-lech-ke	Chwileczkę.
Look!	pro-she spoy-zhech!	Proszę spojrzeć! (pol)
	pach!	Patrz! (inf)
Listen (to this)!	pro-she po-swoo-hach!	Proszę posłuchać! (pol)
	swoo-hay!	Słuchaj! (inf)
Let's go.	hoch-mi	Chodźmy.
Wait!	pro-she za-che-kach!	Proszę zaczekać! (pol)
	za-che-kay!	Zaczekaj! (inf)

POLISH

Are you ready?
chi yest pan/*pa*-nee
go-*to*-vi/a?
chi *yes*-tesh go-*to*-vi/a?

*Czy jest pan/pani
gotowy/a?* (pol)
Czy jesteś gotowy/a? (inf)

I'm ready.	*yes*-tem go-*to*-vi/a	*Jestem gotowy/a.*
Good luck!	po-vo-*dze*-nya!	*Powodzenia!*
It's (not) important.	to (nye-)*vazh*-ne	*To (nie)ważne.*
It's (not) possible.	to (nye-)mozh-*lee*-ve	*To (nie)możliwe.*
That's strange.	to *djeev*-ne	*To dziwne.*
That's funny. (amusing)	to za-*bav*-ne	*To zabawne.*
It doesn't matter.	to nye-*vazh*-ne	*To nieważne.*

ALL THE BEST!

Polish has many ways of congratulating people. The
following are some of the most popular universal
expressions used for birthdays, saint's days and other
occasions, in both formal and informal situations. They
all roughly mean 'all the best'.

nay-lep-*she*-go!
fshis-*tkye*-go
fshis-*tkye*-go do-*bre*-go!
po-mishl-*nosh*-chee!
doo-zho *shchen*-shcha!
doo-zho *zdro*-vya!
po-vo-*dze*-nya!

Najlepszego!
Wszystkiego
Wszystkiego dobrego!
Pomyślności!
Dużo szczęścia!
Dużo zdrowia!
Powodzenia!

POLISH

BREAKING THE LANGUAGE BARRIER

Do you speak English?

	chi pan/*pa*-nee *moo*-vee po an-*gyel*-skoo?	*Czy pan/pani mówi po angielsku?*

Yes, I do.	tak, *moo*-vye	*Tak, mówię.*
No, I don't.	nye, nye *moo*-vye	*Nie, nie mówię.*
I speak a little.	*moo*-vye swa-bo	*Mówię słabo.*

Does anyone here speak English?

	chi ktosh too *moo*-vee po an-*gyel*-skoo?	*Czy ktoś tu mówi po angielsku?*

Do you understand?

	chi pan/*pa*-nee ro-*zoo*-mye?	*Czy pan/pani rozumie?*

I (don't) understand.

	(nye) ro-*zoo*-myem	*(Nie) rozumiem.*

Please speak more slowly.

	pro-she *moo*-veech *vol*-nyey	*Proszę mówić wolniej.*

Please repeat that.

	pro-she to pof-*too*-zhich	*Proszę to powtórzyć.*

Please write it down.

	pro-she to na-*pee*-sach	*Proszę to napisać.*

How do you say ...?

	yak she *moo*-vee ...?	*Jak się mówi ...?*

What does it mean?

	tso to *zna*-chi?	*Co to znaczy?*

BODY LANGUAGE

Body language in Poland is much the same as in most Western countries, so can be easily understood. For example, 'yes' is commonly indicated by nodding the head down and up, while 'no' is expressed by shaking the head from side to side.

POLISH

PAPERWORK

address	a-dres	adres
age	vyek	wiek
date of birth	da-ta	data urodzenia
	oo-ro-dze-nya	
date of expiry	da-ta	data ważności
	vazh-nosh-chee	
date of issue	da-ta vi-da-nya	data wydania
driver's licence	pra-vo yaz-di	prawo jazdy
given names	ee-myo-na	imiona
marital status	stan tsi-veel-ni	stan cywilny
single	ka-va-ler	kawaler (m)
	pan-na	panna (f)
	nye-zho-na-ti	nieżonaty (m)
	nye-za-men-zhna	niezamężna (f)
married	zho-na-ti	żonaty (m)
	za-men-zhna	zamężna (f)
divorced	roz-vye-djo-ni/a	rozwiedziony/a
widowed	vdo-vyets	wdowiec (m)
	vdo-va	wdowa (f)
nationality	na-ro-do-voshch	narodowość
passport	pash-port	paszport
passport number	noo-mer	numer paszportu
	pash-por-too	
place of birth	myey-stse	miejsce urodzenia
	oo-ro-dze-nya	
profession	za-voot	zawód
purpose of visit	tsel vee-zi-ti	cel wizyty
business	pra-tsa	praca
tourism	too-ris-ti-ka	turystyka
sex	pwech	płeć
signature	pot-pees	podpis
surname	naz-vees-ko	nazwisko
visa	vee-za	wiza

POLISH

GETTING AROUND

Where's the ...?	gdje yest ...?	Gdzie jest ...?
bus station	dvo-zhets	dworzec
	aw-to-boo-so-vi	autobusowy
bus stop	pshis-ta-nek	przystanek
	aw-to-boo-so-vi	autobusowy
city centre	tsen-troom	centrum
road to ...	dro-ga do ...	droga do ...
taxi stand	pos-tooy tak-soo-vek	postój taksówek
ticket office	ka-sa bee-le-to-va	kasa biletowa
train station	dvo-zhets ko-le-yo-vi	dworzec kolejowy

How do I get there?
yak she tam dos-tach? *Jak się tam dostać?*
Is it far from here?
chi to da-le-ko stont? *Czy to daleko stąd?*
Please show me (on the map).
pro-she mee po-ka-zach *Proszę mi pokazać (na mapie).*
(na ma-pye)

Directions

Go straight ahead.	pro-she eeshch pros-to	Proszę iść prosto.
Turn left/right at the ...	pro-she skren-cheech fle-vo/fpra-vo na ...	Proszę skręcić w lewo/prawo na ...
next corner	nay-bleesh-shim ro-goo	najbliższym rogu
traffic lights	shfya-twah	światłach
roundabout	ron-dje	rondzie
end of the street	kon-tsoo oo-lee-tsi	końcu ulicy

behind	za	*za*
in front of	pshet	*przed*
far	da-*le*-ko	*daleko*
near	*blees*-ko	*blisko*
opposite	na-pshe-*cheef*-ko	*naprzeciwko*
here	too	*tu*
there	tam	*tam*

POLISH

north	*poow*-nots	*północ*
south	po-*wood*-nye	*południe*
east	fs-hoot	*wschód*
west	za-hoot	*zachód*

SIGNS

CIĄGNĄĆ	PULL
NIE PALIĆ	NO SMOKING
OTWARTE	OPEN
PCHAĆ	PUSH
TOALETY	TOILETS
WEJŚCIE	ENTRANCE
WSTĘP WOLNY	FREE ADMISSION
WSTĘP WZBRONIONY	NO ENTRY
WYJŚCIE	EXIT
WYJŚCIE AWARYJNE/	EMERGENCY EXIT
BEZPIECZEŃSTWA	
WZBRONIONY	PROHIBITED
ZAMKNIĘTE	CLOSED
ZAREZERWOWANY	RESERVED

POLISH

Booking Tickets

Excuse me, where's the
ticket office?
pshe-*pra*-sham, gdje yest   *Przepraszam, gdzie jest kasa*
ka-sa bee-le-*to*-va?   *biletowa?*

Where can I buy a ticket?
gdje *mo*-ge *koo*-peech *bee*-let?   *Gdzie mogę kupić bilet?*

I want to go to ...
htse po-*ye*-hach do ...   *Chcę pojechać do ...* (bus, train)
htse po-*le*-chech do ...   *Chcę polecieć do ...* (plane)

Do I need to book?
chi *moo*-she re-zer-*vo*-vach?   *Czy muszę rezerwować?*

I'd like to book a seat to ...
htse za-re-zer-*vo*-vach   *Chcę zarezerwować miejsce do ...*
myey-stse do ...

How much is the ticket?
ee-le kosh-*too*-ye *bee*-let?   *Ile kosztuje bilet?*

I'd like ...	po-*pro*-she ...	*Poproszę ...*
a one-way ticket	*bee*-let *fyed*-nom *stro*-ne	*bilet w jedną stronę*
a return ticket	*bee*-let po-*vrot*-ni	*bilet powrotny*
two tickets	dva bee-*le*-ti	*dwa bilety*
a window seat	*myey*-stse pshi *ok*-nye	*miejsce przy oknie*

1st class	*pyer*-fshom *kla*-se	*pierwszą klasę*
2nd class	*droo*-gom *kla*-se	*drugą klasę*
for (non)smokers	dla (nye)pa-*lon*-tsih	*dla (nie)palących*

Is there a discount for ...?	chi yest *zneesh*-ka dla ...?	*Czy jest zniżka dla ...?*
children	*dje*-chee	*dzieci*
pensioners	ren-*chees*-toof	*rencistów*
students	stoo-*den*-toof	*studentów*

Air

Poland's only commercial carrier, *LOT* Polish Airlines, services all domestic routes. It has regular flights from Warsaw, the country's aviation hub, to half a dozen major cities. Tickets can be booked and bought at *LOT* offices and from travel agencies.

POLISH

Is there a flight to ...?
    chi yest lot do ...?   *Czy jest lot do ...?*
When's the next flight to ...?
    kye-di yest   *Kiedy jest*
    nas-*temp*-ni lot do ...?   *następny lot do ...?*
What time does the plane
leave/arrive?
    o *ktoo*-rey od-la-*too*-ye/   *O której odlatuje/przylatuje*
    pshi-la-*too*-ye sa-*mo*-lot?   *samolot?*
What's the flight number?
    ya-kee yest *noo*-mer *lo*-too?   *Jaki jest numer lotu?*
How long does the flight take?
    ee-le trfa lot?   *Ile trwa lot?*
What time do I have to check
in at the airport?
    o *ktoo*-rey *moo*-she bich   *O której muszę być na lotnisku?*
    na lot-*nees*-koo?
Is there a bus to the airport?
    chi yest *ya*-keesh aw-*to*-bus   *Czy jest jakiś autobus na*
    na lot-*nees*-ko?   *lotnisko?*

airport	lot-*nees*-ko	*lotnisko*
airport tax	o-*pwa*-ta lot-nees-*ko*-va	*opłata lotniskowa*
boarding pass	*kar*-ta po-kwa-*do*-va	*karta pokładowa*
flight	lot	*lot*
hand luggage	*ba*-gash pod-*rench*-ni	*bagaż podręczny*
plane	sa-*mo*-lot	*samolot*

POLISH

Bus

Poland's intercity buses are cheap but rather slow. Buses mostly service medium and short-distance regional routes (long-distance travel is faster and more convenient by train).

Most domestic buses are operated by the state bus company commonly known as PKS. Tickets can be bought at the bus terminal or directly from the bus driver.

Where's the bus terminal?
    gdje yest *dvo*-zhets   *Gdzie jest dworzec*
    aw-to-boo-*so*-vi?   *autobusowy?*

Which bus goes to ...?
    ktoo-ri aw-*to*-boos   *Który autobus*
    ye-dje do ...?   *jedzie do ...?*

Does this bus go to ...?
    chi ten aw-*to*-boos   *Czy ten autobus*
    ye-dje do ...?   *jedzie do ...?*

How often do buses go to ...?
    yak *chen*-sto *ho*-dzom   *Jak często chodzą*
    aw-to-*boo*-si do ...?   *autobusy do ...?*

What time does the
bus leave/arrive?
    o *ktoo*-rey ot-*ho*-djee/   *O której odchodzi/*
    pshi-*ho*-djee aw-*to*-boos?   *przychodzi autobus?*

Please let me know
when we get to ...
    pro-she mi po-*vye*-djech gdi   *Proszę mi powiedzieć gdy*
    do-ye-*dje*-mi do ...   *dojedziemy do ...*

Where do I get the bus for ...?
    skont vzhonch   *Skąd wziąć*
    aw-*to*-boos do ...?   *autobus do ...?*

What time's the ... bus?	o *ktoo*-rey yest ... aw-*to*-boos?	*O której jest ...* *autobus?*
first	*pyer*-fshi	*pierwszy*
last	os-*tat*-ni	*ostatni*
next	nas-*temp*-ni	*następny*

Train

Railway networks and trains are administered by the Polish State Railways, commonly referred to as *PKP*. Services include EuroCity (EC), InterCity (IC), express (Ex), fast and ordinary.

Almost all trains have seats in two classes – 1st and 2nd – and some night trains have cars with couchettes and sleepers. Tickets can be purchased at train stations or from some travel agencies.

POLISH

Where's the train station?
  gdje yest *dvo*-zhets ko-le-*yo*-vi?   *Gdzie jest dworzec kolejowy?*
Which platform does the train
leave from?
  sktoo-*re*-go pe-*ro*-noo   *Z którego peronu odjeżdża*
  ot-*yesh*-dja po-chonk?   *pociąg?*
What station is this?
  ***ya*-ka to *sta*-tsya?**   *Jaka to stacja?*
What's the next station?
  ***ya*-ka yest nas-*temp*-na *sta*-tsya?**   *Jaka jest następna stacja?*
Does this train stop at ...?
  chi ten *po*-chonk   *Czy ten pociąg zatrzymuje się*
  za-tshi-*moo*-ye she f ...?   *w...?*
I want to get off at ...
  htse *vi*-shonshch f ...   *Chcę wysiąść w ...*
How long does the trip take?
  yak *dwoo*-go trfa *po*-droosh?   *Jak długo trwa podróż?*
Is that seat taken?
  chi to *myey*-stse yest za-*yen*-te?   *Czy to miejsce jest zajęte?*
Is this seat free?
  chi to *myey*-stse yest *vol*-ne?   *Czy to miejsce jest wolne?*

... train	**po**-chonk ...	*pociąg ...*
fast	**pos-*pyesh*-ni**	*pospieszny*
long-distance	**da-le-ko-*byezh*-ni**	*dalekobieżny_*
slow	**o-so-*bo*-vi**	*osobowy*
suburban	**pod-*myey*-skee**	*podmiejski*

POLISH

Taxi

Where's the nearest taxi rank?
  gdje yest nay-*bleesh*-shi
  pos-tooy tak-*soo*-vek?

Gdzie jest najbliższy postój taksówek?

Are you free?
  chi yest pan/*pa*-nee *vol*-ni/a?

Czy jest pan/pani wolny/a?

How much does it cost to go to ...?
  ee-le *ben*-dje kosh-*to*-vach do ...?

Ile będzie kosztować do ...?

Please take me to ...	*pro*-she mnye *za*-vyeshch ...	*Proszę mnie zawieźć ...*
the airport	na lot-*nees*-ko	*na lotnisko*
this address	pot ten *a*-dres	*pod ten adres*
the city centre	do *tsen*-troom	*do centrum*
this hotel	do *te*-go ho-*te*-loo	*do tego hotelu*
a cheap hotel	do ta-*nye*-go ho-*te*-loo	*do taniego hotelu*
the train station	na *dvo*-zhets ko-le-*yo*-vi	*na dworzec kolejowy*

How much do I owe you?
  ee-le *pwa*-tse?

Ile płacę?

Please give me the change.
  pro-she mee *vi*-dach *resh*-te

Proszę mi wydać resztę.

Please keep the change.
  pro-she za-*tshi*-mach
  so-bye *resh*-te

Proszę zatrzymać sobie resztę.

Continue straight ahead.
  pro-she *ye*-hach *da*-ley *pros*-to

Proszę jechać dalej prosto.

The next street to the left/right.
  nas-*temp*-na oo-*lee*-tsa na
  le-vo/*pra*-vo

Następna ulica na lewo/prawo.

Please slow down.
  pro-she *zvol*-neech

Proszę zwolnić.

Please wait here.
  pro-she too za-*che*-kach

Proszę tu zaczekać.

Please stop here.

    pro-she she too za-*tshi*-mach   *Proszę się tu zatrzymać.*

Please stop at the corner.

    pro-she she za-*tshi*-mach   *Proszę się zatrzymać*
    na *ro*-goo   *na rogu.*

Car

Where can I rent a car?

    gdje *mo*-ge vi-po-*zhi*-chich   *Gdzie mogę wypożyczyć*
    sa-*mo*-hoot?   *samochód?*

How much is it daily/weekly?

    ee-le kosh-*too*-ye *djen*-nye/   *Ile kosztuje dziennie/*
    ti-god-*nyo*-vo?   *tygodniowo?*

Does that include insurance?

    chi oo-bes-pye-*che*-nye   *Czy ubezpieczenie*
    yest vlee-*cho*-ne?   *jest wliczone?*

Where's the nearest petrol station?

    gdje yest nay-*bleesh*-sha   *Gdzie jest najbliższa stacja*
    sta-tsya ben-zi-*no*-va?   *benzynowa?*

Can I park here?

    chi *mozh*-na too par-*ko*-vach?   *Czy można tu parkować?*

How long can I park here?

    yak *dwoo*-go *mozh*-na too   *Jak długo można tu*
    par-*ko*-vach?   *parkować?*

Does this road lead to ...?

    chi ta *dro*-ga pro-*va*-djee do ...?   *Czy ta droga prowadzi do ...?*

I need a mechanic.

    pot-she-*boo*-ye me-ha-*nee*-ka   *Potrzebuję mechanika.*

The radiator's leaking.

    hwod-*nee*-tsa *chek*-nye   *Chłodnica cieknie.*

I've got a flat tyre.

    zwa-*pa*-wem/wam *goo*-me   *Złapałem/łam gumę.*

I've lost my car keys.

    zgoo-*bee*-wem/wam   *Zgubiłem/łam kluczyki.*
    kloo-*chi*-kee

I've run out of petrol.

    za-*brak*-wo mee ben-*zi*-ni   *Zabrakło mi benzyny.*

POLISH

air	po-*vyet*-she	*powietrze*
battery	a-koo-moo-*la*-tor	*akumulator*
brakes	ha-*mool*-tse	*hamulce*
clutch	*spshen*-gwo	*sprzęgło*
drivers licence	*pra*-vo *yaz*-di	*prawo jazdy*
engine	*sheel*-neek	*silnik*
garage	*var*-shtat	*warsztat*
indicator	kye-roon-*kof*-skas	*kierunkowskaz*
headlights	*shfya*-twa	*światła*
motorway	aw-to-*stra*-da	*autostrada*
oil	*o*-ley	*olej*
radiator	hwod-*nee*-tsa	*chłodnica*
roadmap	*ma*-pa dro-*go*-va	*mapa drogowa*
seatbelts	*pa*-si bes-pye-*chen*-stfa	*pasy bezpieczeństwa*
self-service	sa-mo-op-*swoo*-ga	*samoobsługa*
speed limit	o-gra-nee-*che*-nye	*ograniczenie*
	prent-*kosh*-chee	*prędkości*
tyre	o-*po*-na	*opona*
windscreen	*pshe*-dnya *shi*-ba	*przednia szyba*

... petrol	ben-*zi*-na ...	*benzyna* ...
leaded	o-wo-*vyo*-va	*ołowiowa*
regular	*zvik*-wa	*zwykła*
unleaded	be-so-wo-*vyo*-va	*bezołowiowa*

ACCOMMODATION

Where can I find a ...?	gdje *mo-ge zna-leshch* ...?	*Gdzie mogę znaleźć ...?*
camping ground	*kam*-peenk	*camping*
guesthouse	pen-*syo*-nat	*pensjonat*
hotel	*ho*-tel	*hotel*
motel	*mo*-tel	*motel*
youth hostel	sro-*nees*-ko mwo-dje-*zho*-ve	*schronisko młodzieżowe*

POLISH

Can you recommend a ...?	chi *mo-zhe* mee pan/ *pa*-nee po-*le*-cheech ...?	*Czy może mi pan/pani polecić ...?*
cheap hotel	*ta*-nee *ho*-tel	*tani hotel*
clean hotel	*chis*-ti *ho*-tel	*czysty hotel*
good hotel	*do*-bri *ho*-tel	*dobry hotel*

Where's the ... hotel?	gdje yest ... *ho*-tel?	*Gdzie jest ... hotel?*
best	nay-*lep*-shi	*najlepszy*
cheapest	nay-*tan*-shi	*najtańszy*
nearest	nay-*bleesh*-shi	*najbliższy*

What's the address?
ya-kee yest *a*-dres?   *Jaki jest adres?*

At the Hotel

For (three) nights.
na (tshi) *no*-tse   *Na (trzy) noce.*

How much does it cost per night?
ee-le kosh-*too*-ye za nots?   *Ile kosztuje za noc?*

Do you have any rooms available?
chi som *vol*-ne po-*ko*-ye?   *Czy są wolne pokoje?*

SIGNS

BRAK MIEJSC	NO VACANCIES
WOLNE POKOJE	ROOMS AVAILABLE

POLISH

I'd like a ... room.	po-*pro*-she o *po*-kooy ...	*Poproszę o pokój ...*
single	yed-no-o-so-*bo*-vi	*jednoosobowy*
double	dvoo-o-so-*bo*-vi	*dwuosobowy*
triple	tshi-o-so-*bo*-vi	*trzyosobowy*

I'd like a bed in a dorm.
po-*pro*-she o *woosh*-ko *fsa*-lee zbyo-*ro*-vey

Poproszę o łóżko w sali zbiorowej.

I want a room with a ...	po-*pro*-she o *po*-kooy s ...	*Poproszę o pokój z ...*
bathroom	wa-*zhen*-kom	*łazienką*
double bed	pod-*vooy*-nim *woosh*-kyem	*podwójnym łóżkiem*
phone	te-le-*fo*-nem	*telefonem*
shower	prish-*ni*-tsem/ na-*tris*-kyem	*prysznicem/ natryskiem*
TV	te-le-vee-*zo*-rem	*telewizorem*
twin beds	dvo-ma *woosh-ka*-mi	*dwoma łóżkami*
view	vee-*do*-kyem	*widokiem*
window	*ok*-nem	*oknem*

POLISH

Can I see it?
chi *mo*-ge go zo-*ba*-chich?   *Czy mogę go zobaczyć?*

Are there any others?
chi som *een*-ne?   *Czy są inne?*

Where's the bathroom?
gdje yest wa-*zhen*-ka?   *Gdzie jest łazienka?*

Is there hot water (all day)?
chi yest *chep*-wa *vo*-da   *Czy jest ciepła woda (przez*
(pshes *tsa*-wi djen)?   *cały dzień)?*

How much is the
room per night?
ee-le kosh-*too*-ye ten   *Ile kosztuje ten pokój za noc?*
po-kooy za nots?

Is there a discount for
children/students?
chi yest *ya*-kash *zneesh*-ka   *Czy jest jakaś zniżka dla*
dla *dje*-chee/*stoo-den*-toof?   *dzieci/studentów?*

It's fine. I'll take it.
do-bzhe. *vez*-me go   *Dobrze. Wezmę go.*

Requests & Complaints

Can I deposit my valuables here?
chi *mozh*-na too zde-po-*no*-   *Czy można tu zdeponować*
vach *zhe*-chi var-tosh-*cho*-ve?   *rzeczy wartościowe?*

Is there somewhere
here to wash clothes?
chi *mozh*-na too *oo*-prach   *Czy można tu uprać*
oo-*bra*-nye?   *ubranie?*

Can I use the telephone?
chi *mozh*-na sko-*zhis*-tach   *Czy można skorzystać*
ste-le-*fo*-noo?   *z telefonu?*

I don't like this room.
nye po-*do*-ba mee she ten   *Nie podoba mi się ten*
po-kooy   *pokój.*

POLISH

I can't open/close the
window/door.

> nye *mo*-ge ot-*fo*-zhich/
> *zam*-knonch *ok*-na/dzhvee

Nie mogę otworzyć/
zamknąć okna/drzwi.

The toilet doesn't flush.

> *vo*-da she nye *spoosh*-cha

Woda się nie spuszcza.

There's no hot water.

> nye ma *chep*-wey *vo*-di

Nie ma ciepłej wody.

Can I pay by credit card?

> chi *mo*-ge za-*pwa*-cheech
> *kar*-tom kre-di-*to*-vom?

Czy mogę zapłacić
kartą kredytową?

air conditioning	klee-ma-ti-*za*-tsya	*klimatyzacja*
bed	*woosh*-ko	*łóżko*
bedclothes	*posh*-chel	*pościel*
blanket	kots	*koc*
chair	*kshe*-swo	*krzesło*
key	klooch	*klucz*
lamp	*lam*-pa	*lampa*
light bulb	zha-*roof*-ka	*żarówka*
lock	za-mek	*zamek*
mattress	ma-*te*-rats	*materac*
mirror	*loos*-tro	*lustro*
padlock	*kwoot*-ka	*kłódka*
pillow	po-*doosh*-ka	*poduszka*
soap	*mi*-dwo	*mydło*
suitcase	va-*lees*-ka	*walizka*
swimming pool	*ba*-sen	*basen*
table	stoow	*stół*
toilet	to-a-*le*-ta	*toaleta*
towel	*rench*-neek	*ręcznik*
washbasin	oo-mi-*val*-ka	*umywalka*
... water	... *vo*-da	*... woda*
cold	*chep*-wa	*ciepła*
hot	*zheem*-na	*zimna*

AROUND TOWN

Where's a/the ...?	gdje yest ...?	*Gdzie jest ...?*
bank	**bank**	*bank*
city centre	*tsen*-troom	*centrum*
consulate	kon-*soo*-lat	*konsulat*
embassy	am-ba-*sa*-da	*ambasada*
hotel	*ho*-tel	*hotel*
police station	pos-te-*roo*-nek	*posterunek*
	po-*lee*-tsyee;	*policji;*
	ko-mee-*sa*-ryat	*komisariat*
post office	*poch*-ta	*poczta*
public telephone	aw-*to*-mat	*automat*
	te-le-fo-*neech*-ni	*telefoniczny*
public toilet	to-a-*le*-ta	*toaleta publiczna*
	poo-*bleech*-na	
tourist	*byoo*-ro	*biuro informacji*
information	een-for-*ma*-tsyee	*turystycznej*
office	too-ris-*tich*-ney	

POLISH

What time does it
open/close?
  o *ktoo*-rey she ot-*fye*-ra/   *O której się otwiera/*
  za-*mi*-ka?   *zamyka?*

At the Post Office

In Poland, postal services and telecommunications facilities are usually combined under one roof, in a *poczta*, 'post office'. Large cities have plenty of post offices, of which the *poczta główna*, 'main post office', will usually have the widest range of facilities, including poste restante and fax.

I want to buy ...	htse *koo*-peech ..	*Chcę kupić ...*
postcards	poch-*toof*-kee	*pocztówki*
stamps	*znach*-kee	*znaczki*

POLISH

How much does it cost
to send this to ...?

ee-le kosh-*too*-ye vi-*swa*-nye *te*-go do ...?	*Ile kosztuje wysłanie tego do ...?*

Where can I collect poste
restante mail?

gdje *mo*-ge o-*de*-brach post res-tant?	*Gdzie mogę odebrać poste restante?*

Is there any mail for me?

chi yest *ya*-kash *poch*-ta dla mnye?	*Czy jest jakaś poczta dla mnie?*

I want to send a ...	**htse *vi*-swach ...**	*Chcę wysłać ...*
letter	**leest**	*list*
parcel	***pach*-ke**	*paczkę*

address	*a*-dres	adres
airmail	*poch*-ta lot-*nee*-cha	poczta lotnicza
envelope	ko-*per*-ta	koperta
letter	leest	list
mail box	*skshin*-ka poch-*to*-va	skrzynka pocztowa
parcel	*pach*-ka	paczka
postcard	poch-*toof*-ka	pocztówka
postcode	kot poch-*to*-vi	kod pocztowy
postal worker	lees-*to*-nosh	listonosz
	lees-to-*nosh*-ka	listonoszka
post office	*poch*-ta	poczta
postage stamp	*zna*-chek poch-*to*-vi	znaczek pocztowy
registered letter	leest po-le-*tso*-ni	list polecony
sender	na-*daf*-tsa	nadawca

Telephone

Could I please use the telephone?

chi *mo*-ge sko-*zhis*-tach ste-le-*fo*-noo?	*Czy mogę skorzystać z telefonu?*

Can I place a (phone) call?

chi *mo*-ge za-*moo*-vich roz-*mo*-ve (te-le-fo-*neech*-nom)?	*Czy mogę zamówić rozmowę (telefoniczną)?*

POLISH

I want to make a call to ...
 htse za-*dzvo*-neech do ... *Chcę zadzwonić do ...*
The number is ...
 to yest *noo*-mer ... *To jest numer ...*
I want to speak for
(three) minutes.
 htse roz-*ma*-vyach (tshi) *Chcę rozmawiać (trzy)*
 mee-*noo*-ti *minuty.*
How much does a three-minute
call cost?
 ee-le kosh-*too*-ye roz-*mo*-va *Ile kosztuje rozmowa*
 tshi-mee-noo-*to*-va? *trzyminutowa?*
I want to make a
reverse-charges call.
 htse za-*dzvo*-neech na kosht *Chcę zadzwonić na koszt*
 a-bo-*nen*-ta *abonenta.*
What's the area code for ...?
 ya-kee yest *noo*-mer *Jaki jest numer*
 kye-roon-*ko*-vi do ...? *kierunkowy do ...?*
It's engaged.
 yest za-*yen*-te *Jest zajęte.*
I've been cut off.
 roz-won-*cho*-no mnye *Rozłączono mnie.*
Can you put me through to ...?
 pro-she mnye po-*won*-chich s ... *Proszę mnie połączyć z ...*
Can I speak to ...?
 chi *mo*-ge *moo*-veech s ...? *Czy mogę mówić z ...?*

operator	te-le-fo-*nees*-ta	*telefonista* (m)
	te-le-fo-*neest*-ka	*telefonistka* (f)
phonecard	*kar*-ta te-le-fo-*neech*-na	*karta telefoniczna*
public	aw-*to*-mat	*automat*
telephone	te-le-fo-*neech*-ni	*telefoniczny*
telephone	te-*le*-fon	*telefon*
token	*zhe*-ton	*żeton*

Hello. (making a call)	*ha*-lo	*Halo.*
Hello. (answering a call)	*swoo*-ham/ *pro*-she	*Słucham/Proszę.*

POLISH

Internet

Is there an Internet cafe
around here?

    chi yest too *ya*-kash
    ka-*vyar*-nyaeen-ter-ne-*to*-va?   *Czy jest tu jakaś kawiarnia
                                     internetowa?*

I want to get access to the Internet.

    shoo-kam dɔs-*tem*-poo do   *Szukam dostępu do
    een-ter-*ne*-too   internetu.*

I want to check my email.

    htse *sprav*-djeech *mo*-yom   *Chcę sprawdzić moją pocztę
    poch-te e-lek-tro-*neech*-nom   *elektroniczną.*

At the Bank

The usual place to change foreign cash in Poland is the *kantor*, or
the private currency exchange office. They are ubiquitous in cities
and towns and change most major currencies. They accept cash
only, so if you want to change travellers cheques you'll need a
bank.

Many major banks will cash travellers cheques, though they'll
usually charge a commission. An increasing number of banks have
ATMs which accept international credit cards.

Can I exchange money here?

    chi *mo*-ge too vi-*mye*-neech   *Czy mogę tu wymienić
    pye-*nyon*-dze?   *pieniądze?*

I want to change …	htse vi-*mye*-neech …	*Chcę wymienić …*
cash	go-*toof*-ke	*gotówkę*
Deutschmarks	*mar*-kee	*marki niemieckie*
	nye-*myets*-kye	
foreign currency	*op*-tsom va-*loo*-te	*obcą walutę*
pounds sterling	*foon*-ti bri-*tiy*-skye	*funty brytyjskie*
travellers cheques	*che*-kee	*czeki*
	po-*droozh*-ne	*podróżne*
US dollars	do-*la*-ri	*dolary*
	a-me-ri-*kan*-skye	*amerykańskie*

Can I get a cash advance on
my credit card?

    chi *mo*-ge *dos*-tach za-*leech*-ke   *Czy mogę dostać zaliczkę na*
    na *mo*-yom *kar*-te kre-di-*to*-wom?   *moją kartę kredytową?*

Can I use my credit card
in the ATM?

    chi *mo*-ge oo-*zhi*-vach *mo*-yom   *Czy mogę używać moją*
    kar-te kre-di-*to*-vom   *kartę kredytową*
    vban-ko-*ma*-che?   *w bankomacie?*

The ATM has swallowed my card.

    ban-*ko*-mat *powk*-now   *Bankomat połknął*
    mo-yom *kar*-te   *moją kartę.*

Can you give me smaller notes?

    po-*pro*-she o *mnyey*-she   *Poproszę o mniejsze*
    ban-*kno*-ti   *banknoty.*

What's the exchange rate?

    ya-kee yest koors vi-*mya*-ni?   *Jaki jest kurs wymiany?*

Is there a commission?

    chi yest *ya*-kash pro-*vee*-zya?   *Czy jest jakaś prowizja?*

ATM (automatic teller machine)	ban-*ko*-mat	*bankomat*
bank account	ra-*hoo*-nek	*rachunek*
banknote	*ban*-knot	*banknot*
cash	go-*toof*-ka	*gotówka*
cashier	*ka*-syer	*kasjer*
	ka-*syer*-ka	*kasjerka*
coin	mo-*ne*-ta	*moneta*
commission	pro-*vee*-zya	*prowizja*
credit card	*kar*-ta kre-di-*to*-va	*karta kredytowa*
currency	va-*loo*-ta	*waluta*
exchange office	*kan*-tor	*kantor*
exchange rate	koors vi-*mya*-ni	*kurs wymiany*
money	pye-*nyon*-dze	*pieniądze* (pl)
signature	*pot*-pees	*podpis*
travellers cheque	chek po-*droozh*-ni	*czek podróżny*

POLISH

INTERESTS & ENTERTAINMENT
Sightseeing

Can I get a guidebook/city map?
chi dos-*ta*-ne pshe-*vod*-neek/ *Czy dostanę przewodnik/*
plan *mya*-sta? *plan miasta?*

What are the tourist
attractions here?
ya-kye too som a-*trak*-tsye *Jakie tu są atrakcje turystyczne?*
too-ris-*tich*-ne?

Are there organised tours?
chi som zor-ga-nee-zo-*va*-ne *Czy są zorganizowane*
vi-*chech*-kee? *wycieczki?*

What's that?
tso to yest? *Co to jest?*

Is there an admission charge?
chi *pwa*-chee she za fstemp? *Czy płaci się za wstęp?*

STREET WALKING		
What's this?	tso to yest?	Co to jest?
What's happenning?	tso she *dje*-ye?	Co się dzieje?
What happened?	tso she *sta*-wo?	Co się stało?
What's he/ she doing?	tso on/ *o*-na *ro*-bee?	Co on/ ona robi?
festival	fes-*tee*-val	festiwal
flea market	phlee targ	pchli targ
newspaper kiosk	kyosk sga-ze-*ta*-mee	kiosk z gazetami
	kyosk *roo*-hoo	kiosk Ruchu
street	oo-*lee*-tsa	ulica
street demonstration	de-mon-*stra*-tsya oo-*leech*-na	demonstracja uliczna
street market	targ oo-*leech*-ni	targ uliczny
street theatre	*te*-atr oo-*leech*-ni	teatr uliczny

Can I take photographs?

> chi *mo*-ge *ro*-beech *zdyen*-cha?   *Czy mogę robić zdjęcia?*

What's the name of this
street/suburb?

> yak she na-*zi*-va ta   *Jak się nazywa ta ulica/*
> oo-*lee*-tsa/djel-*nee*-tsa?   *dzielnica?*

POLISH

art gallery	ga-*le*-rya *shtoo*-kee	*galeria sztuki*
botanic gardens	*o*-groot bo-ta-*neech*-ni	*ogród botaniczny*
castle	*za*-mek	*zamek*
cathedral	ka-*te*-dra	*katedra*
cemetery	*tsmen*-tash	*cmentarz*
church	*kosh*-choow	*kościół*
concert hall	*sa*-la kon-tser-*to*-va	*sala koncertowa*
monastery	*klash*-tor	*klasztor*
monument	*pom*-neek	*pomnik*
museum	*moo*-ze-oom	*muzeum*
old town	*sta*-re *mya*-sto	*stare miasto*
old town square	*ri*-nek	*rynek*
palace	*pa*-wats	*pałac*
stadium	*sta*-dyon	*stadion*
synagogue	si-na-*go*-ga	*synagoga*
tourist	*byoo*-ro	*biuro informacji*
information	een-for-*ma*-tsyee	*turystycznej*
office	too-ris-*tich*-ney	
university	oo-nee-*ver*-si-tet	*uniwersytet*

POLISH

Going Out

What's on tonight?
tso *gra*-yom djeesh vye-*cho*-rem?   *Co grają dziś wieczorem?*

Are there any tickets for ...?
chi som bee-*le*-ti na ...?   *Czy są bilety na ...?*

I feel like going to a cinema/theatre.
mam o-*ho*-te pooyshch do   *Mam ochotę pójść do*
***kee*-na/te-*a*-troo**   *kina/teatru.*

Is there a jazz club around here?
chi yest too gdjesh kloop   *Czy jest tu gdzieś klub*
dje-*zo*-vi?   *jazzowy?*

Where can you go to hear folk
music?
gdje too *mozh*-na   *Gdzie tu można*
pos-*woo*-hach *moo*-zi-kee   *posłuchać muzyki*
loo-*do*-vey?   *ludowej?*

Let's go to the philharmonic.
***hoch*-mi na *kon*-tsert do**   *Chodźmy na koncert do*
feel-har-*mo*-nee   *filharmonii.*

What a great concert/film!
tso za fspa-*nya*-wi *kon*-tsert/   *Co za wspaniały koncert/*
feelm!   *film!*

band	*groo*-pa/*zes*-poow	*grupa/zespół*
cinema	*kee*-no	*kino*
comedy	ko-*me*-dya	*komedia*
concert	*kon*-tsert	*koncert*
documentary	feelm	*film*
	do-koo-men-*tal*-ni	*dokumentalny*
drama	*dra*-mat	*dramat*
orchestra	or-*kyes*-tra	*orkiestra*
performance	pshet-sta-*vye*-nye	*przedstawienie*
play	*shtoo*-ka (te-a-*tral*-na)	*sztuka (teatralna)*
show	spek-takl	*spektakl*

Sports & Interests

Besides soccer, there's no particular sport that drives the nation crazy. Cycling is reasonably popular in some circles, as are basketball, athletics, boxing, tennis and skiing.

POLISH

What do you do in your spare time?

tso pan/*pa*-nee *ro*-bee *vvol*-nim *cha*-she?	*Co pan/pani robi w wolnym czasie?* (pol)
tso *ro*-beesh *vvol*-nim *cha*-she?	*Co robisz w wolnym czasie?* (inf)

Which kind of music do you like?

ya-kom *moo*-zi-ke pan/*pa*-nee *loo*-bee?	*Jaką muzykę pan/pani lubi?* (m/f, pol)
ya-kom *moo*-zi-ke *loo*-beesh?	*Jaką muzykę lubisz?* (inf)

Do you like sport?

chi pan/*pa*-nee *loo*-bee sport?	*Czy pan/pani lubi sport?* (pol)
chi *loo*-beesh sport?	*Czy lubisz sport?* (inf)

I play sport.

oo-*pra*-vyam sport	*Uprawiam sport.*

I prefer to watch rather than play sport.

vo-le o-*glon*-dach sport neesh go oo-*pra*-vyach	*Wolę oglądać sport niż go uprawiać.*

Which sport do you like?

ya-kee sport pan/*pa*-nee *loo*-bee?	*Jaki sport pan/pani lubi?* (pol)
ya-kee sport *loo*-beesh?	*Jaki sport lubisz?* (inf)

What sport do you play?

ya-kee sport pan/*pa*-nee oo-*pra*-vya?	*Jaki sport pan/pani uprawia?* (pol)
ya-kee sport oo-*pra*-vyash?	*Jaki sport uprawiasz?* (inf)

POLISH

Do you like ...?	chi pan/	*Czy pan/*
	pa-nee *loo*-bee ...?	*pani lubi ...?* (pol)
	chi *loo*-beesh ...?	*Czy lubisz ...?* (inf)
I like ...	*loo*-bye ...	*Lubię ...*
arts	*shtoo*-ke	*sztukę*
athletics	lek-ko-a-tle-*ti*-ka	*lekkoatletyka*
basketball	ko-shi-*koof*-ka	*koszykówka*
boxing	boks	*boks*
dance	*ta*-nyets	*taniec*
diving	noor-ko-*va*-nye	*nurkowanie*
film	*kee*-no	*kino*
gymnastics	geem-nas-*ti*-ka	*gimnastyka*
hockey	*ho*-key	*hokej*
horseriding	*yaz*-da *kon*-na	*jazda konna*
horse racing	vish-*chee*-gee	*wyścigi konne*
	kon-ne	
literature	lee-te-ra-*too*-re	*literaturę*
music	*moo*-zi-ke	*muzykę*
photography	fo-to-*gra*-fye	*fotografię*
skiing	nar-*char*-stfo	*narciarstwo*
soccer	*peew*-ka *nozh*-na	*piłka nożna*
sports	sport	*sport*
swimming	pwi-*va*-nye	*pływanie*
tennis	*te*-nees	*tenis*
theatre	*te*-atr	*teatr*
travel	po-*droo*-zhe	*podróże*
TV	te-le-*vee*-zye	*telewizję*

POLISH

Festivals

Wielkanoc **vyel-ka-nots**
Easter (March/April)
Easter is one of Poland's most important religious feasts. Celebrations start on Palm Sunday (*Niedziela Palmowa*) and go for the whole Holy Week (*Wielki Tydzień*) until Easter Monday (*Poniedziałek Wielkanocny*). A solemn breakfast on Easter Sunday (*Niedziela Wielkanocna*) features the consecrated food, including the painted Easter eggs (*jajka wielkanocne*).

Święto Konstytucji 3-go Maja
  shfyen-to kon-sti-too-tsyee tshe-che-go ma-ya
3 May Constitution Day
This holiday commemorates the constitution of 1791, passed in Warsaw on the 3 of May (and commonly referred to as such). It was the world's first fully liberal constitution after the one in the US.

Boże Ciało **bo-zhe cha-wo**
Corpus Christi (a Thursday in May or June)
This important religious day features church masses and processions all over the country, with the most elaborate celebrations taking place in Łowicz, near Warsaw

Wniebowzięcie **vnye-bo-vzhen-che**
Assumption (15 August)
Another major religious day, it culminates at Częstochowa, Poland's spiritual capital, where mass pilgrimages from all around the country come for this holy day

Święto Zmarłych **shfyen-to zmar-wih**
All Souls' Day (1 November)
A day of remembrance and prayer for the souls of the dead, when people visit cemeteries to leave flowers, wreaths and lit candles on the graves of their relatives

POLISH

Święto Niepodległości   shfyen-to nye-pod-leg-*wosh*-chee
Independence Day (11 November)
This holiday is held to commemorate 11 November 1918,
the day Poland regained its independence after 123 years under foreign occupation

Boże Narodzenie   *bo*-zhe na-ro-*dze*-nye
Christmas (25 December)
Arguably the most important religious event of the year.
Unlike in English-speaking countries, the most celebrated day
is Christmas Eve (*Wigilia*), featuring a solemn family supper
which traditionally should consist of 12 courses.
     After the meal, Santa Claus (*Święty Mikołaj*) will hand out
gifts from under the Christmas tree (*choinka*). Many people
will then go to church for the midnight mass (*pasterka*).

IN THE COUNTRY
Weather
Poland has a transitional climate, influenced by a continental
climate from the east and a maritime climate from the west. It's
characterised by four clearly differentiated seasons and changing
weather, with significant differences from day to day, season to
season and year to year.

What's the weather like?
     ya-ka yest po-*go*-da?   *Jaka jest pogoda?*
The weather's fine/bad.
     yest *wad*-nye/*bzhit*-ko   *Jest ładnie/brzydko.*
It's raining.
     pa-da deshch   *Pada deszcz.*
Fortunately, it's not raining.
     tsa-we *shchen*-shche zhe   *Całe szczęście że nie pada.*
     nye *pa*-da
It's snowing.
     pa-da shnyek   *Pada śnieg.*

POLISH

What a lovely day!
    tso za tsoo-*dov*-ni djen!   *Co za cudowny dzień!*
What's the temperature?
    ***ya*-ka yest tem-pe-ra-*too*-ra?** *Jaka jest temperatura?*
What's the weather
forecast for tomorrow?
    ***ya*-ka yest pro-*gno*-za**   *Jaka jest prognoza pogody na*
    po-*go*-di na *yoo*-tro?   *jutro?*

Today it's ...	djeesh yest ...	*Dziś jest ...*
Tomorrow it'll be ...	*yoo*-tro ben-dje ...	*Jutro będzie ...*
cloudy	poh-*moor*-nye	*pochmurnie*
cold	*zheem*-no	*zimno*
hot	go-*ron*-tso	*gorąco*
sunny	swo-*nech*-nye	*słonecznie*
warm	*chep*-wo	*ciepło*
windy	*vyech*-nye	*wietrznie*

climate	*klee*-mat	*klimat*
cloud	*hmoo*-ra	*chmura*
fog	mgwa	*mgła*
forecast	pro-*gno*-za	*prognoza*
frost	mroos	*mróz*
hail	grat	*grad*
heat	*oo*-paw	*upał*
ice	loot	*lód*
lightning	bwis-ka-*vee*-tsa	*błyskawica*
rain	deshch	*deszcz*
snow	shnyek	*śnieg*
storm	*boo*-zha	*burza*
sun	*swon*-tse	*słońce*
sunrise	fs-hoot *swon*-tsa	*wschód słońca*
sunset	za-hoot *swon*-tsa	*zachód słńca*
temperature	tem-pe-ra-*too*-ra	*temperatura*
thunder	gzhmot	*grzmot*
weather	po-*go*-da	*pogoda*
wind	vyatr	*wiatr*

POLISH

Camping

Camping is fairly popular in Poland. There are plenty of campsites throughout the country, in cities, towns and the countryside. Camping's also possible outside official sites, on private and public land, after asking proprietors or administrators for permission.

Is there a campsite nearby?
chi yest *ya*-keesh *kam*-peenk   *Czy jest jakiś camping w*
fpob-*lee*-zhoo?   *pobliżu?*

Where's the nearest campsite?
gdje yest nay-*bleesh*-shi   *Gdzie jest najbliższy camping?*
kam-peenk?

Where can we pitch our tent?
gdje *mozh*-na *roz*-beech   *Gdzie można rozbić namiot?*
na-myot?

Are there shower facilities?
chi som prish-*nee*-tse?   *Czy są prysznice?*

Is there hot water?
chi yest *chep*-wa *vo*-da?   *Czy jest ciepła woda?*

How much is it for a ...?	*ee*-le kosh-*too*-ye za ...?	*Ile kosztuje za ...?*
car	sa-*mo*-hoot	*samochód*
caravan	pshi-*che*-pe	*przyczepę*
night	nots	*noc*
person	o-*so*-be	*osobę*
tent	*na*-myot	*namiot*

camping	*kam*-peenk	*camping*
campsite	*kam*-peenk	*camping*
caravan (trailer)	pshi-*che*-pa	*przyczepa*
	(kam-peen-*go*-va)	*(campingowa)*
mattress	ma-*te*-rats	*materac*
penknife	stsi-*zo*-rik	*scyzoryk*
sleeping bag	*shpee*-voor	*śpiwór*
tent	*na*-myot	*namiot*
torch (flashlight)	la-*tar*-ka	*latarka*

POLISH

FOOD

Poland has for centuries been a cosmopolitan country, and its food has been influenced by various cuisines. The Jewish, Lithuanian, Belarusian, Ukrainian, Russian, Hungarian and German traditions have all made their mark. Polish food is hearty and filling – with thick soups and sauces, potatoes and dumplings – and is rich in meat, if not in vegetables.

Some of the better-known dishes include *bigos* (sauerkraut cooked with different kinds of meat); *pierogi* (ravioli-like dumplings stuffed with a variety of fillings); and *barszcz* (red beetroot soup). Favourite ingredients and herbs include dill, marjoram, caraway seeds and wild mushrooms.

Table for (four), please.
   po-*pro*-she *sto*-leek dla   *Poproszę stolik dla (czterech*
   (*chte*-reh *o*-soop)   *osób).*
Can I/we see the menu?
   chi *mozh*-na *pro*-sheech   *Czy można prosić o kartę?*
   o *kar*-te?

OBIAD

Poles start off their day with *śniadanie*, 'breakfast', which is roughly similar to its Western counterpart. For some people, the second meal is the *drugie śniadanie* (lit: second breakfast), which is often just a sandwich or other snack eaten somewhere between 10 am and noon. (See page 246 for breakfast foods.)

The most important and substantial meal of the day is the *obiad*, which is normally eaten somewhere between 1 and 5 pm. *Obiad* has no direct equivalent in English – judging by its contents, it's closer to Western dinner, but the timing is closer to lunch. Put simply, it's a dinner at lunch time.

The last meal is *kolacja*, 'supper', which is usually much lighter than the *obiad*. It often consists of foods similar to those eaten at breakfast.

POLISH

What's the speciality here?
ya-ka yest spe-*tsyal*-noshch zak-*wa*-doo? — *Jaka jest specjalność zakładu?*

What do you recommend?
tso pan/*pa*-nee po-*le*-tsa? — *Co pan/pani poleca?*

Are the accompaniments included in the price?
chi do-*dat*-ki som vlee-*cho*-ne *ftse*-ne? — *Czy dodatki są wliczone w cenę.*

Can I have the bill, please?
po-*pro*-she o ra-*hoo*-nek? — *Poproszę o rachunek.*

ashtray	po-pyel-*neech*-ka	*popielniczka*
bill	ra-*hoo*-nek	*rachunek*
cup	fee-lee-*zhan*-ka	*filiżanka*
fork	vee-*de*-lets	*widelec*
glass (for tea, water, soft drinks)	*shklan*-ka	*szklanka*
glass (for wine and spirits)	kye-*lee*-shek	*kieliszek*
knife	noosh	*nóż*
menu	*kar*-ta dan; ya-*dwos*-pees	*karta dań; jadłospis*
napkin	ser-*vet*-ka	*serwetka*
plate	*ta*-lesh	*talerz*
spices	pshi-*pra*-vi	*przyprawy* (f, pl)
spoon	*wish*-ka	*łyżka*
tablecloth	*o*-broos	*obrus*
teaspoon	wi-*zhech*-ka	*łyżeczka*
tip	na-*pee*-vek	*napiwek*
waiter	*kel*-ner	*kelner*
waitress	kel-*ner*-ka	*kelnerka*

Vegetarian Meals

The overwhelming majority of Poles are avid meat-eaters and don't consider a lunch or dinner a serious meal if it comes without a chunk of meat. This said, vegetarians won't starve in Poland, as most restaurants and cafes offer a selection of vegetarian dishes, called *dania jarskie*, though this isn't always an inspiring choice.

Exclusively vegetarian restaurants are rare, but there will almost always be a cafeteria, bistro, salad bar or other eatery around which will sport some veggie fare.

POLISH

I'm a vegetarian.
   yes-tem ya-*ro*-shem/   *Jestem jaroszem/jaroszką.* (m/f)
   ya-*rosh*-kom

I don't eat meat.
   nye *ya*-dam *myen*-sa   *Nie jadam mięsa.*

I don't eat chicken or fish.
   nye *ya*-dam *dro*-byoo   *Nie jadam drobiu*
   a-*nee* rip   *ani ryb.*

I can't eat dairy products.
   nye *mo*-ge yeshch   *Nie mogę jeść produktów*
   pro-*dook*-toof *mlech*-nih   *mlecznych.*

Do you have any
vegetarian dishes?
   chi som *ya*-kyesh *da*-nya   *Czy są jakieś dania jarskie?*
   yar-skye?

Does this dish have meat?
   chi to *da*-nye za-*vye*-ra   *Czy to danie zawiera mięso?*
   myen-so?

Can I get this
without meat?
   chi *mo*-ge to *dos*-tach bes   *Czy mogę to dostać bez*
   myen-sa?   *mięsa?*

Does it contain eggs?
   chi to za-*vye*-ra *yay*-ka?   *Czy to zawiera jajka?*

POLISH

MENU DECODER

Appetisers

barszcz (czerwony) ...	beetroot broth ...
ukraiński	with beans and potatoes
zabielany	with sour cream
z pasztecikiem	with a savoury pastry filled with minced meat
z uszkami	with small, ravioli-style dumplings stuffed with meat
befsztyk tatarski	raw minced sirloin served with onion, raw egg yolk and often chopped dill cucumber
botwinka	summertime soup made from the stems and leaves of baby beetroot
bukiet z jarzyn	mixed raw and pickled vegetables
grzyby (marynowane)	(marinated) wild mushrooms
kapuśniak	sauerkraut soup with potatoes
krupnik	thick barley soup with a variety of vegetables and small chunks of meat
jajko w majonezie	boiled egg in mayonnaise
łosoś wędzony	smoked salmon
mizeria	sliced, fresh cucumber in sour cream
sałatka jarzynowa	salad made with potato, vegetable and mayonnaise
zapiekanka	half bread roll with cheese and mushrooms, baked and served hot
zupa ...	... soup
cebulowa	onion
grochowa	lentil
jarzynowa	vegetable
ogórkowa	dill cucumber
pomidorowa	tomato
rybna	fish
ziemniaczana	potato

Main Meals

bigos	thick stew made of sauerkraut, cabbage and various kinds of meat and seasonings
gołąbki	cabbage leaves stuffed with minced beef and rice

POLISH

kaczka ...	duck ...
pieczona	roasted
z jabłkami	roasted and stuffed with apples
karp ...	carp ...
po grecku	served cold in an onion and tomato sauce
kurczak ...	... chicken
pieczony	roasted
z rożna	spit-roasted
naleśniki	crepes served with various fillings
pasztecik	savoury pastry stuffed with minced meat
pierogi ...	dumplings ...
ruskie	with soft, white cheese and potatoes
z kapustą i grzybami	with sauerkraut and wild mushrooms
z serem	with cottage cheese
placki kartoflane/ ziemniaczane	pancakes made with grated potatoes, egg and flour. Usually served with sour cream and/or sugar.
polędwica pieczona	roasted sirloin steak
pyzy	potato dumplings, steamed
sałatka ...	... salad
jarzynowa	potato, vegetable and mayonnaise
owocowa	fruit
z pomidorów	tomato
schab pieczony	roasted pork seasoned with prunes
sos ...	... sauce/gravy
chrzanowy	horseradish
grzybowy	mushroom
pomidorowy	tomato
zrazy zawijane	beef rolls stuffed with mushrooms and/or bacon, stewed and served in a sour-cream sauce
sztuka mięsa	boiled beef served with horseradish

Breakfast

Polish breakfast usually includes bread with butter, cheese, jam, and sausage or ham. Eggs are fairly popular, and can be prepared in a variety of guises such as soft-boiled, fried and scrambled. All this is washed down with a glass of tea or a cup of coffee with milk.

bacon	*bo*-chek	boczek
butter	*ma*-swo	masło
cheese	ser	ser
coffee	*ka*-va	kawa
ham	*shin*-ka	szynka
honey	myoot	miód
jam	djem	dżem
margarine	mar-ga-*ri*-na	margaryna
milk	*mle*-ko	mleko
sandwich	ka-*nap*-ka	kanapka
sausage	kyew-*ba*-sa	kiełbasa
tea	her-*ba*-ta	herbata
bread	hlep	chleb
bread roll	boo-*wech*-ka	bułeczka
dark rye bread	hlep ra-*zo*-vi	chleb razowy
white bread	*boow*-ka	bułka
toast	*gzhan*-ka	grzanka
eggs	*yay*-ka	jajka
with bacon/	na *boch*-koo/	na boczku/
ham	*shin*-tse	szynce
fried eggs	*yay*-ka sa-*dzo*-ne	jajka sadzone (pl)
hard-boiled egg	*yay*-ko na *tfar*-do	jajko na twardo
scrambled eggs	ya-yech-*nee*-tsa	jajecznica
soft-boiled egg	*yay*-ko na *myenk*-ko	jajko na miękko

POLISH

POLISH

Basics

bread	*hlep*	*chleb*
butter	*ma*-swo	*masło*
cheese	*ser*	*ser*
egg	*yay*-ko	*jajko*
flour	*mon*-ka	*mąka*
ham	*shin*-ka	*szynka*
margarine	mar-ga-*ri*-na	*margaryna*
milk	*mle*-ko	*mleko*
salt	*sool*	*sól*
sugar	*tsoo*-kyer	*cukier*
yogurt	*yo*-goort	*jogurt*

Meat & Poultry

beef	vo-wo-*vee*-na	*wołowina*
chicken	*koor*-chak	*kurczak*
ham	*shin*-ka	*szynka*
lamb	ba-ra-*nee*-na	*baranina*
meat	*myen*-so	*mięso*
pork	vyep-sho-*vee*-na	*wieprzowina*
sausage	kyew-*ba*-sa	*kiełbasa*
turkey	*een*-dik	*indyk*
veal	che-len-*chee*-na	*cielęcina*

Seafood

fish	*ri*-ba	*ryba*
lobster	*ho*-mar	*homar*
mussels	*maw*-zhe	*małże*
oysters	os-*tri*-gee	*ostrygi*
shrimp	kre-*vet*-ka	*krewetka*

POLISH

Vegetables

(green) beans	fa-*so*-la shpa-*ra*-go-va	*fasola (szparagowa)*
beetroot	boo-*ra*-kee	*buraki*
cabbage	ka-*poos*-ta	*kapusta*
capsicum	pa-*pri*-ka	*papryka*
carrot	*mar*-hef	*marchew*
cauliflower	ka-*la*-fyor	*kalafior*
celery	*se*-ler	*seler*
cucumber	o-*goo*-rek	*ogórek*
lettuce	sa-*wa*-ta	*sałata*
onion	tse-*boo*-la	*cebula*
peas	*gro*-shek	*groszek*
potato	*zhem*-nyak	*ziemniak*
	kar-*to*-fel	*kartofel*
pumpkin	*di*-nya	*dynia*
spinach	*shpee*-nak	*szpinak*
tomato	po-*mee*-dor	*pomidor*
vegetables	va-*zhi*-va	*warzywa*
	ya-*zhi*-ni	*jarzyny*

Fruit

apple	*yap*-ko	*jabłko*
apricot	mo-*re*-la	*morela*
banana	*ba*-nan	*banan*
fig	*fee*-ga	*figa*
grape	vee-no-*gro*-no	*winogrono*
lemon	tsi-*tri*-na	*cytryna*
orange	po-ma-*ran*-cha	*pomarańcza*
peach	bzhos-*kfee*-nya	*brzoskwinia*
pear	*groosh*-ka	*gruszka*
plum	*shleef*-ka	*śliwka*
wild stawberry	po-*zhom*-ka	*poziomka*

POLISH

Herbs, Spices & Condiments

garlic	*chos*-nek	czosnek
ginger	*eem*-beer	imbir
parsley	pyet-*roosh*-ka	pietruszka
pepper	pyepsh	pieprz
salt	sool	sól

OUT TO EAT

The main place for a meal with table service is the *restauracja*, 'restaurant'. You'll come across many, especially in major cities, which range from unpretentious budget eateries up to a la carte.

Another place to eat is a *kawiarnia*, 'cafe'. Unlike in communist Poland, when cafes provided little apart from sweets and drinks, most now offer meals which may be more attractive and often cheaper than those of some restaurants.

The cheapest place to eat is a *bar mleczny* (lit: milk bar), a sort of no-frills, self-service cafeteria. They were created to provide cheap food for the less affluent, and were once subsidised by the state. The free-market economy forced many to close, but a number have survived and do a good job. They offer mostly vegetarian fare, including Polish specialities, but also feature a choice of meat dishes. They are smoke-free, no-alcohol territory.

Another type of budget eatery, the *jadłodajnia*, is roughly similar to a *bar mleczny* (self-service, non-smoking, non-alcohol), though a little more expensive. Many have a family atmosphere and the food usually tastes home-cooked. Some of these places are excellent value.

For a dessert or a sweet snack, try a *cocktail bar* which, in contrast to its Western counterpart, serves not alcohol but milkshakes (in Polish, *cocktails*, hence the name), ice cream, cakes, pastries, coffee, tea and the like.

POLISH

Desserts

apple cake	shar-*lot*-ka	*szarlotka*
apple strudel	yab-*wech*-neek	*jabłecznik*
cream cake	tort;	*tort;*
	chas-tko tor-*to*-ve	*ciastko tortowe*
dumplings filled with plums/cherries/apples	*kne*-dle	*knedle*
fruit cake	keks	*keks*
fruit compote	*kom*-pot	*kompot*
ginger bread	*pyer*-neek	*piernik*
ice cream	*lo*-di	*lody*
ice cream with fruit and whipped cream	*mel*-ba	*melba*
marble cake	*bap*-ka	*babka*
milk pudding	*boo*-din	*budyń*
pastry; small cake	*chas*-tko	*ciastko*
poppyseed strudel	ma-*ko*-vyets	*makowiec*
waffles	*gof*-ri	*gofry*

Non-Alcoholic Drinks

black coffee	*char*-na *ka*-va	*czarna kawa*
coffee (with milk)	*ka*-va (*zmle*-kyem)	*kawa (z mlekiem)*
herbal tea	her-*ba*-ta zho-*wo*-va	*herbata ziołowa*
tea with milk	ba-*var*-ka	*bawarka*
tea ...	her-*ba*-ta ...	*herbata ...*
with sugar	*stsoo*-krem	*z cukrem*
without sugar	bes *tsoo*-kroo	*bez cukru*
with a slice of lemon	stsi-*tri*-nom	*z cytryną*
... juice	sok ...	*sok ...*
fruit	o-vo-*tso*-vi	*owocowy*
tomato	po-mee-do-*ro*-vi	*pomidorowy*
milk	*mle*-ko	*mleko*
milkshake	*kok*-tail	*cocktail*
(mineral) water	*vo*-da	*woda*
	(mee-ne-*ral*-na)	*(mineralna)*

POLISH

Alcoholic Drinks

Cheers!	na *zdro*-vye!	*Na zdrowie!*
beer	*pee*-vo	*piwo*
brandy	*ko*-nyak	*koniak*
champagne	*sham*-pan	*szampan*
liqueur	*lee*-kyer	*likier*
mead	myoot *peet*-ni	*miód pitny*
mulled beer	*gzha*-nyets *spee*-va	*grzaniec z piwa*
mulled wine	*gzha*-nyets *zvee*-na	*grzaniec z wina*
plum brandy	shlee-vo-*vee*-tsa	*śliwowica*
rum	room	*rum*
vodka	*voot*-ka	*wódka*
... wine	*vee*-no ...	*wino ...*
dry	vi-*trav*-ne	*wytrawne*
red	cher-*vo*-ne	*czerwone*
sweet	*swot*-kye	*słodkie*
white	*bya*-we	*białe*

NA ZDROWIE!

Vodka is Poland's national drink, and Poles claim it was invented here. Polish vodka comes in a number of colours and flavours, from very sweet to extra-dry.

bimber	*beem*-ber	home-distilled vodka
jarzębiak	ya-*zhem*-byak	vodka flavoured with rowanberry
ŵmyśliwska	mish-*leef*-ska	vodka flavoured with juniper berries
nalewka	na-*lef*-ka	home-made spirit made from vodka flavoured with herbs and berries
wiśniówka	veesh-*nyoof*-ka	cherry-flavoured vodka
wódka (f)	*voot*-ka	vodka
żubrówka	zhoo-*broof*-ka	bison vodka (flavoured with grass from the Białowieża forest on which bison feed)
żytnia	*zhit*-nya	dry vodka

POLISH

AT THE MARKET

Basics

bread	hlep	chleb
butter	*ma*-swo	masło
cheese	ser	ser
egg	*yay*-ko	jajko
flour	*mon*-ka	mąka
ham	*shin*-ka	szynka
margarine	mar-ga-*ri*-na	margaryna
milk	*mle*-ko	mleko
salt	sool	sól
sugar	*tsoo*-kyer	cukier
yogurt	*yo*-goort	jogurt

Meat & Poultry

beef	vo-wo-*vee*-na	wołowina
chicken	*koor*-chak	kurczak
ham	*shin*-ka	szynka
lamb	ba-ra-*nee*-na	baranina
meat	*myen*-so	mięso
pork	vyep-sho-*vee*-na	wieprzowina
sausage	kyew-*ba*-sa	kiełbasa
turkey	*een*-dik	indyk
veal	che-len-*chee*-na	cielęcina

Seafood

fish	*ri*-ba	ryba
lobster	*ho*-mar	homar
mussels	*maw*-zhe	małże
oysters	os-*tri*-gee	ostrygi
shrimp	kre-*vet*-ka	krewetka

Vegetables

(green) beans	fa-*so*-la	fasola
	shpa-*ra*-go-va	(szparagowa)
beetroot	boo-*ra*-kee	buraki
cabbage	ka-*poos*-ta	kapusta

AT THE MARKET

POLISH

capsicum	pa-*pri*-ka	papryka
carrot	*mar*-hef	marchew
cauliflower	ka-*la*-fyor	kalafior
celery	*se*-ler	seler
cucumber	o-*goo*-rek	ogórek
lettuce	sa-*wa*-ta	sałata
onion	tse-*boo*-la	cebula
peas	*gro*-shek	groszek
potato	*zhem*-nyak	ziemniak
	kar-*to*-fel	kartofel
pumpkin	*di*-nya	dynia
spinach	*shpee*-nak	szpinak
tomato	po-*mee*-dor	pomidor
vegetables	va-*zhi*-va	warzywa
	ya-*zhi*-ni	jarzyny

Fruit

apple	*yap*-ko	jabłko
apricot	mo-*re*-la	morela
banana	*ba*-nan	banan
fig	*fee*-ga	figa
grape	vee-no-*gro*-no	winogrono
lemon	tsi-*tri*-na	cytryna
orange	po-ma-*ran*-cha	pomarańcza
peach	bzhos-*kfee*-nya	brzoskwinia
pear	*groosh*-ka	gruszka
plum	*shleef*-ka	śliwka
wild stawberry	po-*zhom*-ka	poziomka

Herbs, Spices & Condiments

garlic	*chos*-nek	czosnek
ginger	*eem*-beer	imbir
parsley	pyet-*roosh*-ka	pietruszka
pepper	pyepsh	pieprz
salt	sool	sól

POLISH

SHOPPING

Where's the ...?	gdje yest ...?	*Gdzie jest ...?*
bakery	pye-*kar*-nya	*piekarnia*
bookshop	kshen-*gar*-nya	*księgarnia*
chemist (pharmacy)	ap-*te*-ka	*apteka*
delicatessen	de-lee-ka-*te*-si	*delikatesy* (pl)
greengrocer	sklep o-vo-*tso*-vo va-*zhiv*-ni	*sklep owocowo-warzywny*
grocer	sklep spo-*zhif*-chi	*sklep spożywczy*
laundry	*pral*-nya	*pralnia*
pharmacy	ap-*te*-ka	*apteka*
photographic shop	fo-to-*op*-ti-ka	*fotooptyka*
stationers	sklep pa-pyer-*nee*-chi	*sklep papierniczy*
travel agency	*byoo*-ro po-*droo*-zhi	*biuro podróży*

Do you have ...?
  chi som ...?   *Czy są ...?*
Can I pay by credit card?
  chi *mo*-ge za-*pwa*-cheech   *Czy mogę zapłacić kartą*
  kar-tom kre-di-*to*-vom?   *kredytową?*

Essential Groceries

bread	hlep	*chleb*
butter	*ma*-swo	*masło*
cheese	ser	*ser*
chocolate	che-ko-*la*-da	*czekolada*
eggs	*yay*-ka	*jajka*
flour	*mon*-ka	*mąka*
fruit	o-*vo*-tse	*owoce*
ham	*shin*-ka	*szynka*
margarine	mar-ga-*ri*-na	*margaryna*
matches	za-*paw*-kee	*zapałki*

POLISH

milk	*mle*-ko	*mleko*
salt	sool	*sól*
shampoo	*sham*-pon	*szampon*
soap	*mi*-dwo	*mydło*
sugar	*tsoo*-kyer	*cukier*
toilet paper	*pa*-pyer to-a-le-*to*-vi	*papier toaletowy*
toothpaste	*pas*-ta do *zem*-boof	*pasta do zębów*
washing powder	*pro*-shek do *pra*-nya	*proszek do prania*
yogurt	*yo*-goort	*jogurt*

Souvenirs

amber	*boor*-shtin	*bursztyn*
glassware	shkwo	*szkło*
handicrafts	vi-*ro*-bi shtoo-kee	*wyroby sztuki*
	loo-*do*-vey	*ludowej*
jewellery	bee-zhoo-*te*-rya	*biżuteria*
posters	pla-*ka*-ti	*plakaty*

Clothing

belt	*pa*-sek	*pasek*
bra	byoos-*to*-nosh	*biustonosz*
clothing	oo-*bra*-nye	*ubranie*
coat	pwashch	*płaszcz*
dress	soo-*kyen*-ka	*sukienka*
jacket	*koor*-tka	*kurtka*
jumper	*sfe*-ter	*sweter*
shirt	ko-*shoo*-la	*koszula*
shoes	*boo*-ti	*buty*
skirt	spood-*nee*-tsa	*spódnica*
socks	skar-*pet*-kee	*skarpetki*
sweater	*sfe*-ter	*sweter*
trousers	*spod*-nye	*spodnie*
T-shirt	pot-ko-*shool*-ka	*podkoszulka*
underpants (men)	*slee*-pi	*slipy*
underpants (women)	*fee*-gee	*figi*

POLISH

Materials

ceramic	tse-ra-*mee*-ka	*ceramika*
cotton	ba-*veoo*-na	*bawełna*
glass	shkwo	*szkło*
gold	*zwo*-to	*złoto*
leather	*skoo*-ra	*skóra*
linen	*pwoot*-no	*płótno*
silk	*yet*-vap	*jedwab*
silver	*sre*-bro	*srebro*
wood	*dzhe*-vo	*drzewo*
wool	*veoo*-na	*wełna*

Colours

beige	be-*zho*-vi	*beżowy*
black	*char*-ni	*czarny*
blue	nye-*byes*-kee	*niebieski*
brown	bron-*zo*-vi	*brązowy*
green	zhe-*lo*-ni	*zielony*
orange	po-ma-ran-*cho*-vi	*pomarańczowy*
pink	roo-*zho*-vi	*różowy*
purple	fyo-le-*to*-vi	*fioletowy*
red	cher-*vo*-ni	*czerwony*
white	*bya*-wi	*biały*
yellow	*zhoow*-ti	*żółty*

POLISH

Toiletries

comb	*gzhe*-byen	*grzebień*
condoms	pre-zer-va-*ti*-vi/	*prezerwatywy*
	kon-*do*-ni	*kondony*
moisturiser	krem	*krem*
	na-veel-zha-*yon*-tsi	*nawilżający*
razor	ma-*shin*-ka do	*maszynka do*
	go-*le*-nya	*golenia*
sanitary napkins	pot-*pas*-kee	*podpaski*
	hee-gye-*neech*-ne	*higieniczne*
shaving cream	krem do go-*le*-nya	*krem do golenia*
tampons	tam-*po*-ni	*tampony*
toothbrush	shcho-*tech*-ka do	*szczoteczka do*

Stationery & Publications

Is there an English-language
bookshop here?
    chi yest too kshen-*gar*-nya   *Czy jest tu księgarnia*
    an-glo-yen-*zich*-na?   *anglojęzyczna?*
Where's the English-language section?
    gdje yest sek-tsya   *Gdzie jest sekcja*
    an-glo-yen-*zich*-na?   *anglojęzyczna?*

book	*kshon*-shka	*książka*
city map	plan *mya*-sta	*plan miasta*
dictionary	*swov*-neek	*słownik*
envelope	ko-*per*-ta	*koperta*
magazine	ma-*ga*-zin	*magazyn*
map	*ma*-pa	*mapa*
newspaper	ga-*ze*-ta	*gazeta*
notebook	no-*tat*-neek	*notatnik*
paper	*pa*-pyer	*papier*
pen (ballpoint)	dwoo-*go*-pees	*długopis*
pencil	o-*woo*-vek	*ołówek*
postcard	poch-*toof*-ka	*pocztówka*
stamp	*zna*-chek	*znaczek*
weekly	ti-*god*-neek	*tygodnik*

POLISH

Photography

Can I have this film processed here?
*chi mo-ge too vi-vo-wach
ten feelm?*

*Czy mogę tu wywołać
ten film?*

How much is it to process this film?
*ee-le kosh-too-ye vi-vo-wa-nye
te-go feel-moo?*

*Ile kosztuje wywołanie
tego filmu?*

When will it be ready?
kye-di ben-dje go-to-vi?

Kiedy będzie gotowy?

I'd like a set of prints from this film.
*po-pro-she o kom-plet
ot-bee-tek ste-go feel-moo*

*Poproszę o komplet
odbitek z tego filmu.*

I need new batteries for this camera.
*pot-she-boo-ye no-ve ba-te-rye
do te-go a-pa-ra-too*

*Potrzebuję nowe baterie
do tego aparatu.*

My camera doesn't work.
mooy a-pa-rat nye dja-wa

Mój aparat nie działa.

Where can I have it fixed?
gdje go mo-ge na-pra-veech?

Gdzie go mogę naprawić?

battery	ba-*te*-rya	*bateria*
B&W film	feelm char-no-*bya*-wi	*film czarno-biały*
camera	a-*pa*-rat (fo-to-gra-*feech*-ni)	*aparat (fotograficzny)*
colour film	feelm ko-lo-*ro*-vi	*film kolorowy*
enlargement	po-vyenk-*she*-nye	*powiększenie*
lens	o-*byek*-tiv	*obiektyw*
light meter	shvya-*two*-myesh	*światłomierz*
slides	*slay*-di	*slajdy*
videotape	*tash*-ma vee-*de*-o	*taśma video*

Smoking

A packet of cigarettes, please.
*po-pro-she pach-ke
pa-pye-ro-soof*

*Poproszę paczkę
papierosów.*

Are these cigarettes strong or mild?
chi te pa-pye-*ro*-si som
***mots*-ne chi wa-*god*-ne?**
Czy te papierosy są mocne czy łagodne?

Do you have a light?
chi *mo*-ge *pro*-sheech o *o*-gyen?
Czy mogę prosić o ogień.

Please don't smoke here.
pro-she too nye *pa*-leech
Proszę tu nie palić.

Can I smoke here?
chi *mo*-ge too *pa*-leech?
Czy mogę tu palić?

Do you smoke?
chi pan/*pa*-nee *pa*-lee?
Czy pan/pani pali? (pol)
chi *pa*-leesh?
Czy palisz? (inf)

POLISH

cigarettes	pa-pye-*ro*-si	*papierosy*
cigarette paper	bee-*boow*-ka do	*bibułka do*
	pa-pye-*ro*-soof	*papierosów*
lighter	za-pal-*neech*-ka	*zapalniczka*
matches	za-*paw*-kee	*zapałki*
pipe	*fay*-ka	*fajka*
tobacco	*ti*-ton	*tytoń*
with filter	*sfeel*-trem	*z filtrem*
without filter	bes *feel*-tra	*bez filtra*

Sizes & Comparisons

small	*ma*-wi/a	*mały/a*
big	*doo*-zhi/a	*duży/a*
heavy	*chensh*-kee/a	*ciężki/a*
light	*lek*-kee/a	*lekki/a*
little (amount)	*ma*-wo	*mało*
a little bit	*tro*-he	*trochę*
too little	za *ma*-wo	*za mało*
much/many	*doo*-zho	*dużo*
too much/many	za *doo*-zho	*za dużo*
more	*vyen*-tsey	*więcej*
less	mnyey	*mniej*
enough	vis-*tar*-chi	*wystarczy*
also	*tak*-zhe	*także*

POLISH

HEALTH

Where's the nearest ...?	gdje yest nay-bleesh-shi/a ...?	Gdzie jest najbliższy/a ...?
doctor	le-kash	lekarz
dentist	den-tis-ta	dentysta
chemist	ap-te-ka	apteka
hospital	shpee-tal	szpital
outpatient clinic	pshi-hod-nya	przychodnia

I'm sick.
> yes-tem ho-ri/a   Jestem chory/a.

My friend is sick.
> mooy pshi-ya-chel yest ho-ri   Mój przyjaciel jest chory.
> mo-ya pshi-ya-choow-ka   Moja przyjaciółka
> yest ho-ra   jest chora.

I need a doctor who speaks English.
> pot-she-boo-ye le-ka-zha   Potrzebuję lekarza
> ktoo-ri moo-vee po   który mówi po
> an-gyel-skoo   angielsku.

It hurts here.
> too-tay mnye bo-lee   Tutaj mnie boli.

I feel better/worse.
> choo-ye she le-pyey/go-zhey   Czuję się lepiej/gorzej.

This is my usual medicine.
> to yest lek ktoo-ri   To jest lek który
> nor-mal-nye byo-re   normalnie biorę.

I've been vaccinated.
> yes-tem zash-che-pyo-ni/a   Jestem zaszczepiony/a.

I don't want a blood transfusion.
> nye htse trans-foo-zyee   Nie chcę transfuzji.

Can I have a receipt for my insurance?
> po-pro-she o ra-hoo-nek dla   Poproszę o rachunek dla
> mo-ye-go oo-bes-pye-che-nya   mojego ubezpieczenia.

POLISH

Parts of the Body

My ... hurts.	*bo-*lee mnye ...	*Boli mnie ...*
ankle	*kos-*tka	*kostka*
appendix	*shle-*pa *keesh-*ka	*ślepa kiszka*
arm	*ra-*mye	*ramię*
back	*ple-*tsi	*plecy*
chest	pyersh	*pierś*
ear	*oo-*ho	*ucho*
eye	*o-*ko	*oko*
finger	*pa-*lets	*palec*
foot	*sto-*pa	*stopa*
hand	*ren-*ka	*ręka*
head	*gwo-*va	*głowa*
heart	*ser-*tse	*serce*
kidney	*ner-*ka	*nerka*
knee	ko-*la-*no	*kolano*
leg	*no-*ga	*noga*
liver	von-*tro-*ba	*wątroba*
mouth	*oos-*ta	*usta*
muscle	*myen-*shen	*mięsień*
nose	nos	*nos*
rib	*zhe-*bro	*żebro*
shoulder	*ra-*mye	*ramię*
skin	*skoo-*ra	*skóra*
stomach	zho-*won-*dek	*żołądek*
throat	*gar-*dwo	*gardło*
tooth	zomp	*ząb*

Ailments

I'm ill.	*yes-*tem *ho-*ri/a	*Jestem chory/a.* (m/f)
I feel nauseous.	mam *mdwosh-*chee	*Mam mdłości.*
I've been vomiting.	vi-*myo-*to-*va-*wem/wam	*Wymiotowałem/łam.* (m/f)
I can't sleep.	nye *mo-*ge spach	*Nie mogę spać.*
I feel dizzy.	mam za-*vro-*ti *gwo-*vi	*Mam zawroty głowy.*
I feel shivery.	mam *dresh-*che	*Mam dreszcze.*
I feel weak.	*choo-*ye she *swa-*bo	*Czuję się słabo.*

POLISH

I have (a/an) ...	**mam ...**	*Mam ...*
allergy	oo-choo-*le*-nye	*uczulenie*
burn	o-pa-*zhe*-nye	*oparzenie*
cancer	*ra*-ka	*raka*
cold	pshe-zhem-*bye*-nye	*przeziębienie*
constipation	zat-far-*dze*-nye	*zatwardzenie*
cough	*ka*-shel	*kaszel*
diarrhoea	bye-*goon*-ke/	*biegunkę/*
	roz-vol-*nye*-nye	*rozwolnienie*
fever	go-*ronch*-ke	*gorączkę*
headache	bool *gwo*-vi	*ból głowy*
indigestion	nye-*strav*-noshch	*niestrawność*
infection	za-ka-*zhe*-nye	*zakażenie*
influenza	*gri*-pe	*grypę*
lice	fshi	*wszy*
low/high blood	*nees*-kye/vi-*so*-kye	*niskie/wysokie*
pressure	cheesh-*nye*-nye	*ciśnienie*
migraine	mee-*gre*-ne	*migrenę*
pain	bool	*ból*
rash	vi-*sip*-ke	*wysypkę*
sore throat	bool *gar*-dwa	*ból gardła*
sprain	zveeh-*nyen*-che	*zwichnięcie*
stomachache	bool zho-*won*-tka	*ból żołądka*
thrush	gzhi-*bee*-tse	*grzybicę*
travel sickness	ho-*ro*-be	*chorobę*
	lo-ko-mo-*tsiy*-nom	*lokomocyjną*
venereal disease	ho-*ro*-be	*chorobę*
	ve-ne-*rich*-nom	*weneryczną*
worms	ro-*ba*-kee	*robaki*

POLISH

Women's Health

The usual Polish terms for 'doctor' are *lekarz* (m) and *lekarka* (f), but the old-fashioned, formal *doktor* and *doktór* remain in common use. Both nouns are masculine, so if you're addressing or talking about a female doctor, you should use *pani doktor* or *pani doktór* (lit: madam doctor).

Could I have an appointment
with a female doctor?
    chi *mo*-ge za-*moo*-veech   *Czy mogę zamówić wizytę u*
    vee-*zi*-te oo *pa*-nee *dok*-toor? *pani doktór?*

I'm pregnant.
    yes-tem *fchon*-zhi   *Jestem w ciąży.*

I think I'm pregnant.
    vi-*da*-ye mee she, zhe   *Wydaje mi się, że jestem w*
    yes-tem *fchon*-zhi   *ciąży.*

I'm on the Pill.
    byo-re pee-*goow*-kee   *Biorę pigułki antykoncepcyjne.*
    an-ti-kon-tsep-*tsiy*-ne

I haven't had my period for
... weeks.
    nye mam mye-*shonch*-kee   *Nie mam miesiączki od ...*
    ot ... ti-*god*-nee   *tygodni.*

menstruation	men-stroo-*a*-tsya/	*menstruacja*
	mye-*shonch*-ka	*miesiączka*
miscarriage	po-ro-*nye*-nye	*poronienie*
period pain	bool mye-shonch-*ko*-vi	*ból miesiączkowy*
the Pill	pee-*goow*-ka	*pigułka*
	an-ti-kon-tsep-*tsiy*-na	*antykoncepcyjna*
pregnancy test	test chon-*zho*-vi	*test ciążowy*
premenstrual	na-*pyen*-che pshe-	*napięcie przed-*
tension	dmye-shonch-*ko*-ve	*miesiączkowe*

POLISH

At the Chemist

Where's the nearest (all-night) chemist?

gdje yest nay-*bleesh*-sha (tsa-wo-*nots*-na) ap-*te*-ka?	*Gdzie jest najbliższa (całonocna, apteka?*

Please give me something for ...

po-*pro*-she tsosh na ...	*Poproszę coś na ...*

antibiotic	an-ti-*byo*-tik	*antybiotyk*
antiseptic	an-ti-*sep*-tik	*antyseptyk*
aspirin	as-pee-*ri*-na	*aspiryna*
bandage	*ban*-dash	*bandaż*
Band-aids	plas-ter zo-pa-*troon*-kyem	*plaster z opatrunkiem*
condom	pre-zer-va-*ti*-va/ *kon*-don	*prezerwatywa/ kondon*
contraceptive	*shro*-dek an-ti-kon-tsep-*tsiy*-ni	*środek antykoncepcyjny*
cough medicine	lek na *ka*-shel	*lek na kaszel*
laxative	*shro*-dek pshe-chish-cha-*yon*-tsi	*środek przeczyszczający*
painkiller	*shro*-dek pshe-cheef-boo-*lo*-vi	*środek przeciwbólowy*
sleeping pills	*prosh*-kee na-*sen*-ne	*proszki nasenne*

At the Dentist

I have a toothache.	*bo*-lee mnye zomp	*Boli mnie ząb.*
I have a cavity.	mam *djoo*-re	*Mam dziurę.*

I've lost a filling.

vi-*pad*-wa mee *plom*-ba	*Wypadła mi plomba.*

I've broken my tooth.

zwa-maw mee she zomp	*Złamał mi się ząb.*

My gums hurt.

djon-swa mnye *bo*-lom	*Dziąsła mnie bolą.*

I don't want it extracted.

nye htse go *vir*-vach	*Nie chcę go wyrwać.*

Please give me an anaesthetic.

pro-she o znye-choo-*le*-nye	*Proszę o znieczulenie.*

POLISH

TIME & DATES

What time is it?
  ktoo-ra (yest) go-djee-na?   *Która (jest) godzina?*
(It's) one o'clock.
  (yest) *pyer*-fsha   *(Jest) pierwsza.*
(It's) ten o'clock.
  (yest) dje-*shon*-ta   *(Jest) dziesiąta.*
Half past one.
  fpoow do *droo*-gyey   *Wpół do drugiej.*
Half past three.
  fpoow do *chfar*-tey   *Wpół do czwartej.*
Five past one.
  pyench po *pyer*-fshey   *Pięć po pierwszej.*

in the morning	*ra*-no	*rano*
in the afternoon	po po-*wood*-nyoo	*po południu*
in the evening	vye-*cho*-rem	*wieczorem*
at night	*vno*-tsi	*w nocy*

Days

Monday	po-nye-*dja*-wek	*poniedziałek*
Tuesday	*fto*-rek	*wtorek*
Wednesday	*shro*-da	*środa*
Thursday	*chfar*-tek	*czwartek*
Friday	*pyon*-tek	*piątek*
Saturday	so-*bo*-ta	*sobota*
Sunday	nye-*dje*-la	*niedziela*

POLISH

Months

January	*sti*-chen	*styczeń*
February	*loo*-ti	*luty*
March	*ma*-zhets	*marzec*
April	*kfye*-chen	*kwiecień*
May	may	*maj*
June	*cher*-vyets	*czerwiec*
July	*lee*-pyets	*lipiec*
August	*sher*-pyen	*sierpień*
September	*vzhe*-shen	*wrzesień*
October	pazh-*djer*-neek	*październik*
November	lees-*to*-pat	*listopad*
December	*groo*-djen	*grudzień*

Seasons

spring	*vyos*-na	*wiosna*
summer	*la*-to	*lato*
autumn	*ye*-shen	*jesień*
winter	*zee*-ma	*zima*

Present

now	*te*-ras	*teraz*
today	djeesh/*djee*-shay	*dziś/dzisiaj*
this morning	djeesh *ra*-no	*dziś rano*
this afternoon	djeesh po po-*wood*-nyoo	*dziś po południu*
tonight	djeesh vye-*cho*-rem	*dziś wieczorem*
this week	ftim ti-*god*-nyoo	*w tym tygodniu*
this month	ftim mye-*shon*-tsoo	*w tym miesiącu*
this year	ftim *ro*-koo	*w tym roku*

Past

yesterday	*fcho*-ray	*wczoraj*
day before yesterday	pshet-*fcho*-ray	*przedwczoraj*
yesterday ...	*fcho*-ray ...	*wczoraj ...*
morning	*ra*-no	*rano*
afternoon	po po-*wood*-nyoo	*po południu*

POLISH

last ...	*vzesh*-wim ...	*w zeszłym ...*
week	ti-*god*-nyoo	*tygodniu*
month	mye-*shon*-tsoo	*miesiącu*
year	ro-koo	*roku*

... ago	... te-moo	*... temu*
half an hour	poow go-*djee*-ni	*pół godziny*
(three) days	(tshi) dnee	*(trzy) dni*
(five) years	(pyench) lat	*(pięć) lat*
a long time	*dav*-no	*dawno*

a moment ago	pshet *hfee*-lom	*przed chwilą*
since (May)	ot (*ma*-ya)	*od maja*
last night	*fcho*-ray vye-*cho*-rem	*wczoraj wieczorem*

Future

tomorrow	*yoo*-tro	*jutro*
day after tomorrow	po-*yoo*-tshe	*pojutrze*

tomorrow ...	*yoo*-tro ...	*jutro ...*
morning	*ra*-no	*rano*
afternoon	po po-*wood*-nyoo	*po południu*
evening	vye-*cho*-rem	*wieczorem*

next ...	*fpshish*-wim ...	*w przyszłym ...*
week	ti-*god*-nyoo	*tygodniu*
month	mye-*shon*-tsoo	*miesiącu*
year	ro-koo	*roku*

in (five) minutes	za (pyench) *mee*-noot	*za (pięć) minut*
in (four) days	za (*chte*-ri) dni	*za (cztery) dni*
within an hour	*fchon*-goo go-*djee*-ni	*w ciągu godziny*
until (December)	do (*grood*-nya)	*do (grudnia)*

POLISH

During the Day

dawn	shfeet	*świt*
day	djen	*dzień*
early	*fchesh*-nye	*wcześnie*
hour	go-*djee*-na	*godzina*
midnight	*poow*-nots	*północ*
minute	mee-*noo*-ta	*minuta*
morning	*ra*-no	*rano*
night	nots	*noc*
noon	po-*wood*-nye	*południe*
second	se-*koon*-da	*sekunda*
sunrise	fs-hoot *swon*-tsa	*wschód słońca*
sunset	*za*-hoot *swon*-tsa	*zachód słońca*

NUMBERS & AMOUNTS

0	*ze*-ro	*zero*
1	*ye*-den	*jeden*
2	dva	*dwa*
3	tshi	*trzy*
4	*chte*-ri	*cztery*
5	pyench	*pięć*
6	sheshch	*sześć*
7	*she*-dem	*siedem*
8	*o*-shem	*osiem*
9	*dje*-vyench	*dziewięć*
10	*dje*-shench	*dziesięć*
11	ye-de-*nash*-che	*jedenaście*
12	dva-*nash*-che	*dwanaście*
13	tshi-*nash*-che	*trzynaście*
14	chter-*nash*-che	*czternaście*
15	pyent-*nash*-che	*piętnaście*
16	shes-*nash*-che	*szesnaście*
17	she-dem-*nash*-che	*siedemnaście*
18	o-shem-*nash*-che	*osiemnaście*
19	dje-vyet-*nash*-che	*dziewiętnaście*
20	dva-*djesh*-cha	*dwadzieścia*
21	dva-*djesh*-cha *ye*-den	*dwadzieścia jeden*
22	dva-*djesh*-cha dva	*dwadzieścia dwa*

POLISH

30	tshi-*djesh*-chee	*trzydzieści*
31	tshi-*djesh*-chee *ye*-den	*trzydzieści jeden*
32	tshi-*djesh*-chee dva	*trzydzieści dwa*
40	chter-*djesh*-chee	*czterdzieści*
41	chter-*djesh*-chee *ye*-den	*czterdzieści jeden*
50	pyen-*dje*-shont	*pięćdziesiąt*
51	pyen-*dje*-shont *ye*-den	*pięćdziesiąt jeden*
60	shesh-*dje*-shont	*sześćdziesiąt*
70	she-dem-*dje*-shont	*siedemdziesiąt*
80	o-shem-*dje*-shont	*osiemdziesiąt*
90	dje-vyen-*dje*-shont	*dziewięćdziesiąt*
100	sto	*sto*
101	sto *ye*-den	*sto jeden*
110	sto *dje*-shench	*sto dziesięć*
200	*dvyesh*-che	*dwieście*
300	*tshis*-ta	*trzysta*
400	chte-*ris*-ta	*czterysta*
500	*pyen*-tset	*pięćset*
600	*shesh*-set	*sześćset*
700	she-*dem*-set	*siedemset*
800	o-*shem*-set	*osiemset*
900	dje-*vyen*-tset	*dziewięćset*
1000	*ti*-shonts	*tysiąc*
1100	*ti*-shonts sto	*tysiąc sto*
2000	dva ti-*shon*-tse	*dwa tysiące*
5000	pyench ti-*shen*-tsi	*pięć tysięcy*
10,000	*dje*-shench ti-*shen*-tsi	*dziesięć tysięcy*
100,000	sto ti-*shen*-tsi	*sto tysięcy*
one million	*mee*-lyon	*milion*

48	chter-*djesh*-chee o-shem	*czterdzieści osiem*
335	*tshis*-ta tshi-*djesh*-chee pyench	*trzysta trzydzieści pięć*
1280	*ti*-shonts *dvyesh*-che o-shem-*dje*-shont	*tysiąc dwieście osiemdziesiąt*
14,500	chter-*nash*-che ti-*shen*-tsi *pyen*-tset	*czternaście tysięcy pięćset*

POLISH

Useful Words

dozen	*too-*zheen	*tuzin*
few	*keel-*ka	*kilka*
less	mnyey	*mniej*
a little (amount)	nye-*doo-*zho	*niedużo*
many/much	*doo-*zho	*dużo*
more	*vyen-*tsey	*więcej*
once	ras	*raz*
pair	*pa-*ra	*para*
percent	*pro-*tsent	*procent*
some	*tro-*he	*trochę*
too little	za *ma-*wo	*za mało*
too much/many	za *doo-*zho	*za dużo*
twice	dva *ra-*zi	*dwa razy*

ABBREVIATIONS

al	avenue
dr	doctor
godz	hour
inż	engineer
itp	etc
LOT	LOT Polish Airlines
mgr	MA, MSc
min	minute
ONZ	United Nations
PKP	Polish State Railways
PKS	Polish State Bus Company
PTSM	Polish Youth Hostel Association
PTTK	Polish Tourist Association
PZM	Polish Motoring Association
ul	street

EMERGENCIES

Help!	ra-*toon*-koo!;	*Ratunku!;*
	po-*mo*-tsi!;	*Pomocy!;*
	na *po*-mots!	*Na pomoc!*
Stop!	stach!	*Stać!*
Go away!	*pro*-she o-*deysh*ch!	*Proszę odejść!* (pol)
	o-*deych*!	*Odejdź!* (inf)
Thief!	*zwo*-djey!	*Złodziej!*
Fire!	po-*zhar*!;	*Pożar!;*
	pa-lee she!	*Pali się!*
Watch out!	*pro*-she oo-*va*-zhach!	*Proszę uważać!* (pol)
	oo-*va*-zhay!	*Uważaj!* (inf)
Call a/an ...!	*pro*-she *vez*-vach ...!	*Proszę wezwać ...!*
ambulance	ka-*ret*-ke	*karetkę*
doctor	le-*ka*-zha	*lekarza*

POLISH

I'm ill.
yes-tem *ho*-ri/a — *Jestem chory/a.*

My friend is ill.
mooy pshi-*ya*-chel yest *ho*-ri — *Mój przyjaciel jest chory.*
mo-ya pshi-ya-*choow*-ka yest *ho*-ra — *Moja przyjaciółka jest chora.*

I have medical insurance.
mam oo-bes-pye-*che*-nye me-*dich*-ne — *Mam ubezpieczenie medyczne.*

Please call the police!
pro-she *vez*-vach po-*lee*-tsye! — *Proszę wezwać policję!*

Where's the police station?
gdje yest pos-te-*roo*-nek po-*lee*-tsye? — *Gdzie jest posterunek policji?*

It's an emergency.
to yest *na*-gwi pshi-*pa*-dek — *To jest nagły przypadek.*

Could you help me please?
pro-she mee *po*-moots? — *Proszę mi pomóc.*

I'm lost.
zgoo-*bee*-wem/wam she — *Zgubiłem/łam się.* (m/f)

Where are the toilets?
gdje som to-a-*le*-ti? — *Gdzie są toalety?*

POLISH

Dealing with the Police

I want to report a/an ...	htse *zgwo*-sheech ...	*Chcę zgłosić ...*
accident	vi-*pa*-dek	*wypadek*
attack	*na*-pat	*napad*
loss	*zgoo*-be	*zgubę*
theft	*kra*-djesh	*kradzież*

I've lost ...	zgoo-*bee*-wem/wam ...	*Zgubiłem/łam* (m/f) ..
My ... has/have been stolen.	skra-*djo*-no mee ...	*Skradziono mi ...*
backpack	*ple*-tsak	*plecak*
camera	a-*pa*-rat (fo-to-gra-*feech*-ni)	*aparat (fotograficzny)*
car	sa-*mo*-hoot	*samochód*
credit card	*kar*-te kre-di-*to*-vom	*kartę kredytową*
money	pye-*nyon*-dze	*pieniądze*
passport	*pash*-port	*paszport*
travellers cheques	*che*-kee po-*droozh*-ne	*czeki podróżne*
wallet	*por*-tfel	*portfel*

I've been assaulted.
  na-pad-*nyen*-to na mnye　　*Napadnięto na mnie.*
I've been robbed.
  o-bra-bo-*va*-no mnye　　*Obrabowano mnie.*
I've been raped.
  zgvaw-*tso*-no mnye　　*Zgwałcono mnie.*
My possessions are insured.
  mo-ye *zhe*-chi son　　*Moje rzeczy są ubezpieczone.*
  oo-bes-pye-*cho*-ne

SLOVAK

QUICK REFERENCE

SLOVAK

English	Pronunciation	Slovak
Hello.	doh-bree dyien	Dobrý deň.
Goodbye.	doh vidyeny-nyiah	Do videnia.
Yes./No.	aa-noh/nyieh	Áno./Nie.
Excuse me.	prepaach-tyeh	Prepáčte.
May I?	smyiem?	Smiem?
Sorry.	prepaach-tyeh	Prepáčte
Please.	proh-seem	Prosím.
Thank you.	dyakuh-yem	Ďakujem.
You're welcome.	proh-seem	Prosím.
What time is it?	koly-koh yeh hoh-dyeen?	Koľko je hodín?
Where's the ...	gdyeh yeh ...?	Kde je ...?

Where are the toilets?
    dyeh soo tuh zaa-khodih?　　Kde sú tu záchody?
Go straight ahead.
    poh-krachuy-tyeh v yaz-dyeh!　Pokračujte v jazde!
Turn to the left/right.
    za-boch-tyeh　　　　　　　Zabočte
    vlyah-voh/fprah-voh　　　　vľavo/vpravo.
I don't understand.
    nyeh-rozuh-miehm　　　　　Nerozumiem.
Do you speak English?
    hovoh-ree-tyeh poh
    ahnglits-kih?　　　　　　　Hovoríte po anglicky?
How much is it?
    koly-koh toh stoh-yee?　　　Koľko to stojí?

I'd like ...	poh-trebuhyem ...	Potrebujem ...
a single room	yednoh-luozhkoh-voo izbuh	jednolôžkovú izbu
a ticket	leas-tok	lístok
one-way	yednoh-smernee	jednosmerný
return	spyiatoch-nee	spiatočný

1	yeh-den	jeden	6	shesty	šesť
2	dvah	dva	7	seh-dyem	sedem
3	trih	tri	8	oh-sem	osem
4	shtih-rih	štyri	9	dye-vety	deväť
5	pety	päť	10	dye-sahty	desať

SLOVAK

The Slovak language belongs to the Western branch of the Slavonic languages, and is the standard language of the six million people living in Slovakia, as well as nearly two million people living beyond the country's borders.

Slovak evolved between the 9th and the 15th centuries, and was associated with the development of a national Slovak culture at a time when Slovakia's territory and the surrounding regions were dominated by Latin at all levels – religious, administrative and literary. In the 17th century Slovakia was at the eastern border of Christian Europe, and the rules of Slovak were written down for the first time. However, Slovak didn't emerge as a uniform literary language until the mid-19th century, during the course of a national revival.

The language that bears the closest resemblance to Slovak is Czech. This should come as no surprise, since ties between the two countries date back to the 9th century and the Great Moravian Empire, where one common language (Old Church Slavonic) was in use. Although modern Slovak and Czech are, in general, mutually understandable, it's advisable not to substitute one for the other. The linguistic territory of each language includes many regional dialects, and these form a continuum across present and past political boundaries, so that, for example, the East Slovak dialect is closer to the West Ukrainian dialect than to the standard Czech language.

SLOVAK

PRONUNCIATION

Slovak is written as it sounds, and isn't as difficult as it looks. It may help to remember that Slovak makes use of only four diacritical marks. The most common are – *é*, which lengthens a vowel, and *ď*, which softens a vowel. The other two are limited to the letters *ä* and *ô*.

Vowels

Slovak has six short and five long vowels and one long and one short semi-vowel. It's important to observe their different pronunciation, as detailed below, since vowel length may determine the meaning of a word.

Short Vowels		**Long Vowels**	
a	as the 'u' in 'cup'	*á*	as the 'a' in 'father'
ä	as the 'a' in 'fat'	*é*	as the 'ea' in 'bear'
e	as in 'bed'	*í*	as the 'ee' in 'feet'
i	as the 'i' in 'machine'	*ó*	as the 'o' in 'shore'
o	as in 'pot'	*ú*	as the 'oo' in 'choose'
u	as the 'oo' in 'book'	*ý*	as the 'ee' in 'feet'
y	as the 'i' in 'bit'		

Vowel Combinations

There are four vowel combinations in Slovak:

ia	as the 'i' in 'machine' followed by the 'u' in 'cup'
ie	as the 'i' in 'machine' followed by the 'e' in 'bed'
iu	as the 'i' in 'machine' followed by the 'oo' in 'book'
ô	as the 'wa' in 'swan'

Consonants

Consonants not described are pronounced as they are in English.

c	as the 'ts' in 'lots'
č	as the 'ch' in 'China'
c	as the 'ch' in Scottish 'loch'
dz	as the 'ds' in 'roads'
dž	as the 'j' in 'jeans'

d̕, t̕, ň, ľ	followed by a 'y' sound, as in 'during', 'tutor', 'new', 'million'
h	as the 'h' in 'hand' but pronounced more forcefully
j	as the 'y' in 'yes'
k, p, t	pronounced without a puff of air following
ĺ, ŕ	semi-vowels, found in words such as *stĺp, vŕba, tŕň* (very hard to pronounce)
q, w, x	only exist in words of foreign origin and are pronounced approximately as in their original language
r	trilled
š	as the 'sh' in 'shoe'

Slovak speakers refer to their language lovingly as *ľúbozvučná slovenčina*, 'sweet sounding Slovak', in recognition of its melodious quality. Slovak doesn't allow two consecutive long syllables, and avoids heavy emphasis on any word. Stress always falls on the first syllable, but is far less strong than in other languages.

Subject Pronouns

Standard Slovak recognises two forms of address corresponding to the English 'you' – the formal *Vy* and the more familiar *ty*. This phrasebook uses the more polite form *Vy*, since in Slovak it's the appropriate form to use when addressing strangers.

SUBJECT PRONOUNS		
SG		
I	yah	ja
you (sg, inf)	tih	ty
you (sg, pol)	vih	Vy
he/she/it	ohn/ohnah/ohnoh	on/ona/ono
PL		
we	mih	my
you (pl)	vih	vy
they (m)	onyih	oni
they (f)	onih	ony

SLOVAK

GREETINGS & CIVILITIES
Top Useful Phrases

Hello.	doh-bree dyien	*Dobrý deň.*
Goodbye.	doh vidyeny-nyiah	*Do videnia.*
Yes./No.	aa-noh/nyieh	*Áno./Nie.*
Excuse me.	prepaach-tyeh	*Prepáčte.*
May I?	smyiem?	*Smiem?*
Do you mind?	dovoh-leetyeh?	*Dovolíte?*
Sorry. (Forgive me.)	prepaach-tyeh, proh-seem	*Prepáčte, prosím.*
Please.	proh-seem	*Prosím.*
Thank you.	dyakuh-yem	*Ďakujem.*
Many thanks.	dyakuh-yem vely-mih pek-neh	*Ďakujem veľmi pekne.*
That's fine.	nyieh yeh zah cho	*Nie je za čo.*
You're welcome.	proh-seem	*Prosím.*

SLOVAK

Greetings

Good morning.	doh-brair raano	*Dobré ráno.*
Good afternoon.	doh-bree dyeny	*Dobrý deň.*
Good evening.	doh-bree veh-cher	*Dobrý večer.*
Good night.	doh-broo nots	*Dobrú noc.*
How are you?	akoh sah maa-tyeh?	*Ako sa máte?*
Well, thanks.	dyakuh-yem dobreh	*Ďakujem, dobre.*

Forms of Address

Madam/Mrs/Ms	pah-nyih	*pani*
Sir/Mr	paan	*pán*
Miss	slech-nah	*slečna*
friend	pryiah-tyely	*priateľ* (m)
	pryiah-tyely-kah	*priateľka* (f)

SMALL TALK
Meeting People
What's your name?
    akoh sah voh-laa-tyeh?   *Ako sa voláte?*
My name's ...
    voh-laam sah ...   *Volám sa ...*
I'd like to introduce you to ...
    dovoly-tyeh abih som   *Dovolte, aby som Vás*
    vaas predstah-vil totoh yeh ...   *predstavil. Toto je ...*
Pleased to meet you.
    tyeshee mah   *Teší ma.*
How old are you?
    koly-koh maa-teh rokohw?   *Koľko máte rokov?*

Nationalities
Where are you from? odkyialy styeh?   *Odkiaľ ste?*

I'm from ...	som z ...	*Som z ...*
Australia	ahwstraa-lyieh	*Austrálie*
Canada	kanah-dih	*Kanady*
England	anglitz-kah	*Anglicka*
Ireland	eer-skah	*Írska*
New Zealand	novair-hoh	*Nového*
	zair-landuh	*Zélandu*
Scotland	shkawht-skah	*Škótska*
USA	oo-es-ah	*USA*
	(spoyeh-neekh	*(Spojených*
	shtaa-tohw	*štátov*
	ameritz-keekh)	*amerických)*
Wales	wheyl-suh	*Walesu*

Occupations
What do you do?
    choh robee-tyeh?   *Čo robíte?*
I'm unemployed.
    som nyeh-zah-mest-nah-nee   *som nezamestnaný* (m)
    som nyeh-zah-mest-nah-naa   *som nezamestnaná* (f)

SLOVAK

SLOVAK

I'm a/an ...	(yah) som ...	(Ja) som ...
artist	oomeh-lets	umelec (m)
	oomel-kinya	umelkyňa (f)
businessperson	podnyih-kah-tyely	podnikateľ (m)
	podnyih-kah-tyely-kah	podnikateľka (f)
computer programmer	proh-grah-maa-tor	programátor (m)
	proh-grah-maa-tor-kah	programátorka (f)
doctor	dok-tor	doktor (m)
	dok-tor-kah	doktorka (f)
engineer	inzhih-nyier	inžinier (m)
	inzhih-nyier-kah	inžinierka (f)
farmer	roly-nyeek	roľník (m)
	roly-nyeech-kah	roľníčka (f)
journalist	novih-naar	novinár (m)
	novih-naar-kah	novinárka (f)
lawyer	praav-nyik	právnik (m)
	praav-nyich-kah	právnička (f)
manual worker	robot-nyeek	robotník (m)
	robot-nyeech-kah	robotníčka (f)
mechanic	mekhah-nik	mechanik (m)
	mekhah-nich-kah	mechanička (f)
nurse	osheh-trovah-tyely	ošetrovateľ (m)
	osheh-trovah- tyely-kah	ošetrovateľka (f)
office worker	oorad-nyeek	úradník (m)
	oorad-nyeech-kah	úradníčka (f)
scientist	vedyets-kee	vedecký
	pratsov-nyeek	pracovník (m)
	vedyets-kaa	vedecká
	pratsov-nyeech-kah	pracovníčka (f)
student	shtuh-dent	študent (m)
	shtuh-dent-kah	študentka (f)
teacher	oochih-tyely	učiteľ (m)
	oochih-tyely-kah	učiteľka (f)
waiter	chash-nyeek	čašník (m)
	chash-nyeech-kah	čašníčka (f)
writer	spisoh-vah-tyely	spisovateľ (m)
	spisoh-vah-tyely-kah	spisovateľka (f)

Religion

What's your religion?
akair-hoh styeh (vyieroh) *Akého ste (viero-)vyznania?*
viznah-nyiah?

I'm not religious.
som bez viznah-nyiah *Som bez vyznania.*

I'm ...	(yah) som ...	(Ja) som ...
Buddhist	boodhih-stah	*budhista* (m)
	bood-hist-kah	*budhistka* (f)
Catholic	kahtoh-leek	*katolík* (m)
	kahtoh-leech-kah	*katolíčka* (f)
Protestant	evanyieh-lik	*evanjelik* (m)
	evanyieh-lich-kah	*evanjelička* (f)
Christian	kres-tyan	*krestan* (m)
	kres-tyan-kah	*krestanka* (f)
Hindu	hindoo-istah	*hinduista* (m)
	hindoo-ist-kah	*hinduistka* (f)
Jewish	zhid	*žid* (m)
	zhidohv-kah	*židovka* (f)
Muslim	mos-lim	*moslim* (m)
	mos-lim-kah	*moslimka* (f)

SLOVAK

Family

Are you married?
steh zhenah-tee? *Ste ženatý?* (m)
steh vidah-taa? *Ste vydatá?* (f)

I'm single.
som slobod-nee *Som slobodný.* (m)
som slobod-naa *Som slobodná.* (f)

I'm married.
som zhenah-tee *Som ženatý.* (m)
som vidah-taa *Som vydatá.* (f)

Is your husband here?
vaash man-zhel yeh tuh? *Váš manžel je tu?*

Is your wife here?
vaa-shah man-zhel-kah *Vaša manželka je tu?*
yeh tuh?

I'm ...	yah som ...	*Ja som ...*
a widow	vdoh-vah	*vdova*
a widower	vdoh-vets	*vdovec*
divorced	roz-veh-dye-nee	*rozvedený* (m)
	roz-veh-dye-naa	*rozvedená* (f)

I'm separated.
nye-zhi-yem zoh svoh-yeem	*Nežijem so svojím*
part-nehr-rom	*partnerom.* (m)
nye-zhi-yem zoh svoh-yow	*Nežijem so svojou*
part-nehr-kow	*partnerkou.* (f)

How many children do you have?
koly-koh maa-tyeh dyeh-tyee?	*Koľko máte detí?*

I don't have any children.
nye-maam dyeh-tih	*Nemám deti.*

I have a daughter/son.
maam tsair-ruh/sinah	*Mám dcéru/syna.*

How many brothers/ sisters do you have?
koly-koh maa-teh brah-tohw/	*Koľko máte bratov/*
seh-styier?	*sestier?*

Do you have a boyfriend/girlfriend?
maa-teh priah-tyeh-lyah/	*Máte priateľa/priateľku?*
priah-tyely-kuh?	

brother	braht	*brat*
daughter	tsair-rah	*dcéra*
family	rodyih-nah	*rodina*
father	oh-tyets	*otec*
grandfather	stah-ree oh-tyets	*starý otec*
grandmother	stah-raa mat-kah	*stará matka*
husband	man-zhel	*manžel*
mother	mat-kah	*matka*
sister	seh-strah	*sestra*
son	sin	*syn*
wife	manzhel-kah	*manželka*

Kids' Talk

What's your name?
akoh sah volaash?   *Ako sa voláš?*

How old are you?
kolyikoh maash roh-kohv?   *Koľko máš rokov?*

When's your birthday?
**kedih maash
nahroh-dyieh-nyinih?**   *Kedy máš narodeniny?*

What grade are you in?
**doh ktoh-rey trye-dih
kho-dyeesh?**   *Do ktorej triedy chodíš?*

How many brothers and
sisters do you have?
**kolyih-koh maash brah-tohv
ah sehs-tyierh?**   *Koľko máš bratov
a sestier?*

Do you have your own room?
maash svoh-yiuh ihz-buh?   *Máš svoju izbu?*

I share my room.
nye-maam svoh-yiuh ihz-buh   *Nemám svoju izbu.*

I have my own room.
maam svoh-yiuh ihz-buh   *Mám svoju izbu.*

What are your favourite
games/hobbies?
choh tyah bah-vee?   *Čo ťa baví?*

SLOVAK

I have a ...	(yah) maam ...	(Ja) mám ...
budgerigar	**ahndul-kuh**	*andulku*
canary	**kahnaa-rihkah**	*kanárika*
cat	**mahtch-kuh**	*mačku*
cow	**krah-vuh**	*kravu*
dog	**psah**	*psa*
donkey	**soh-maa-rah**	*somára*
duck	**kach-kuh**	*kačku*
frog	**zha-buh**	*žabu*
mouse	**mishich-kuh**	*myšičku*
rabbit	**zah-yats**	*zajac*

collecting things	zbyie-ratyh vet-sih	*zbierať veci*
making things	viraah-batyh vet-sih	*vyrábať veci*
playing outside	hratyih sah vohn-kuh	*hrať sa vonku*
sports	shpohrt	*šport*
video games	videoh hrih	*video hry*
watching TV	pohzeh-ratyih	*pozerať*
	teleh-vee-zyiuh	*televíziu*

SLOVAK

Feelings

I'm ...

cold/hot	yeh mih zimah/	*Je mi zima/*
	tyep-loh	*teplo.*
hungry	maam hlahd	*Mám smäd.*
in a hurry	ponaa-hlyam sah	*Ponáhľam sa.*
right	maam prahv-duh	*Mám pravdu.*
sleepy	som ospah-lee/	*Som ospalý/*
	ospah-laa	*ospalá.* (m/f)
thirsty	maam smed	*Mám smäd.*

I'm ...

angry	hnye-vaam sah	*Hnevám sa.*
happy	sohm shtyast-nee/	*Som šťastný/*
	shtyast-naa	*šťastná.* (m/f)
sad	sohm smut-nee/	*Som smutný/*
	smut-naa	*smutná.* (m/f)
tired	sohm oonah-vehnee/	*Som unavený/*
	oonah-vehnaa	*unavená.* (m/f)
well	tsee-tyim sah dob-reh	*Cítim sa dobre.*
worried	ohbaa-vam sah	*Obávam sa.*

I like ...
   maam raad/radah...   *Mám rád/rada ...* (m/f)
I don't like ...
   nyeh-maam raad/radah...   *Nemám rád/rada ...* (m/f)

I'm sorry. (condolence)
   lyutuh-yem   *L'utujem.*
I'm grateful.
   sohm vdyach-nee/vdyach-naa *Som vďačný/vďačná.* (m/f)

QUESTION WORDS

How?	ah-koh?	Ako?
When?	kedy?	Kedy?
Where?	gdyeh?	Kde?
Which?	ktoh-ree?	Ktorý?
Who?	gdoh?	Kto?
Why?	preh-choh?	Prečo?

SLOVAK

Useful Phrases

Sure!	oorchih-tyeh!	*Určite!*
Just a minute.	ohkam-zhik	*Okamžik.*

It's (not) important.
   oh (nyieh) yeh   *To (nie) je dôležité.*
   duoleh-zhitair
It's (not) possible.
   toh (nyieh) yeh   *To (nie) je možné.*
   mozh-nair
Wait!
   pochkay!/pochkay-tyeh! *Počkaj!* (sg)/*Počkajte!* (pl)
Good luck!
   fshet-koh naylep-shyieh! *Všetko najlepšie!*

BREAKING THE LANGUAGE BARRIER

Do you speak English?
hovoh-ree-tyeh poh ahnglits-kih? *Hovoríte po anglicky?*

Does anyone (here) speak English?
hovoh-ree (tuh) nyiek-toh poh ahnglits-kih? *Hovorí (tu) niekto po anglicky?*

I speak a little ...
yah hovoh-reehm tro-kha (poh) ... *Ja hovorím trocha (po) ...*

I don't speak ...
nyeh-hovoh-reehm (poh) ... *Nehovorím (po) ...*

I understand.
rozuh-miehm *Rozumiem.*

I don't understand.
nyeh-rozuh-miehm *Nerozumiem.*

Could you speak more slowly, please?
muoh-zhetyeh proh-seem hoh-vohrity pohmal-shyieh? *Môžete prosím hovoriť pomalšie?*

Could you repeat that?
muoh-zhetyeh toh zopa-kovaty? *Môžete to zopakovať?*

How do you say ...?
akoh sah povyieh? *Ako sa povie ...?*

What does ... mean?
choh znameh-naa ...? *Čo znamená ...?*

I speak ...	**hovoh-reehm poh ...**	*Hovorím po ...*
Arabic	**arab-skih**	*arabsky*
Danish	**daan-skih**	*dánsky*
Dutch	**holand-skih**	*holandsky*
English	**anglits-kih**	*anglicky*
Finnish	**feen-skih**	*fínsky*
French	**fran-tsooz-kih**	*francúzsky*
German	**nyemetz-kih**	*nemecky*
Italian	**talyian-skih**	*taliansky*
Japanese	**yapohn-skih**	*japonsky*

SLOVAK

BODY LANGUAGE

The body language or gesticulation of Slovaks has nothing typical which might distinguish them from other Central Europeans.

SIGNS	
HORÚCA/STUDENÁ (VODA)	HOT/COLD (WATER)
INFORMÁCIE	INFORMATION
NÚDZOVÝ VÝCHOD	EMERGENCY EXIT
OTVÁRACIE HODINY	OPENING HOURS
OTVORENÉ/ZATVORENÉ	OPEN/CLOSED
REZERVOVANÉ	RESERVED
TELEFÓN	TELEPHONE
VCHOD	ENTRANCE
VOL'NÝ (BEZPLATNÝ) VSTUP	FREE ADMISSION
VÝCHOD	EXIT
ZÁCHODY/WC/TOALETY	TOILETS
ZAKÁZANÉ	PROHIBITED
ZÁKAZ FAJČENIA	NO SMOKING
ZÁKAZ VSTUPU/VSTUP ZAKÁZANÝ	NO ENTRY

PAPERWORK

address	adreh-sah	*adresa*
age	vek	*vek*
birth certificate	rodnee list	*rodný list*
car owner's title	doklah-dih oh	*doklady o*
	vlast-nyeetst-veh	*vlastníctve*
	motor o h-vair-hoh	*motorového*
	vozid-lah	*vozidla*
citizenship	shtaat-nah pree-slush-nosty	*štátna príslušnosť*

SLOVAK

date of birth	daatum	*dátum narodenia*
	naroh-dyenyiah	
driver's licence	vodyich-skee	*vodičský*
	preh-oo-kahz	*preukaz*
identification	preh-oo-kahz	*preukaz*
	totozh-nostih	*totožnosti*
marital status	(rohdin-nee) stav	*(rodinný) stav*
name	menoh	*meno*
nationality	naarod-nosty	*národnosť*
passport	tses-tohv-nee pahs	*cestovný pas*
passport number	cheesloh tses-tohv-	*číslo cestovného*
	nairhoh pahsuh	*pasu*
place of birth	myiestoh	*miesto*
	naroh-dyenyiah	*narodenia*
profession	povoh-lanyieh	*povolanie*
religion	vyieroh-vizna-nyieh	*vierovyznanie*
reason for travel	oochel tses-tih	*účel cesty*
business	ob-khod-nee stick	*obchodný styk*
holiday	doh-voh-len-kah/	*dovolenka/*
	praazd-nyi-nih	*prázdniny*
sex	poh-hlavyieh	*pohlavie*
tourist card	toorist itskee	*turistický*
	preh-oo-kahz	*preukaz*
visa	veezum	*vízum*

GETTING AROUND

What time	kedih ot-khaa-dzah/	*Kedy odchádza/*
does the ...	pri-khaa-dzah ...?	*prichádza ...?*
leave/arrive?		
aeroplane	lyieh-tadloh	*lietadlo*
boat	lody	*loď*
city/	mest-skee/	*mestský/*
intercity bus	medzih-mest-skee	*medzimestský*
	owtoh-buhs	*autobus*
train	vlakh	*vlak*
tram	elek-trich-kah	*električka*

SIGNS

AUTOBUSOVÁ ZASTÁVKA	**BUS STOP**
CESTOVNÝ PORIADOK	**TIMETABLE**
COLNICA (COLNÁ KONTROLA)	**CUSTOMS**
ODBAVOVANIE CESTUJÚCICH	**CHECK-IN COUNTER**
ODCHODY	**DEPARTURES**
PODAJ BATOŽÍN	**BAGGAGE COUNTER**
PODZEMNÁ DRÁHA/ METRO	**SUBWAY**
PRÍCHODY	**ARRIVALS**
PREDAJ CESTOVNÝCH LÍSTKOV	**TICKET OFFICE**
STANICA	**STATION**
ŽELEZNIČNÁ STANICA	**TRAIN STATION**

SLOVAK

Directions

Where's ...?
   gdyeh yeh ...?   *Kde je ...?*

How do I get to ...?
   akoh sah dostah-
   nyem doh ...?   *Ako sa dostanem do ...?*

Is it far/closeby?
   yeh toh od-tyialy-toh
   dya-lekoh/bleez-koh?   *Je to odtiaľto ďaleko/blízko?*

Can I walk there?
   daa sah tam easty peshih?   *Dá sa tam ísť peši?*

Can you show me (on the map)?
   muo-zhetyeh mih
   uh-kaazaty (nah mapeh)?   *Môžete mi ukázať (na mape)?*

I want to go to ...
   khtsehm easty doh ...   *Chcem ísť do ...*

Are there other means of getting there?

	akoh sah tam	*Ako sa tam*
	daa eshtyeh dos-taty?	*dá ešte dostať?*

Go straight ahead.

	khody-tyeh rovnoh dya-lay	*Choďte rovno ďalej.*

It's two blocks down.

	soo toh od-tyialy-toh	*Sú to odtiaľto dve ulice.*
	dveh uhlih-tse	

Turn left/right	zaboch-tyeh vlya-voh/	*Zabočte vľavo/*
at the ...	fpra-voh nah ...	*vpravo na ...*
next corner	nasleh- duh-yootsom rohuh	*nasledu júcom rohu*
traffic lights	krizho-vatkeh zoh svetlah-mih	*križovatke so svetlami*

SLOVAK

behind	zah	*za*
far	dyah-leh-koh	*ďaleko*
near	bleez-koh	*blízko*
in front of	pred	*pred*
opposite	oh-protyih	*oproti*

north	seh-ver	*sever*
south	yukh	*juh*
east	vee-khod	*východ*
west	zaa-pahd	*západ*

Booking Tickets

Excuse me, where's the ticket office?

	gdyeh yeh pre-dai	*Kde je predaj*
	tses-tohv-neekh	*cestovných*
	least- kohw proh-seem?	*lístkov, prosím?*

Where can I buy a ticket?

	gdyeh sih muo-zhem koo-pity	*Kde si môžem kúpiť*
	tses-tohv-nee leas-tok?	*cestovný lístok?*

I want to go to ...

	khtsem easty do ...	*Chcem ísť do ...*

Do I need to book?
  potreh-buyem   *Potrebujem*
  myies-tyenkuh?   *miestenku?*

I'd like to book a seat to ...
  myies-tyenkuh do ...   *Miestenku do ...*
  proh-seem   *prosím.*

Can I reserve a place?
  muo-zhem sih rezer-vohvaty *Môžem si rezervovať*
  myiestyen-kuh?   *miestenku?*

How long does the trip take?
  akoh dlhoh tr-vaa tsestah? *Ako dlho trvá cesta?*

Is it a direct route?
  yeh toh pryiah-meh   *Je to priame spojenie?*
  spoyeh-nyieh?

Is it completely full?
  nyieh yeh tuh nich voly-nee? *Nie je tu nič voľné?*

Can I get a stand-by ticket?
  muo-zhem dos-taty   *Môžem dostať*
  stend-baay leas-tok?   *'stand by' lístok?*

SLOVAK

I'd like ...	proh-seem sih ...	*Prosím si ...*
a one-way ticket	yednoh-smernee leas-tok	*jednosmerný lístok*
a return ticket	spyiatoch-nee leas-tok	*spiatočný lístok*
two tickets	dvah least-kih	*dva lístky*
tickets for all of us	least-kih preh naas fshet-keekh	*lístky pre nás všetkých*
a student's fare	shtudent-skee leas-tok	*študentský lístok*
a child's fare	dyet-skee leas-tok	*detský lístok*
pensioner's fare	leas-tok preh duo-khod-tsohw	*lístok pre dôchodcov*
1st class	prvaa tryieh-dah	*prvá trieda*
2nd class	dru-haa tryieh-dah	*druhá trieda*

SLOVAK

Air

Is there a flight to ...?
   yeh let doh ...?   *Je let do ...?*
When's the next flight to ...?
   kedih yeh nai- blizh-shee   *Kedy je najbližší*
   let doh ...?   *let do ...?*
How long does the flight take?
   akoh dlhoh tr-vaa tentoh let?   *Ako dlho trvá tento let?*
What's the flight number?
   akair chees-loh maa tentoh let?   *Aké číslo má tento let?*
You must check in at ...
   pred od-letom sah   *Pred odletom sa musíte*
   muh-seetye dos-tavity   *dostaviť k prezentácii ku ...*
   k prezen-taatsiyi kuh ...

SIGNS

ODBAVOVANIE CESTUJÚCICH;	**CHECK-IN**
PREZENTÁCIA	
REGISTRÁCIA	**REGISTRATION**
VÝDAJ BATOŽÍN	**BAGGAGE**
	COLLECTION

airport tax	letisht-nee poh-platok	*letištný poplatok*
boarding pass	palub-nee leas-tok	*palubný lístok*
customs	tsol-naa kon-trolah	*colná kontrola*

Bus & Tram

Where's the bus/tram stop?
   gdyeh yeh tuh zas-taavkah   *Kde je tu zastávka*
   owtoh-buhsuh/elek-trichkih?   *autobusu/električky?*
Which bus goes to ...?
   ktoh-reem owtoh-buhsom   *Ktorým autobusom*
   sah dos-tanyem doh ...?   *sa dostanem do ...?*

Does this bus go to ...?
  idyeh tentoh owtoh-buhs   *Ide tento autobus do ...?*
  doh ...?
How often do buses pass by?
  akoh chas-toh tuh yaz-dyiah   *Ako často tu jazdia*
  owtoh-buhsih?   *autobusy?*
Could you let me know
when we get to ...?
  muo-zhetyeh mah proh-seem   *Môžete ma prosím*
  upoh-zornyity kedih   *upozorniť keď*
  buh-dyemeh v ...?   *budeme v ...?*
I want to get off!
  khtsem vih-stoopyity!   *Chcem vystúpiť!*

SLOVAK

SIGNS

ZASTÁVKA AUTOBUSOV	**BUS STOP**
ZASTÁVKA ELEKTRIČIEK	**TRAM STOP**

What time's   kedih pree-dyeh ...   *Kedy príde ...*
the ... bus?   owtoh-buhs?   *autobus?*
  first   pr-vee   *prvý*
  last   poh-slednee   *posledný*
  next   nasleh-duhyoo-tsih   *nasledujúci*

Train & Metro
dining car   yedaa-lenskee vozeny   *jedálenský vozeň*
express   eks-pres/reekh-lick   *expres/rýchlik*
local   lokaal-nih vlakh   *lokálny vlak*
sleeping car   spah-tsee vozeny   *spací vozeň*

Which line takes me to ...?
  ktoh-rohw lin-kohw sah   *Ktorou linkou sa*
  dos-tahnyem doh ...?   *dostanem do ...?*

SIGNS

DROBNÉ	CHANGE (for coins)
K VÝCHODU	WAY OUT
NÁSTUPIŠTE ČÍSLO	PLATFORM NUMBER
PODZEMNÁ DRÁHA	UNDERGROUND
TÝMTO SMEROM	THIS WAY TO

SLOVAK

What's the next station?
akoh sah volaa
nah-sleduh-yoo-tsah
stanyi-tsah?

*Ako sa volá nasledujúca
stanica?*

Is this the right platform for ...?
yeh toh spraav-neh
naah-stupish-tyeh doh ...?

*Je to správne
nástupište do ...?*

THEY MAY SAY ...

vlak od-khaatzah z naah-stupish-tyah ...
 The train leaves from platform ...

tsestuh-yootsih
muhsyiah ...
 pres-toopity nah ...
 preysty nah inair
 naah-stupish-tyeh

Passengers
must ...
 change trains at ...
 change platforms

vlak maa meshkah-nyieh
 The train is delayed.

vlak bol zruh-sheh-nee
 The train is cancelled.

meshkah-nyieh budyeh ...
 There's a delay of ... hours.

Taxi

Can you take me to ...?
   muo-zhetyeh mah
   zavyiesty doh ...?
   Môžete ma
   zaviesť do ...?

Please take me to ...
   zavestyeh mah
   proh-seem doh ...
   Zavezte ma
   prosím do ...

How much does it cost to go to ...?
   koly-koh toh budyeh
   staaty doh ...?
   Koľko to bude
   stáť do ...?

Here's fine, thank you.
   potyialy-toh toh stachee
   Potiaľ to to stačí.

The next corner, please.
   azh poh nai-blizh-shee rokh
   proh-seem
   Až po najbližší roh,
   prosím.

SLOVAK

Continue!
   poh-krachuy-tyeh v yaz-dyeh!
   Pokračujte v jazde!

The next street to the left/right.
   nah-sleduyoo-tsa ulitsa
   vlyah-voh/fprah-voh
   Nasledujúca ulica
   vľavo/vpravo.

Stop here, please.
   zah-stavtyeh tuh proh-seem
   Zastavte tu, prosím.

Please slow down.
   spomal-tyeh proh-seem
   Spomaľte, prosím.

Please wait here.
   pochkay-tyeh tuh proh-seem
   Počkajte tu, prosím.

Useful Phrases

How long will it be delayed?
    akoh dlhoh budyeh meshkaty?   *Ako dlho bude meškať?*
Is that seat taken?
    ob-sadyenair?   *Obsadené?*
I want to get off at ...
    khtsem vih-stoopity v ...   *Chcem vystúpiť v ...*
Where can I hire a bicycle?
    gdyeh sah daa poh-zhichaty   *Kde sa dá požičať*
    bih-tsih-kehl?   *bicykel?*

SLOVAK

Car

Where can I hire a car?
    gdyeh sih muo-zhem   *Kde si môžem*
    preh-nayaty owtoh?   *prenajať auto?*
How much is it daily/weekly?
    koly-koh toh stoh-yee nah   *Koľko to stojí na*
    dyeny/nah teezh-dyeny?   *deň/na týždeň?*
Does that include insurance/
mileage?
    yeh v tse-nyeh za-hrnuh-tai   *Je v cene zahrnuté*
    poh-istyeh-nyieh/   *poistenie/*
    kiloh-metraazh?   *kilometráž?*

What make is it?
  akaa yeh toh znach-kah   *Aká je to značka (auta)?*
  (owtah)?
Where's the next petrol station?
  gdyeh yeh nai-blizh-shyieh   *Kde je najbližšie*
  benzee-novair cher-pahd-loh? *benzínové čerpadlo?*
Please fill the tank.
  pl-noo naa-drzh proh-seem   *Plnú nádrž, prosím.*
I want ... litres of petrol (gas).
  potreh-buyem ... lit-rohw   *Potrebujem ... litrov*
  ben-zeenuh   *benzínu.*
Please check the oil and water.
  skon-troluy-tyeh proh-seem   *Skontrolujte prosím*
  hlah-dyinuh aw-leyah ah vodih *hladinu oleja a vody.*
How long can I park here?
  akoh dlhoh tuh muo-zhem   *Ako dlho tu môžem*
  par-kovaty?   *parkovat?*
Does this road lead to ...?
  veh-dyieh taa-toh tses-tah   *Vedie táto cesta do ...?*
  doh ...?

I need a mechanic.
  potreh-buyem pomots   *Potrebujem pomoc*
  owtoh-mekhah-nikah   *automechanika.*
The battery is flat.
  bah-tair-ryiah yeh vih-bihtaa *Batéria je vybitá.*
The radiator is leaking.
  khlah-dyich tyeh-chyieh   *Chladič tečie.*
I have a flat tyre.
  maam preh-pikh-nutoo   *Mám prepichnutú*
  pneu-mah-tikuh   *pneumatiku.*
  maam deh-fekt   *Mám defekt.* (inf)
It's overheating.
  moh-tor sah preh-hryieh-vah *Motor sa prehrieva.*
It's not working.
  neh-fuhn-guhyeh toh   *Nefunguje to.*

SLOVAK

SLOVAK

air (for tyres)	stlah-cheh-nee vz-dukh/ kom-preh-sor	*stlačený vzduch/ kompresor*
battery	bah-tair-ryiah	*batéria*
brakes	brz-dih	*brzdy*
clutch	spoy-kah	*spojka*
driver's licence	voh-dyich-skee preh-oo-kaz	*vodičský preukaz*
engine	moh-tor	*motor*
lights	sveht-laa	*svetlá*
oil	aw-ley	*olej*
petrol (gas)	ben-zeenuh	*benzínu*
puncture	deh-fekt	*defekt*
radiator	khlah-dyich	*chladič*
road map	owtoh-mapah	*automapa*
tyres	pneu-mah-tikih	*pneumatiky*
windscreen	pred-nair skloh	*predné sklo*

SIGNS

AUTOOPRAVY	*REPAIRS*
AUTOOPRAVOVŇA	*GARAGE/ WORKSHOP*
DAJ PREDNOSŤ V JAZDE	*GIVE WAY*
DIAL'NICA	*FREEWAY*
JEDNOSMERNÁ DOPRAVA/ PREMÁVKA	*ONE WAY*
NATURÁL	*UNLEADED*
OBCHÁDZKA	*DETOUR*
SAMOOBSLUHA	*SELF SERVICE*
ZÁKAZ PARKOVANIA	*NO PARKING*
ZÁKAZ VJAZDU	*NO ENTRY*

ACCOMMODATION

Where's a ... hotel?	Gdyeh yeh ... hoh-tel?	Kde je ... hotel?
cheap	lats-nee	lacný
clean	chis-tee	čistý
good	dob-reeh	dobrý
nearby	nah-blees-kuh	nablízku

Could you write the address, please?
muo-zhe-tyeh mih proh-seem
nah-pee-saty too ah-dreh-suh?   *Môžete mi prosím*
napísaš tú adresu?

SLOVAK

At the Hotel

Do you have any rooms available?
maa-tyeh voly-nair izbih?   *Máte voľné izby?*

I'd like ...	poh-trebuhyem ...	Potrebujem ...
a single room	yednoh-luozhkoh-voo izbuh	jednolôžkovú izbu
a double room	izbuh preh dveh ohsoh-bih	izbu pre dve osoby
a room with a bathroom	izbuh s koo-pely-nyohw	izbu s kúpeľňou
to share a dorm	(spoloch-noo) izbuh nah uhbitov-nyih	(spoločnú) izbu na ubytovni
a bed	pos-tyely	posteľ

SLOVAK

SIGNS

PENZIONÁT	GUEST HOUSE
TÁBORISKO	CAMPING GROUND
TURISTICKÁ UBYTOVŇA MLÁDEŽE	YOUTH HOSTEL

I want a room with a ...	muo-zhetyeh mih daty izbuh ...	*Môžete mi daťizbu ...*
bathroom	s koo-pelynyohw	*s kúpeľňou*
shower	zoh spr-khohw	*so sprchou*
television	s teleh-veeznim prih-yeemachom	*s televíznym prijímačom*
window	s oknom	*s oknom*

I'm not sure how long I'm staying.
nyeh-vyiem eshtyeh akoh
dlhoh tuh zoh-stanyem

Neviem ešte ako dlho tu zostanem.

THEY MAY SAY ...

maa-tyeh preh-oo-kaz totozh-nostyih?
  Do you have identification?

vaash chlen-skee preh-oo-kaz proh-seem
  Your membership card, please.

zhyialy smeh plnyieh obsah-dyieh-nee
  Sorry, we're full.

akoh dlhoh tuh zoh-stanyeh-tyeh?
  How long will you be staying?

koly-koh nohtsee?
  How many nights?

stoh-yee toh ... nah dyeny/oh-sobuh
  It's ... per day/per person.

I'm going to stay for ...	zoh-stanyem tuh ...	*Zostanem tu ...*
one day	yeden dyeny	*jeden deň*
two days	dvah dnyih	*dva dni*
one week	yeden teezh-dyeny	*jeden týždeň*

How much is it per night/person?
koly-koh toh stoh-yee nah *Koľko to stojí na*
dyeny/oh-sobuh? *deň/osobu?*

Can I see it, please?
muo-zhem toh proh-seem *Môžem to (prosím) vidieť?*
vi-dyiety?

Are there any others?
maa-tyeh eshtyeh ih-nair *Máte ešte iné na výber?*
nah vee-ber?

Do you have any cheaper rooms?
maa-tyeh ih lats- *Máte aj lacnejšie izby?*
nyey-shyieh izbih?

Can I see the bathroom?
muo-zhem vih-dyiety *Môžem vidieť kúpeľňu?*
koo-pelynyu?

Is there a reduction for
(students/children)?
mah-yoo (shtuden-tyih/ *Majú (študenti/deti) zľavu?*
dyetyih) zlyah-vuh?

Does it include breakfast?
soo rah-nyaikih *Sú raňajky zahrnuté v cene?*
zahrh-nuhtair f tse-nyeh?

It's fine, I'll take it.
doh-breh, beh-ryiem toh *Dobre, beriem to.*

Is there a lift?
yeh tam vee-tyakh? *Je tam výťuh?*

Is there hot water all day?
yeh horoo-tsah vodah *Je horúca voda po celý deň?*
poh tselee dyeny?

Requests & Complaints

Do you have a safe where I can
leave my valuables?

    maa-tyeh treh-zor (saife)   *Máte trezor (safe) na*
    nah uh-lozheh-nyieh   *uloženie cenností?*
    tsen-nos-tyee?

Is there somewhere to wash clothes?

    muo-zhem sih nyiegdyeh   *Môžem si niekde oprať*
    opraty obleh-chenyieh?   *oblečenie?*

Can I use the kitchen?

    muo-zhem poh-uzheevaty   *Môžem používať kuchyňu?*
    kukhih-nyuh?

Can I use the telephone?

    muo-zhem poh-uzheevaty   *Môžem používať telefón?*
    teleh-fawn?

Please wake me up at ...

    zoh-boody-tyeh mah   *Zobuďte ma (prosím) o ...*
    (proh-seem) oh ...

The room needs to be cleaned.

    izbuh trebah vih-chistyity   *Izbu treba vyčistiť.*

Please change the sheets.

    vih-menytyeh (proh-seem)   *Vymeňte (prosím) posteľnú*
    postyely-noo byehlih-zeny   *bielizeň.*

I can't open/close the window.

    nyeh-muo-zhem oh-tvohrity/   *Nemôžem otvoriť/*
    zah-tvohrity oknoh   *zatvoriť okno.*

I've locked myself out of my room.

    vim-kohl/vim-klah   *Vymkol/Vymkla*
    som sah z izbih   *som sa z izby.* (m/f)

The toilet won't flush.

    zaa-khod nyeh-splah-khooyeh   *Záchod nesplachuje.*

I don't like this room.

    taa-toh izbah sah mih   *Táto izba sa mi nepáči.*
    nyeh-paachih

SLOVAK

It's too small.	yeh pree-lish malaa	*Je príliš malá.*
It's noisy.	yeh hlooch-naa	*Je hlučná.*
It's too dark.	yeh pree-lish tmah-vaa	*Je príliš tmavá.*
It's expensive.	yeh drahaa	*Je drahá.*

SLOVAK

Useful Words & Phrases

I'd like to pay the bill.

| khtsel/khtselah bih | *Chcel/Chcela by* |
| som vih-rovnaty ooh-chet | *som vyrovnať účet. (m/f)* |

I'm leaving ...	ot-khaa-dzam ...	*Odchádzam ...*
We're leaving ...	ot-khaa-dzameh ...	*Odchádzame ...*
now/tomorrow	teraz/zai-trah	*teraz/zajtra*

address	adreh-sah	*adresa*
air-conditioned	klimah-tih-zaatsyiah	*klimatizácia*
balcony	bal-koohn	*balkón*
bathroom	koo-pelynyah	*kúpeľňa*
bed	pos-tyely	*posteľ*
bill	ooh-chet	*účet*
blanket	prih-kreev-kah	*prikrývka*
candle	svyiech-kah	*sviečka*
chair	stolich-kah/kres-loh	*stolička/kreslo*
cupboard	ot-kladah-tsee	*odkladací*
	pryieh-stor	*priestor*

double bed	dvoh-yih-taa postyely	*dvojitá posteľ*
electricity	elek-trinah	*elektrina*
excluded	bez ...	*bez ...*
fan	ventih-laator	*ventilátor*
included	vraa-tah-nyeh/	*vrátane/*
	fchee-tah-nyeh	*včítane*
key	klyooch	*kľúč*
lift (elevator)	vee-tyakh	*výťah*
light bulb	zhyiah-rohw-kah	*žiarovka*
lock (n)	zaam-kah	*zámka*
mattress	matrats	*matrac*
mirror	zrkad-loh	*zrkadlo*
name	(krst-nee) menoh	*(krstné) meno*
padlock	vih-satsyiah zaam-kah	*visacia zámka*
pillow	van-koosh	*vankúš*
quiet	tyikhoh	*ticho*
room (in hotel)	iz-bah	*izba*
room number	chees-loh izbih	*číslo izby*
sheet	plakh-tah	*plachta*
shower	spr-khah	*sprcha*
soap	midloh	*mydlo*
suitcase	kufohr	*kufor*
surname	pryieh-zviskoh	*priezvisko*
swimming pool	bazairn	*bazén*
table	stuol	*stôl*
toilet	zaa-khod/toah-letah/	*záchod/toaleta/*
	vair-tsair	*WC*
toilet paper	zaa-khod-ohvee	*záchodový*
	(toah-letnee)	*(toaletný)*
	pah-pyier	*papier*
towel	utyeh-raak	*uterák*
water	vodah	*voda*
cold/hot water	studyeh-naa/	*studená/*
	horoo-tsah vodah	*horúca voda*
window	oknoh	*okno*

SLOVAK

AROUND TOWN

I'm looking for a/the ...	hlyah-daam ...	Hľadám ...
art gallery	galair-ryiuh	galériu
bank	bankuh	banku
church	kostol	kostol
city (centre)	stred (tsen-truhm)	stred (centrum)
	mestah	mesta
... embassy	shtaat-neh	štátne
	zastuh- pityehly-stvoh ...	zastupiteľstvo ...
market	trkh	trh
museum	moo-zeum	múzeum
police	polee-tsyiuh	políciu
post office	posh-tuh	poštu
public toilet	vereih-nair	verejné
	zaa-khodih	záchody
telephone	teleh-fawn-nuh	telefónnu
centre	tsentraa-luh	centrálu
tourist	infor-mahchnair	informačné
information	stredyis-koh preh	stredisko pre
office	turis-tohw	turistov

SLOVAK

What time does it open/close?
od/doh koly-kei yeh   *Od/Do koľkej je*
otvoh-renair?   *otvorené?*

What ... is this?	akoh sah voh-laa ...?	Ako sa volá ...?
street	taa-toh uhli-tsa	táto ulica
suburb	taa-toh shtvr-ty	táto štvrť

For directions, see the Getting Around section, page 289.

SLOVAK

At the Post Office

I'd like to send a/an ...	khtsel/khtseh-lah bih som pos-laty ...	*Chcel/Chcela by som poslať...* (m/f)
aerogram	airoh-grahm	*aerogram*
letter	list	*list*
parcel	bah-leak	*balík*
postcard	pohlyad-nitsu	*pohľadnicu*
telegram	teleh-grahm	*telegram*

I'd like some stamps. khtsel/khtseh-lah bih som koo-pit znaam-kih.	*Chcel/Chcela by som kúpiť známky. (m/f)*
How much is the postage? koly-koh yeh posh-tohv-nair?	*Koľko je poštovné?*

airmail	letyets-kaa posh-tah	*letecká pošta*
envelope	obaal-kah	*obálka*
mailbox	poshtoh-vaa skhraan-kah	*poštová schránka*
registered mail	dopoh-ruche-nyeh	*doporučene*
surface mail	obichai-nohw posh-tohw	*obyčajnou poštou*

Telephone

I want to ring ... khtsem teleh-fohnoh-vaty ...	*Chcem telefonovať...*
The number is ... chees-loh yeh	*Číslo je ...*
I want to make a reverse-charges call. khtsem teleh-fohnoh-vaty nah ooh-chet volah-nair-hoh chees-lah	*Chcem telefonovať na účet volaného čísla.*
It's engaged. yeh op-sadyeh-nair	*Je obsadené.*
I want to speak for three minutes. buh-dyem hoh-vohrity trih minoo-tih	*Budem hovoriť tri minúty.*

How much does a three-minute call cost?

    koly-koh stoh-yee troi-minoo-tohvee hoh-vor?

Koľko stojí trojminútový hovor?

How much does each extra minute cost?

    koly-koh stoh-yee kazh-daa minoo-tah nah-vishe?

Koľko stojí každá minúta navyše?

I'd like to speak to (Mr Perez).

    muo-zhem hoh-vohrity s (paa-nom pe-re-zom)?

Môžem hovoriť s (pánom Perezom)?

I've been cut off.

    muoy hoh-vor bol preh-rushe-nee

Môj hovor bol prerušený.

SLOVAK

Internet

Where can I get Internet access?

    gdyeh yeh tuh inter-net gdis-poh-zee-tsyih?

Kde je tu internet k dispozícii?

How much is it per hour?

    koly-koh toh stoh-yee nah hoh-dyi-nuh?

Koľko to stojí na hodinu?

I want to check my email.

    khtsem sih skon-troh-loh-vaty e-mail?

Chcem si skontrolovať e-mail.

At the Bank

I want to exchange some (money/travellers cheques).

khtsem vih-meh-nyihty (peh-nyiah-zeh/tses-tohv-nair shekih)

Chcem vymeniť (peniaze/cestovné šeky).

What's the exchange rate?

akee yeh vee-men-nee kurz?

Aký je výmenný kurz?

How many crowns per US dollar?

koly-koh koh-roohn dostah-nyem zah yeden doh-laar?

Koľko korún dostanem za jeden dolár?

Can I have money transferred here from my bank?

muo-zhem sem trahns-feroh-vaty peh-nyiah-zeh z mohyay bankih?

Môžem sem transferovať peniaze z mojej banky?

How long will it take to arrive?

kedih toh muo-zhem ocha-kaavaty?

Kedy to môžem očakávať?

Has my money arrived yet?

ob-drzha-lih/dos-tah-lih styeh uzh moyeh peh-nyiah-zeh?

Obdržali/dostali ste už moje peniaze?

bankdraft	bankoh-vaa zmen-kah	*banková zmenka*
banknotes	bankov-kih	*bankovky*
cashier	poklad-nyeek	*pokladník* (m)
	poklad-nyeech-kah	*pokladníčka* (f)
coins	min-tseh	*mince*
credit card	ooveh-rohvaa (kredit-naa) kartah	*úverová (kreditná) karta*
exchange	zmeh-naa-reny	*zmenáreň*
loose change	drob-nair/min-tse	*drobné/mince*
signature	(vlastnoh-ruchnee) pod-pis	*(vlastnoručný) podpis*

INTERESTS & ENTERTAINMENT
Sightseeing

Do you have a guidebook/local map?

maa-tyeh tses-tohv-noo pree-ruchkuh/myiest-nuh mapuh?	*Máte cestovnú príručku/ miestnu mapu?*

What are the main attractions?

akair soo tuh turist-itskair za-ooyee-mah-vostih?	*Aké sú tu turistické zaujímavosti?*

What's that?

cho yeh toh?	*Čo je to?*

How old is it?

akoh yeh toh stah-rair?	*Ako je to staré?*

Can I take photographs?

muo-zhem fotoh-gra- foh-vaty?	*Môžem fotografovať?*

What time does it open/close?

oh koly-kay otvaa-rahyoo/ zah-tvaa-rahyoo?	*O koľkej otvárajú/zatvárajú?*

ancient	staroh-bilee/	*starobylý*
archaeological	arkheoloh-ghi-tskee	*archeologický*
castle	hrad/zaa-mok	*hrad/zámok*
cathedral	kateh-draalah	*katedrála*
church	kostol	*kostol*
concert hall	kon-tsert-naa syieny	*koncertná sieň*
library	knyizh-nyitsa	*knižnica*
main square	hlav-nair-naa-mestyieh	*hlavné námestie*
market	trkh	*trh*
monastery	klaash-tor	*kláštor*
monument	pah-mat-nyeek	*pamätník*
old city	stah-raa chasty mestah	*stará časť mesta*
palace	palaats	*palác*
opera house	operah	*opera*
ruins	zroo-tsa-nyihnih	*zrúcaniny*
statues	sokhih	*sochy*
temple	khraam	*chrám*
university	uhnih-ver-zitah	*univerzita*

SLOVAK

Going Out

What's there to do in the evenings?

kam sah daa easty vecher?	*Kam sa dá ísť večer?*

Are there any nightclubs around here?

soo tuh diskoh-taihkih?	*Sú tu diskotéky?*

Are there places where you can hear local folk music?

daa sah tuh nyieh-gdyeh easty pochoo-vaty lyudoh-voo hoodbuh?	*Dá sa tu niekde ísť počúvať ľudovú hudbu?*

How much does it cost to get in?

koly-koh yeh vstup-nair?	*Koľko je vstupné?*

cinema	kinah	*kina*
concert	kon-tsert	*koncert*
nightclub	diskoh-taihkuh	*diskotéku*
theatre	dyivah-dlah	*divadla*

Sports & Interests

What sports do you play?

a-keehm shpor-tohm sah veh-nuh-yeh-tyeh?	*Akým športom sa venujete?*

What are your interests?

a-keeh maa-tyieh zaau-yee-mih?	*Aké máte záujmy?*

art	uh-meh-nyieh	*umenie*
basketball	basket-bahl	*basketbal*
chess	shah-khih	*šachy*
collecting things	zbeh-rah-telyi-stvoh	*zberateľstvo*
dancing	tah-nyets	*tanec*
food	yed-loh	*jedlo*
football	foot-bahl	*futbal*
hiking	peshyiuh	*pešiu*
	tuh-ris-tih-kuh	*turistiku*

martial arts	boh-yo-veh uh-meh-nyiah	*bojové umenia*
meeting friends	streh-taah-vahtyi sah s pryia-tyiel-mih	*stretávať sa s priateľmi*
movies	fil-mih	*filmy*
music	hood-booh	*hudbu*
nightclubs	notch-neh kloo-bih	*nočné kluby*
photography	phoh-toh-graphoh-vah-nyieh	*fotografovanie*
reading	chee-tah-nyieh	*čítanie*
shopping	nah-kooh-poh-vah-nyieh	*nakupovanie*

SLOVAK

skiing	lee-zhoh-vah-nyieh	*lyžovanie*
swimming	plaah-vah-nyieh	*plávanie*
tennis	tennis	*tenis*
travelling	tses-toh-vah-nyieh	*cestovanie*
TV/videos	teh-leh-vee-zyiuh/ vih-deh-aah	*televíziu/videá*
visiting friends	nah-vshteh-voh-vatyih	*navštevovať*
walking	pryia-tyie-low preh-khaah-tz-kih	*priateľov prechádzky*

Festivals
State Holidays

Cyril a Metod, vierozvestovia
  (July 5) Sts Cyril and Methodius (Apostles) Day

Deň ústavy SR
  (September 1) Constitution Day (1992)

Nový rok a Vznik SR
  (January 1) New Year and Establishment of the Slovak
  Republic (1993)

Výročie Slovenského národného povstania
  (August 29) Slovak National Uprising Anniversary (1944)

Religious Holidays

Druhý sviatok vianočný
  (December 26) Boxing Day

Prvý sviatok vianočný
  (December 25) Christmas Day

Sedembolestná Panna Mária, patrónka Slovenska
  (September 15) Our Lady of Sorrows Day

Štedrý deň
  (December 24) Christmas Eve

Sviatok práce
  (May 1) Labour Day

Traja králi; Zjavenie Pána
  (January 6) Epiphany; Orthodox Christmas Day

Veľkonočný pondelok
  Easter Monday

Veľký piatok
  Easter Friday

Všetkých svätých
  (November 1) All Saints Day

IN THE COUNTRY
Weather
What's the weather like?

akair yeh pocha-syieh?		*Aké je počasie?*

The weather's ... today.	dnyes yeh ...	*Dnes je ...*
Will it be ... tomorrow?	budyeh zai-trah ...?	*Bude zajtra ...?*
cloudy	zamrah-chenair	*zamračené*
cold	zimah	*zima*
foggy	hmlis-toh	*hmlisto*
frosty	mraaz	*mráz*
hot	horoo-tsoh	*horúco*
raining	pr-shaty	*pršať*
snowing	snyeh-zhity	*snežiť*
sunny	sl-nyech-noh	*slnečno*
windy	vetyer-noh	*veterno*

SLOVAK

Camping
Am I allowed to camp here?

muo-zhem tuh stanoh-vaty? *Môžem tu stanovať?*

Is there a campsite nearby?

yeh tuh nableez-kuh taaboh-riskoh? *Je tu nablízku táborisko?*

backpack	plets-nyiak	*plecniak*
can opener	otvaa-rach nah konzer-vih	*otvárač na konzervy*
compass	kom-pahs	*kompas*
crampons	skobih	*skoby*
firewood	palivoh-vair dreh-voh	*palivové drevo*
gas cartridge	naa-plny doh plinoh-vairhoh vahrih-cha	*náplň do plynového variča*
hammock	(visuh-tair) luozh-koh	*(visuté) lôžko* (lit: hanging bed)

ice axe	horoh-lezets-kee	*horolezecký*
	cha-kan	*čakan*
mattress	mah-trahts	*matrac*
penknife	vretskoh-vee nuozh	*vreckový nôž*
rope	poh-vraz/lanoh	*povraz/lano*
tent	stahn	*stan*
tent pegs	stahno-vair kolee-kih	*stanové kolíky*
torch (flashlight)	bater-kah	*baterka*
sleeping bag	spah-tsee vahk	*spací vak*
stove	varich	*varič*
water bottle	flah-sha nah voduh	*fľaša na vodu*

SLOVAK

INCOGNITO

Many Slovak dishes have names that don't offer a clue as to what's in them. One that all Slovaks know is *Španielsky vtáčik* (lit: Spanish Birds), but it is actually beef rolled up with bacon and gherkins, served with rice and sauce.

Another is *Moravský*, 'Moravian Sparrow', which is a fist-sized piece of roasted pork. Other common dishes are *Katův šleh*, 'The Executioner's Lash', which is thinly sliced pieces of pork, capsicum and tomato in a sauce, or *Tajemstvo*, 'A Secret', which is ham wrapped around a slice of cheese in breadcrumbs.

But even the Slovaks will need to ask about the following: *Meč krále Jiřího*, 'King George's Sword', *Tajemství Petra Voka*, Peter Voka's Mystery', *Bašta nadlesního Karáska*, 'Ranger' Karasek's Meal, and *Kotlík rytíre*, 'The Kettle of Rimbaba the Knight'.

FOOD

Food in Slovakia reflects the myriad of influences which has shaped this part of Europe. During your stay you'll find dishes you may have appreciated elsewhere, such as Austrian strudel, Czech dumplings, German sauerkraut, French crepes and Hungarian goulash, but you'll always find them prepared with a special Slovak touch.

You may have already tasted a Slovak speciality without knowing it: *Liptovská bryndza* (*Liptauer* cheese, named after the Liptov region in Central Slovakia). *Medovníky* (honey cakes with ginger) are also eaten throughout the world.

Less well-known but equally delicious are dishes such as *kapustnica* (sauerkraut soup), *lokše* (potato pancakes), *haruľa* (spicy potato puffs), *živánska* (marinated pork roasted with layers of onion, garlic, bacon and vegetables) and many varieties of local freshwater fish such as *sumec*, *zubáč*, *štuka* and *hlavátka*.

Modern Slovak cooks haven't forgotten traditional recipes – they're well worth discovering!

Bon appetit!	doh-broo khuty!	*Dobrú chuť!*
Cheers!	nah zdrah-vyieh!	*Na zdravie!*
breakfast	ranyai-kih	*raňajky*
lunch	obed	*obed*
dinner	vecheh-rah	*večera*

Table for ..., please.
   stuol preh ... proh-seem   *Stôl pre ... prosím.*
Can I see the menu, please?
   muo-zhem dos-taty   *Môžem dostať jedálny*
   yedaal-nih leas-tok?   *lístok?*
I'd like the set lunch, please.
   ponuh-kuh dnyah proh-seem   *Ponuku dňa, prosím.*
Is service included in the bill?
   yeh obslu-hah zahr-nuhtaa   *Je obsluha zahrnutá*
   ftse-nyeh?   *v cene?*
Not too spicy, please.
   meh-nyay koreh-nyiah proh-seem   *Menej korenia, prosím.*

SLOVAK

MENU DECODER

Starters & Snacks

hlávkový šalát s oštiepkom
hlaah-vko-veeh sha-laat z osh-tyiep-kom
green salad with sheep cheese

husacia pečeň
huh-sah-tsyiah peh-tcheny
goose liver

kurací šalát s majonézou
kuh-rah-tseeh sha-laat z mayio-neh-zohw
chicken salad with mayonnaise

obložený chlebíček
ob-loh-zhe-neeh khle-bee-check
open sandwich

praženica
prah-zheh-nitsa
scrambled eggs

salámový tanier s oblohou
sah-laah-moh-vee tanyier z oblo-hohw
salami platter with fresh/pickled vegetables

šalátová misa
sha-laa-toh-vaah mih-sah
salad niçoise

s údeným lososom
z ooh-dyie-neem loh-soh-sohm
smoked salmon

syrový tanier
sih-roh-vih tah-nyier
cheese platter

Main Meals

a s mandľovou plnkou
ah s mand-lyioh-vow pln-kohw
turkey breast stuffed with mushrooms and almonds

cigánska pečienka
tsih-ghan-skah peh-chyien-kah
gypsy style grilled beef; a very common dish on Slovak menus,
which denotes quick preparation similar to barbecuing

kapor na víne
kah-por nah vee-nyieh
carp braised in wine

kurací paprikáš
kuh-rah-tseeh pah-prih-kaash
chicken braised in red (paprika) sauce

morčacie prsíčka na hríboch
mor-chah-tsyieh pr-seech-kah nah hree-bokh

roštenka so šunkou vajcoma
roh-shtyien-kah zoh shun-kohw ah vay-tzoh-ma
roast beef with ham and eggs

vyprážané rybacie filé
vih-praa-zha-neh rih-bah-tsyieh fih-leh
fillet of fish fried in breadcrumbs

zajac na smotane
zah-yats nah smoh-tah-nyieh
rabbit/hare in a cream sauce

SLOVAK

Vegetarian Dishes

karfiolový nákyp
kar-phyio-loh-veeh naah-kip
cauliflower souffle

vyprážaný syr s tatarskou omáčkou
vih-praah-zhah-neeh sihr tah-tar-skohw oh-maatch-kohws
fried cheese with tartare sauce

zeleninové rizoto
zeh-leh-nyi-noh-veh rizo-toh
risotto with vegetables

špagety/makaróny
shpah-gheh-tih/mah-kah-roh-nih

na taliansky spôsob
nah ta-lyian-skih spwoh-sohb
spaghetti or macaroni with tomato sauce and cheese

Vegetarian Meals

Apart from salads, it may be difficult to find food entirely without meat or meat product.

I'm a vegetarian.
    (yah) som veghe-tahryiaan   *(Ja) som vegetarián.*
I don't eat meat.
    nyeh-yem masoh   *Nejem mäso.*
I don't eat chicken, fish or ham.
    nyeh-yem kurah-tsyieh   *Nejem kuracie*
    masoh ribih ahnyih shun-kuh   *mäso, ryby ani šunku.*

Vegetarian dishes are detailed on page 317.

Soups

chicken soup	kuh-rah-tsyiah poh-lyiev-kah	*kuracia polievka*
fish soup	rih-bah-tsyiah poh-lyiev-kah	*rybacia polievka*
pheasant soup	poh-lyiev-kah z bah-zhan-tah	*polievka z bažanta*
vegetable soup	zeh-leh-nyi-noh-veh poh-lyiev-kih	*zeleninové polievky*

with ...	s ...	s ...
dumplings	kned-leetch-kah-mih	*knedlíčkami*
gnocchi	hah-loosh-kah-mih	*haluškami*
rice	rih-zhow	*ryžou*

Side Dishes

bread and pastry	khlyieb ah peh-chih-voh	*chlieb a pečivo*
potato chips	zeh-myiah-koh-veh hrah-nol-kih	*zemiakové hranolky*
roast potatoes	oh-peh-kah-neh zeh-myiah-kih	*opekané zemiaky*

Desserts

apple strudel	yah-bl-koh-veeh zaah-vin	*jablkový závin*
bread pudding	zhem-lyiov-kah	*žemľovka*
cherry souffle	cheh-resh-nyio-vah booh-blah-nyi-nah	*čerešňová bublanina*
chestnut cream	gahsh-tah-noh-veh pih-reh	*gaštanové pyré*
chocolate gateau	choh-koh-laah-doh-vaah tor-tah	*čokoládová torta*
doughnuts	shish-kih	*šišky*
fruit cake	oh-vots-neeh (bis-kup-skeeh) khle-bee-check	*ovocný (biskupský) chlebíček*
rice souffle	rih-zhoh-veeh naah-kip	*ryžový nákyp*
chocolate roulade	choh-koh-laah-doh-vaah roh-laah-dah	*čokoládová roláda*
shortbread	maass-loh-veh (drob-neh cha-yoh-veh) peh-chi-voh	*maslové (drobné čajové) pečivo*

Useful Words

ashtray	popol-nyeek	*popolník*
bill	ooh-chet	*účet*
cup	shaal-kah	*šálka*
dessert	mooch-nyik/ zaa-kuh-sok	*múčnik/ zákusok*
drink	naa-poy	*nápoj*
fork	vidlich-kah	*vidlička*
fresh	cherst-vair	*čerstvé*
glass	poh-haar	*pohár*
knife	nuozh	*nôž*
plate	tah-nyier	*tanier*

SLOVAK

spicy	shtyip-lyah-vaih/	*štipľavé/*
	koreh-nyistair	*korenisté*
spoon	lizhi-tsah	*lyžica*
stale	nyieh tselkom	*nie celkom*
	cherst-vair	*čerstvé*
sweet	slad-kair	*sladké*
teaspoon	lih-zhich-kah	*yžička*
toothpick	shpahraa-tkoh	*šparátko*

Staples

bread	khlyieb	*chlieb*
butter	mahs-loh	*maslo*
cereal	oh-bil-nyi-noh-vair	*obilninové kaše*
	kah-sheh	
cheese	sihr	*syr*
chocolate	choh-koh-laah-duh	*čokoládu*
eggs	vai-tsyiah	*vajcia*
flour	mooh-kuh	*múku*
margarine	mar-gah-reen	*margarín*
marmalade	mar-meh-laah-duh	*marmeládu*
milk	mlyieh-koh	*mlieko*
(olive) oil	(olih-voh-veeh) oh-lei	*(olivový) olej*
pasta	ches-toh-vee-nee	*cestoviny*
pepper	tchyier-neh	*čierne korenie*
	koh-reh-nyieh	
rice	rih-zhah	*ryža*
salt	sol	*soľ*
sugar	tzuh-kor	*cukor*
yogurt	yoh-guhrt	*jogurt*

Meat & Seafood

ham	shoon-kuh	*so šunku*
hamburger	ham-bur-gehr/	*hamburger/*
	fah-sheer-kah	*fašírka*
lamb	yah-nyah-tsye meh-soh	*jahňacie mäso*
lobster	braf-choh-vair meh-soh	*morský rak*

mussels	moosh-leh	*mušle*
oysters	ooh-strih-tseh	*ustrice*
pork	braf-choh-vair meh-soh	*bravčové mäso*
sausage	kloh-baa-sah	*klobása*
shrimp	kreh-veh-tah	*kreveta*
turkey	moh-ryak	*moriak*
veal	tye-lya-tsye meh-soh	*teľacie mäso*

Vegetables

asparagus	shpahr-gloh-vaah	*špargľová*
bean	fah-zoo-loh-vaah	*fazuľová*
beetroot	tsvick-lah	*cvikla*
... capsicum	... pap-rih-kah	*... paprika*
green	zeh-leh-naa	*zelená*
red	cher-veh-naa	*červená*
cabbage	kah-poos-tah	*kapusta*
carrot	mrh-kvah	*mrkva*
cauliflower	kahr-fih-ohl	*karfiol*
celery	zeh-lehr	*zeler*
chillies	feh-feh-rawn-kih	*feferónky*
cucumber	ooh-hor-kah	*uhorka*
eggplant	bah-klah-zhaan	*baklažán*
garlic	tses-nuck	*cesnak*
leek	poh-roh-vaah	*pórová*
lettuce	hlaav-koh-vee shah-laat	*hlávkový šalát*
mushrooms	hree-bih	*hríby*
onion	tsih-buh-lyah	*cibuľa*
pea	hraash	*hráš*
potato	zeh-myi-ak	*zemiak*
spinach	shpeh-naaht	*špenát*
tomato	pah-rah-day-kah	*paradajka*
vegetables	zeh-leh-nyi-nah	*zelenina*
zucchini	tyek-vitch-kih	*tekvičky*

SLOVAK

SLOVAK

Pulses

broad beans	fah-zoo-leh	*fazule*
chick peas	tsih-zr-nah	*cizrna*
kidney beans	vlash-skair	*vlašské fazule*
	fah-zoo-leh	
lentils	sho-sho-vih-tsah	*šošovica*

Salads

beetroot	tzwick-loh-veeh	*cviklový*
cabbage	kah-puss-toh-veeh	*kapustový*
celeriac and carrot	zeh-leh-roh-veeh s mrk-vohw	*zelerový s mrkvou*
cucumber	ooh-hor-koh-veeh	*uhorkový*
lettuce	hlaav-koh-veeh	*hlávkový*
mixed	z myie-shah-nyiey zeh-leh-nyi-nih	*miešanej zeleniny*
potato	zeh-myiah-koh-veeh	*zemiakový*
sauerkraut	zoh suh-doh-vey (kiss-lei) kah-puss-tih	*zo sudovej (kyslej) kapusty*
tomato	ray-tchyia-koh-veeh/ pah-rah-dai-koh-veeh	*rajčiakový/ paradajkový*

Fruit

apple	yah-bl-koh	*jablko*
apricot	mar-hoo-lyah	*marhuľa*
banana	bah-naan	*banán*
figs	fih-gah	*figa*
grapes	hroz-noh	*hrozno*
kiwifruit	kih-vih	*kivi*
lemon	tsit-rawn	*citrón*
orange	poh-mah-rahnch	*pomaranč*
peach	bros-kih-nyah	*broskyňa*
pear	hroosh-kah	*hruška*
plum	slif-kah	*slivka*
strawberry	ya-hoh-dah	*jahoda*

Non-Alcoholic Drinks

carbonated water	saw-dah	*sóda*
... coffee	... kaah-vah	... *káva*
Turkish	two-rets-kaah	*turecká*
Vienna	vyieh-dyien-skaah	*viedenská*
espresso	es-preh-soh	*espresso*
fruit juice	oh-vots-naah	*ovocná*
	shtyah-vah	*štava*
hot chocolate	vah-reh-naah	*varená čokoláda*
	choh-koh-laa-dah	
tea	chai	*čaj*
... water	... voh-dah	... *voda*
boiled	preh-vah-reh-naa	*prevarená*
mineral	mi-neh-raal-nah	*minerálna*

SLOVAK

Alcoholic Drinks

Slovak wine is good and cheap and there are some excellent sparkling wines. Popular brands include *Tokay* from South Slovakia, and *Kláštorné* (a red) and *Venušíno čáro* (a white), both from the Carpathians north of Bratislava.

Special things to try are *demänovka*, a bittersweet Slovak liqueur slightly sweetened with honey, and *slivovice*, 'plum brandy'. *Grog* – rum with hot water and sugar – is a great pick-me-up.

... beer	pih-voh ...	*pivo ...*
bottled	flush-koh-veh	*flaškové*
draught	cha-poh-vah-neh	*čapované*
... wine	vee-noh ...	*víno ...*
white	byieh-leh	*biele*
red	tcher-veh-neh	*červené*
young (green) wine	bur-chyiak	*burčiak*
liqueurs	lih-keh-rih	*likéry*
spirits	deh-stihl-laa-tih	*destiláty*

SLOVAK

AT THE MARKET

Basics

bread	khlyieb	*chlieb*
butter	mahs-loh	*maslo*
cereal	oh-bil-nyi-noh-vair kah-sheh	*obilninové kaše*
cheese	sihr	*syr*
chocolate	choh-koh-laa-duh	*čokoládu*
eggs	vai-tsyiah	*vajcia*
flour	mooh-kuh	*múku*
margarine	mar-gah-reen	*margarín*
marmalade	mar-meh-laah-duh	*marmeládu*
milk	mlyieh-koh	*mlieko*
(olive) oil	(olih-voh-veeh) oh-lei	*(olivový) olej*
pasta	ches-toh-vee-nee	*cestoviny*
pepper	tchyier-neh koh-reh-nyieh	*čierne korenie*
rice	rih-zhah	*ryža*
salt	sol	*sol'*
sugar	tzuh-kor	*cukor*
yogurt	yoh-guhrt	*jogurt*

Meat & Poultry

ham	shoon-kuh	*so šunku*
hamburger	ham-bur-gehr	*hamburger*
lamb	yah-nyah-tsye meh-soh	*jahňacie mäso*
pork	braf-choh-vair meh-soh	*bravčové mäso*
sausage	kloh-baa-sah	*klobása*
turkey	moh-ryak	*moriak*
veal	tye-lya-tsye meh-soh	*teľacie mäso*

Seafood

lobster	braf-choh-vair meh-soh	*morský rak*
mussels	moosh-leh	*mušle*
oysters	ooh-strih-tseh	*ustrice*
shrimp	kreh-veh-tah	*kreveta*

Vegetables

bean	fah-zoo-loh-vaah	*fazuľová*
beetroot	tsvick-lah	*cvikla*
... capsicum	... pap-rih-kah	*... paprika*
green	zeh-leh-naa	*zelená*
red	cher-veh-naa	*červená*

AT THE MARKET

cabbage	kah-poos-tah	*kapusta*
carrot	mrh-kvah	*mrkva*
cauliflower	kahr-fih-ohl	*karfiol*
celery	zeh-lehr	*zeler*
chillies	feh-feh-rawn-kih	*feferónky*
cucumber	ooh-hor-kah	*uhorka*
eggplant	bah-klah-zhaan	*baklažán*
garlic	tses-nuck	*cesnak*
leek	poh-roh-vaah	*pórová*
lettuce	hlaav-koh-vee shah-laat	*hlávkový šalát*
mushrooms	hree-bih	*hríby*
onion	tsih-buh-lyah	*cibuľa*
pea	hraash	*hráš*
potato	zeh-myi-ak	*zemiak*
spinach	shpeh-naaht	*špenát*
tomato	pah-rah-day-kah	*paradajka*
vegetables	zeh-leh-nyi-nah	*zelenina*
zucchini	tyek-vitch-kih	*tekvičky*

SLOVAK

Pulses

broad beans	fah-zoo-leh	*fazule*
chick peas	tsih-zr-nah	*cizrna*
kidney beans	vlash-skair fah-zoo-leh	*vlašské fazule*
lentils	sho-sho-vih-tsah	*šošovica*

Fruit

apple	yah-bl-koh	*jablko*
apricot	mar-hoo-lyah	*marhuľa*
banana	bah-naan	*banán*
figs	fih-gah	*figa*
grapes	hroz-noh	*hrozno*
kiwifruit	kih-vih	*kivi*
lemon	tsit-rawn	*citrón*
orange	poh-mah-rahnch	*pomaranč*
peach	bros-kih-nyah	*broskyňa*
pear	hroosh-kah	*hruška*
plum	slif-kah	*slivka*
strawberry	ya-hoh-dah	*jahoda*

SHOPPING

How much is it?
    koly-koh toh stoh-yee?   *Kolko to stojí?*

bookshop	predai	*predaj kníh*
camera shop	fotoh (potreh-bih)	*foto (potreby)*
chemist (pharmacy)	lekaa-reny	*lekáreň*
clothing store	odyeh-vih	*odevy*
delicatessen	lahuod-kih	*lahôdky*
general store	ob-khod zoh zmyiesha-neem tovah-rom	*obchod so zmiešaným tovarom*
greengrocer	zele-nyinah ah ovoh-tsyieh	*zelenina a ovocie*
laundry	praa-chov-nya	*práčovňa*
market	trkh	*trh*
newsagency	novih-nih ah chahso-pisih	*noviny a časopisy*
stationer's	pahpyier-nitstvoh	*papiernictvo*
shoeshop	obuv	*obuv*
souvenir shop	darche-kih/suveh-neerih	*darčeky/suveníry*
supermarket	samoh-obslu-hah	*samoobsluha*

SLOVAK

THEY MAY SAY ...

cho sih zhelaa-tyeh?
    Can I help you?
toh yeh fshet-koh?
    Will that be all?
zhelaa-tyeh sih toh zabah-lity?
    Would you like it wrapped?
zhyialy ih-nair nyeh-maameh
    Sorry, this is the only one.
koly-koh (kuh-sohw) sih zhelaa-tyeh?
    How much/many do you want?

I'd like to buy ...
    khtsel/khtseh-lah   *Chcel/Chcela*
    bih som koo-pity ...   *by som kúpiť ...* (m/f)
I'd like ... grams/kilos.
    proh-seem sih ...   *Prosím si ... gramov/kíl.*
    grah-mow/keel
Do you have others?
    maa-tyeh ih-nair nah vee-ber?   *Máte iné na výber?*
I don't like it.
    toh sah mih nyeh-pozdaa-vah   *To sa mi nepozdáva.*
Can I look at it?
    muo-zhem toh vih-dyiety?   *Môžem to vidieť?*
I'm just looking.
    len sah tahk pozeh-raam   *Len sa tak pozerám.*
Can you write down the price?
    muo-zhetyeh mih   *Môžete mi napísať*
    napee-saty tsenuh?   *cenu?*
That's too much. (cost)
    toh yeh pree-lish veh-lyah.   *To je príliš veľa.*
Do you accept credit cards?
    muo-zhem plah-tyity   *Môžem platiť úverovou*
    ooveh-rovohw kar- tohw?   *kartou?*

SLOVAK

Souvenirs

Popular souvenirs in Slovakia are wood carvings, lace and
embroidery, glass and leather goods.

earrings	naa-ush-nyitse	*náušnice*
handicrafts	umelets-koh-pryieh-mihsel-nair veerob-kih	*umelecko-priemyselné výrobky*
necklace	naahr-dyelnyeek	*náhrdelník*
pottery	kerah-mikah	*keramika*
ring	prs-tyeny	*prsteň*
rug	prih-kreev-kah/ pokroh-vets	*prikrývka/ pokrovec*

SLOVAK

FOLK ARTS

Folk arts are preserved in many forms – stories and songs, music and dance, skills and handicrafts, food and drink, speech, clothing and architecture. Museums and festivals also keep the traditions alive.

Some of Slovakia's most interesting pockets of traditional culture are in the north-eastern regions – Spiš, Bardejov, Svidník and Humenné. Throughout these places, you'll find:

- traditional clothing such as embroidered skirts, shawls, jackets and fur coats. The most striking feature is usually elaborate embroidery in bright colours and abstract or pictorial designs, which may vary according to the season and the age and marital status of the wearer.

- everyday tools, utensils, musical instruments, linen, furniture and entire buildings decorated with elaborate folk designs

- buildings adorned with carved or moulded plaster, or intricately painted

- polka-like music played with fiddle, brass, clarinet and sometimes dulcimer, trumpet, fujara (a long wooden tube) or accordian

Essential Groceries

I'd like ...	muo-zhem doh-staht ...	*Môžem dostať...*
bread	khlyieb	*chlieb*
butter	mahs-loh	*maslo*
cheese	sihr	*syr*
chocolate	choh-koh-laah-duh	*čokoládu*
eggs	vai-tsyiah	*vajcia*
honey	med	*med*
margarine	mar-gah-reen	*margarín*
marmalade	mar-meh-laah-duh	*marmeládu*
matches	zaah-pal-kih	*zápalky*
milk	mlyieh-koh	*mlieko*
shampoo	shahm-pawn	*šampón*
soap	mid-loh	*mydlo*
toilet paper	zaa-khoh-doh-veeh/	*záchodový/*
	toah-let-neeh pah-pyier	*toaletný papier*
toothpaste	zuhb-nooh pas-tuh	*zubnú pastu*
washing powder	praah-shock nah	*prášok na*
	prah-nyieh	*pranie*

SLOVAK

Toiletries

comb	hreh-beny	*hrebeň*
condoms	prezer-vahtee-vih/	*prezervatívy/*
	kon-doh-mih	*kondómy*
deodorant	dezoh-dorant/	*dezodorant/*
	deoh-dorant	*deodorant*
hairbrush	kefah nah vlasih	*kefa na vlasy*
moisturiser	hidrah-touch-nee	*hydratačný*
	krairm	*krém*
shaving cream	krairm nah	*krém na*
	holeh-nyieh	*holenie*
sunscreen	krairm zoh sl-netch-	*krém so slnečným*
	neehm fil-trom	*filtrom*
tampons	tahm-pohnih	*tampóny*
tissues	vrets-kohw-kih	*vreckovky*
toothbrush	zub-naa kef-kah	*zubná kefka*

SLOVAK

Clothing

coat	kah-baat	*kabát*
dress	shah-tih	*šaty*
jacket	sakoh	*sako*
jumper	sveh-ter	*sveter*
shirt	kosheh-lyah	*košeľa*
shoes	topaan-kih	*topánky*
skirt	suk-nyah	*sukňa*
trousers	nohah-vitseh	*nohavice*
underwear	byeh-lih-zeny	*bielizeň*

It's too big/small.
  yeh toh pree-lish   *Je to príliš veľké/malé.*
  vely-kair/mah-lair

Materials

of brass	moh-sadz	*mosadz*
cotton	bavl-nah	*bavlna*
of gold	zlatoh	*zlato*
handmade	ruch-naa veeroh-bah	*ručná výroba*
leather	kozha	*koža*
silk	hod-vaab	*hodváb*
of silver	stryieh-broh	*striebro*
wool	vl-nah	*vlna*

Colours

black	chyier-nah	*čierna*
blue	behlah-saa/mod-raa	*belasá/modrá*
brown	hnyeh-daa	*hnedá*
green	zeleh-naa	*zelená*
orange	orahn-zhohvaa	*oranžová*
pink	ruzhoh-vaa	*ružová*
purple	nakhoh-vaa	*nachová*
red	cherveh-naa	*červená*
white	byieh-lah	*biela*
yellow	zhl-taa	*žltá*

Stationery & Publications

map	**mahpah**	*mapa*
newspaper	**novih-nih**	*noviny*
paper	**pah-pyier**	*papier*
pen (ballpoint)	**peh-roh**	*pero*
scissors	**nozhnih-tse**	*nožnice*
English-language ...	**... v anglich-tyinyeh**	*... v angličtine*
newspaper	**novih-nih**	*noviny*
novels	**beleh-tryiah**	*beletria*

SLOVAK

Photography

How much is it to process this film?
    koly-koh stoh-yee   *Koľko stojí vyvolanie*
    vivoh-lanyieh   *tohto filmu?*
    tokh-toh fill-muh?

When will it be ready?
    kedih toh buh-dyeh   *Kedy to bude hotové?*
    hotoh-vair?

I'd like a film for this camera.
    maa-tyeh film doh tokh-toh   *Máte film do tohto*
    fotoh-ahpah-raa-tuh?   *fotoaparátu?*

B&W (film)	**chyier-noh-byielih film**	*čiernobiely film*
camera	**fotoh-ahpah-raat**	*fotoaparát*
colour (film)	**fareb-nee film**	*farebný film*
film	**film**	*film*
flash	**blesk**	*blesk*
lens	**obyek-teev**	*objektív*
light meter	**ekspoh-zih-mehter**	*expozimeter*

SLOVAK

Smoking

A packet of cigarettes, please.
 bahlee-chek tsiga-ryiet proh-seem — *Balíček cigariet, prosím.*

Are these cigarettes strong/mild?
 soo toh sil-nair/ yem-nair tsiga-retih? — *Sú to silné/jemné cigarety?*

Do you smoke?
 fy-chee-tyeh? — *Fajčíte?*

Do you have a light?
 maa-teh zaa-palkih/ zapah-lyoh-vach — *Máte zápalky/zapaľovač?*

Please don't smoke
 nye-fy-chithy proh-seem. — *Nefajčiť prosím.*

cigarette papers	tsiga-retoh-vair pah-pyieh-reh	*cigaretové papiere*
cigarettes	tsiga-retih	*cigarety*
filtered	tsiga-retih s fil-trom	*cigarety s filtrom*
lighter	zapah-lyoh-vach	*zapaľovač*
matches	zaa-palkih	*zápalky*
menthol cigarettes	mentoloh-vair tsiga-retih	*mentolové cigarety*
pipe	fy-kah	*fajka*
tobacco (pipe)	fy-koh-vee tabak	*fajkový tabak*

SIGNS

ZÁKAZ FAJČENIA — **NO SMOKING**

Sizes & Comparisons

small	mah-lee	*malý*
big	vely-kee	*veľký*
heavy	tyazh-kee	*ťažký*
light	lyakh-kee	*ľahký*
more	vyiats	*viac*
less	meh-nyeay	*menej*

HEALTH

What's the matter?
  cho vaas traa-pih?   *Čo vás trápi?*

Where does it hurt?
  gdyeh toh boh-lee?   *Kde to bolí?*

It hurts here.
  tuh mah boh-lee   *Tu ma bolí.*

I feel better/worse.
  tsee-tyim sah lep-shyieh/   *Cítim sa lepšie/horšie.*
  hor-shyieh

My friend is sick.
  muoy pryiah-tyely yeh kho-ree   *Môj priateľ je chorý.* (m)
  moh-yah pryiah-tyely-kah   *Moja priateľka je chorá.* (f)
  yeh kho-raa

Parts of the Body

My ... hurts.	boh-lee mah ...	*Bolí ma ...*
ankle	chleh-nok	*členok*
arm	ruh-kah	*ruka*
back	hr-baat	*chrbát*
chest	hrudyi	*hruď*
ear	ukhoh	*ucho*
eye	okoh	*oko*
finger	prst	*prst*
foot	noh-hah/kho-dyid-loh	*noha/chodidlo*
hand	ruh-kah	*ruka*
head	hlah-vah	*hlava*
heart	srd-tse	*srdce*
leg	noh-hah	*noha (celá)*
mouth	oos-tah	*ústa*
nose	nos	*nos*
ribs	reh-braa	*rebrá*
skin	koh-zha/pokozh-kah	*koža/pokožka*
spine	khrb-tyih-tsa	*chrbtica*
stomach	zhaloo-dok	*žalúdok*
teeth	zoobih	*zuby*
throat	hrd-loh	*hrdlo*

SLOVAK

Ailments

I have (a/an) ...

allergy	maam aler-ghiuh	*Mám alergiu.*
blister	maam otlahk	*Mám otlak.*
burn	maam popaa-leh-nyinuh	*Mám popáleninu.*
cold	maam naad-khuh	*Mám nádchu.*
constipation	maam zaap-khuh	*Mám zápchu.*
cough	maam kah-shely	*Mám kašeľ.*
diarrhoea	maam hnach-kuh	*Mám hnačku.*
fever	maam horooch-kuh	*Mám horúčku.*
headache	bohlee mah hla-vah	*Bolí ma hlava.*
hepatitis	maam zhl-touch-kuh	*Mám žltačku.*
indigestion	maam pokah-zenee zhaloo-dok	*Mám pokazený žalúdok.*
infection	maam naa-kaz-livoo khoroh-buh	*Mám nákazlivú chorobu.*
influenza	maam khreep-kuh	*Mám chrípku.*
lice	maam fshih	*Mám vši.*
(low/high) blood pressure	maam (nyeez-kih/ visoh-kee) krv-nee tlak	*Mám (nízky/vysoký) krvný tlak.*
pain	maam boles-tyih	*Mám bolesti.*
sore throat	bohlee mah hrd-loh	*Bolí ma hrdlo.*
stomachache	bohlee mah zhaloo-dok	*Bolí ma žalúdok.*
sunburn	maam ooh-pahl	*Mám úpal.*
veneral disease	maam pohlav-noo khoro-buh	*Mám pohlavnú chorobu.*
worms	maam chrev-neekh parah-zitohw	*Mám črevných parazitov.*

I've sprained my ...
  vitkohl/vitklah som sih ...   *Vytkol/Vytkla som si ...* (m/f)
I'm sick.
  som kho-ree/kho-raa   *Som chorý/chorá..* (m/f)

Women's Health

Could I see a female doctor?
muo-zhem hoh-vohrity zoh
zhe-nohw-lekaar-kohw?   *Môžem hovorit'so*
ženou-lekárkou?

I'm pregnant.
som tyehot-naa   *Som tehotná.*

I'm on the Pill.
pohw-zheevam hormoh-   *Používam hormonálnu*
naal-nuh anti- kon-tseptsyiuh   *antikoncepciu.*

I haven't had my period for
(two) months.
uzh (dvah) mehsiah-tse   *Už (dva) mesiace som*
som nyeh-malah   *nemala menštruáciu.*
men-shtru-aatsyiuh

Useful Words & Phrases

accident	nyeh-hodah	nehoda
addiction	nar-koh-maanyiah/	narkománia/
	toksi-koh-maanyiah	toxikománia
bite (animal)	poh-hriz-nutyieh	pohryznutie
bite (insect)	ushtyip-nutyieh	uštipnutie
blood test	krv-naa skoosh-kah	krvná skúška
injection	in-yek-tsyiah	injekcia
injury	porah-nyeh-nyieh	poranenie
itch	svr-beh-nyieh	svrbenie
menstruation	men-shtru-aatsyiah	menštruácia
nausea	zhaloo-dochnaa	žalúdočná
	nyeh-voly-nosty	nevoľnosť
oxygen	kis-leak	kyslík
Where's the ...?	gdyeh yeh ...?	Kde je ...?
chemist	lekaar-nyik	lekárnik
dentist	zoob-nee lekaar	zubný lekár
doctor	dok-tor/lekaar	doktor/lekár
hospital	nyemots-nyitsah	nemocnica

SLOVAK

SLOVAK

I'm allergic to ...	som aler-ghits-kee/ aler-ghits-kaa nah ...	*Som alergický/ alergická na ...*
antibiotics	antih-biyoh-tihkaa	*antibiotiká*
penicillin	penih-tsileen	*penicilín*

I'm ...	maam ...	*Mám ...*
asthmatic	asth-muh	*astmu*
diabetic	tsuk-rof-kuh	*cukrovku*
epileptic	epi-lepsyiuh	*epilepsiu*

I have my own syringe.
maam vlast-noo
in-yekch-noo stryieh-kach-kuh

Mám vlastnú injekčnú striekačku.

At the Chemist

I need medication for ...
potreh-buyem lyiek nah ...   *Potrebujem liek na ...*
I have a prescription.
maam lekaar-skih   *Mám lekársky*
pred-pis(reh-tsept)   *predpis(recept).*

antiseptic	anti-septih-khum	*antiseptikum*
aspirin	aspih-reen	*aspirín*
bandage	ob-vaz	*obväz*
contraceptives	proh-stryied-kih protih pocha-tyiuh	*prostriedky proti počatiu*
medicine	lyiek	*liek*
vitamins	vitah-meanih	*vitamíny*

At the Dentist

I have a toothache.
    boh-lyiah mah zoobih   *Bolia ma zuby.*

I've lost a filling.
    vih-padlah mih plom-bah   *Vypadla mi plomba.*

I've broken a tooth.
    zloh-mil sa mih zoob   *Zlomil sa mi zub.*

My gums hurt.
    boh-lyiah mah dyas-naa   *Bolia ma ďasná.*

I don't want it extracted.
    nyeh-khtsem sih toh   *Nechcem si to nechať*
    nyeh-khaty vih-trh-nooty   *vytrhnúť.*

Please give me an anaesthetic.
    uh-mrrt-vityeh mih toh   *Umŕtvite mi to, prosím.*
    proh-seem

SLOVAK

FROM ROTTEN EGGS TO RUST

Scattered across Slovakia are hundreds of mineral springs whose waters, taken externally or internally, are said to be beneficial for treating all sorts of ailments. Due to their mineral content, the waters can taste quite odd – ranging from rotten eggs to rust – but you can still convince yourself that they're doing you a power of good.

Locals and foreigners take the cure at dozens of spas. A spa course typically lasts about three weeks.

Some of the better known spa towns and their specialities are:

- *Bardejovské Kúpele* (East Slovakia)
  stomach, gall bladder and respiratory diseases

- *Piešťany* (Central Slovakia)
  rheumatism, nervous diseases

- *Trenčianske Teplice* (West Slovakia)
  rheumatism, motor conditions, respiratory diseases

SLOVAK

TIME & DATES

What date is it today?
koly-kairhoh yeh dnyes?   *Koľkého je dnes?*
What time is it?
koly-koh yeh hoh-dyeen?   *Koľko je hodín?*

Telling the time takes three forms in Slovak:

- 1 o'clock takes the singular form of the verb 'to be' and the singular form of 'hour'

  It's one o'clock.
  yeh jeh-dnah hodih-nah
  Je jedna hodina.
  (lit: it-is one hour)

- 2, 3 and 4 o'clock use the plural form of the verb 'to be' and the plural form of 'hour'

  It's two/three/four o'clock.
  soo dveh/trih/shtih-rih hodyih-nih
  Sú dve/tri/štyri hodiny.
  (lit: they-are two/three/four hours)

- 5 o'clock onwards uses the singular form of the verb 'to be' and plural form of 'hour'

  It's five o'clock.
  yeh petyih hoh-dyeen
  Je päť hodín.
  (lit: it-is five hours)

in the morning
dopoh-luh-dnyah/   *dopoludnia/*
pred-poluh-dnyeem   *predpoludním*
in the afternoon
popoh-ludnyee   *popoludní*
in the evening
veh-cher   *večer*

Days

Monday	pon-dyelok	*pondelok*
Tuesday	uh-torok	*utorok*
Wednesday	stre-dah	*streda*
Thursday	shtvr-tok	*štvrtok*
Friday	piah-tok	*piatok*
Saturday	soboh-tah	*sobota*
Sunday	nye-dye-lya	*nedeľa*

Months

January	yanooh-aar	*január*
February	februh-aar	*február*
March	maretz	*marec*
April	apreel	*apríl*
May	maai	*máj*
June	yoon	*jún*
July	yool	*júl*
August	ow-goost	*august*
September	septem-behr	*september*
October	oktoh-behr	*október*
November	nohvem-behr	*november*
December	detzem-behr	*december*

SLOVAK

Seasons

summer	letoh	*leto*
autumn	yeseny	*jeseň*
winter	zimah	*zima*
spring	yahr	*jar*

Present

now	teras	*teraz*
this morning	dnyes raa-noh	*dnes ráno*
today	dnyes	*dnes*
tonight	dnyes veh-cher	*dnes večer*
this week/year	tentoh	*tento týždeň/*
	teezh-dyeny/rok	*rok*

SLOVAK

Past

yesterday	fcheh-rah	*včera*
day before yesterday	pred-fcheh-rom	*predvčerom*
last night	minuh-loo notz	*minulú noc*
last week/year	minuh-lee teezh-dyeny/rok	*minulý týždeň/rok*

Future

tomorrow	zai-trah	*zajtra*
day after tomorrow	poh-zai-trah	*pozajtra*
tomorrow morning	zai-trah raa-noh	*zajtra ráno*
next week	buhdoo-tzi teezh-dyeny	*budúci týždeň*
next year	buhdoo-tzi rok	*budúci rok*

During the Day

afternoon	popoh-ludnyie	*popoludnie*
dawn	ooh-svit	*úsvit*
day	dyeny	*deň*
early	skoh-roh	*skoro*
early morning	skoh-roh raa-noh	*skoro ráno*
midday	poluh-dnyie	*poludnie*
midnight	pol-notz	*polnoc*
morning	raa-noh	*ráno*
night	notz	*noc*
sunrise	vee-khod sln-kah	*východ slnka*
sunset	zaa-pad sln-kah	*západ slnka*

NUMBERS & AMOUNTS

0	noolah	*nula*
1	yeh-den	*jeden*
2	dvah	*dva*
3	trih	*tri*
4	shtih-rih	*štyri*
5	pety	*päť*
6	shesty	*šesť*
7	seh-dyem	*sedem*
8	oh-sem	*osem*
9	dye-vety	*deväť*
10	dye-sahty	*desať*
20	dvah-tsahty	*dvadsať*
30	trih-tsahty	*tridsať*
40	shtih-rih-tsahty	*štyridsať*
50	pety-dyeh-syiat	*päťdesiat*
60	shez-dyeh-syiat	*šesťdesiat*
70	seh-dyem-dyeh-syiat	*sedemdesiat*
80	oh-sem-dyeh-syiat	*osemdesiat*
90	dyeh-vaty-dyeh-syiat	*deväťdesiat*
100	stoh	*sto*
1000	tyih-seetz	*tisíc*
10 000	dye-sahty tyih-seetz	*desaťtisíc*
100 000	stoh tyih-seetz	*stotisíc*
one million	milih-yawhn	*milión*
1st	pr-ve	*prvý*
2nd	druh-hee	*druhý*
3rd	treh-tyee	*tretí*
1/4	shtvr-tyih-nah	*štvrtina*
1/3	treh-tyih-nah	*tretina*
1/2	poloh-vitzah	*polovica*
3/4	trih shtvr-tyeh	*tri štvrte*

Useful Words

Enough!	**dosty!/stah-cheeh!**	*Dosť!/Stačí!*
double	**dvoy-moh**	*dvojmo*
dozen	**tuhtzet**	*tucet*
few	**maa-loh**	*málo*
less	**meh-nyay**	*menej*
a little bit	**troh-khuh**	*trochu*
many	**mnohoh/veh-lyah**	*mnoho/veľa*
more	**vyiah-tzyey**	*viacej*
once	**yeden-kraat/yeden raz**	*jedenkrát/jeden raz*
pair	**paar**	*pár*
percent	**per-tzen-toh**	*percento*
some	**nyieh-koly-koh**	*niekoľko*
too much	**pree-lish veh-lyah**	*príliš veľa*
twice	**dvah-kraat/dvah razih**	*dvakrát/dva razy*

ABBREVIATIONS

atď.	etcetera
cm/m/km	cm/m/km(s)
D.P.H.	GST (VAT)
EÚ	European Union
h.(hod.)/min./sek.	hr(s)/min/sec
nám	square
nábr	Quay
n.l./pr. n.l.	AD/BC
OSN	UN
Sev./Juž./Záp./Vých.	North/South/West/East
Sk (slovenskákoruna)	crown (unit of currency)
ŠPZ	Car Reg No.
SR	Slovak Republic
t.č.	at present (now)
tel. č.	telephone number
t.j.	i.e.
t.r.	this year
ul.	street

SLOVAK

EMERGENCIES

Help!	pomots!	*Pomoc!*
Thief!	zlodyey!	*Zlodej!*

Call ...	zah-voh-lai-tyeh ...	*Zavolajte ...*
a doctor	leh-kaa-rah	*lekára*
an ambulance	zaa-khran-kuh	*záchranku*
the police	poh-lee-tsyuh	*políciu*

It's an emergency.
  treh-bah pomots   *Treba pomoc.*
There's been an accident.
  stalah sah nyeh-hodah   *Stala sa nehoda.*
Where's the police station?
  gdyeh yeh poli-tsai-naa *Kde je policajná stanica?*
  stanyih-tsa?
Go away!
  khody prech!   *Choď preč!* (sg)
  khody-tyeh prech!   *Choďte preč!* (pl)
I'll call the police.
  zahvoh-laam polee-tsyiuh *Zavolám políciu.*
I'm ill.
  (yah) som khoree/khoraa *(Ja) som chorý/chorá.* (m/f)
My friend is ill.
  muoy pryia-tyely yeh khoree   *Môj priateľ je chorý.* (m)
  moya pryia-tyely-kah yeh khoraa *Moja priateľka je chorá.* (f)
I'm lost.
  nye-viznaahm sah tuh   *Nevyznám sa tu.*
Where are the toilets?
  dyeh soo tuh zaa-khodih? *Kde sú tu záchody?*
Could you help me, please?
  muo-zhetye mih proh-seem *Môžete mi prosím pomôcť?*
  poh-muotsty?
Could I please use the telephone?
  muo-zhem proh-seem   *Môžem prosím*
  pohw-zhity teleh-fawn?   *použiť telefón?*

I'm sorry. I apologise.
    prepaach-tyeh proh-seem   *Prepáčte, prosím.*

I didn't do it.
    yah som toh nyeh-oorobil/   *Ja som to neurobil/*
    nyeh-oorobilah   *neurobila.* (m/f)

I want to contact my embassy/
consulate.
    khtsehm hoh-vohrityi zoh   *Chcem hovoriť so*
    zastuh-pityely-stvom   *zastupiteľstvom*
    svoh-yey krayih-nih   *svojej krajiny.*

I have medical insurance.
    maam nyemotsen-skair   *Mám nemocenské poistenie.*
    poh-istyenyieh

My possessions are insured.
    moyah batoh-zhinah yeh   *Moja batožina je poistená.*
    poh-istyenaa

My ... was stolen.	**ookrad-lih mih**	*Ukradli mi ...*
I've lost my ...	**strahtyil som ...**	*Stratil som ...* (m)
	strahtyil-lah som ...	*Stratila som ...* (f)
bags	**batoh-zhinuh**	*batožinu*
handbag	**tash-kuh/kabel-kuh**	*tašku/kabelku*
money	**penyiah-zeh**	*peniaze*
travellers cheques	**tses-tohv-nair sheh-kih**	*cestovné šeky*
passport	**tses-tohv-nee pahs**	*cestovný pas*
wallet	**peh-nya-zhen-kah**	*peňaženka*

SLOVENE

QUICK REFERENCE

SLOVENE

Hello.	poz-drahw-lyei-ne	Pozdravljeni.
Goodbye.	nahs-vee-dan-yea	Nasvidenje.
Yes.	yah/dah	Ja./Da. (inf/pol)
No.	na	Ne.
Excuse me.	do-vo-lee-tei me, pro-sim	Dovolite mi, prosim.
Maybe	mo-gho-chei	Mogoče.
Sorry.	o-pro-stee-tei	Oprostite.
Please.	pro-sim	Prosim.
Thank you.	hvah-lah	Hvala.
You're welcome.	dob-ro-dosh-le!	Dobrodošli!
May I?	ah-le luh-ko?	Ali lahko?
What time is it?	ko-lick-ko yea oo-rah?	Koliko je ura?

Can I see the room?	
luh-ko vee-dim so-bo?	Lahko vidim sobo?
I (don't) understand.	
(nei) rah-zoom-mam	(Ne) razumem.
Do you speak English?	
go-vo-ree-tei ahn-glesh-ko?	Govorite angleško?
Where's the toilet?	
kye yea strah-neesh-chei/ve-tse?	Kje je stranišče/WC?
I want to go to ...	
zha-leem ee-te ...	Szeretnék ...
Turn left/right.	
o-bur-nee-tei	Obrnite
le-vo/des-no	levo/desno.
Go straight ahead.	
poy-dee-tei nah-rahw-nost nah-pray	Pojdite naravnost naprej.
How much is it?	
ko-lick-ko stah-ne?	Koliko stane?

| one-way (ticket) | an-no-smer-nah (vo-zow-ne-tsah) | enosmerna (vozovnica) |
| return (ticket) | pow-raht-nah (vo-zow-ne-tsah) | povratna (vozovnica) |

1	an-nah	ena	6	shest	šest
2	dve	dve	7	se-dehm	sedem
3	tree	tri	8	o-some	osem
4	shtee-re	štiri	9	de-vet	devet
5	pet	pet	10	de-set	deset

Slovene is the official language of the Republic of Slovenia. The forebears of today's Slovenians brought the language, with its roots in the Slavonic language, from their original homeland beyond the Carpathian Mountains.

The *Brižinski spomeniki* (Monuments of Freising) are the earliest known texts to be written in a language that reveals quite clear features of present-day Slovene. They date from the second half of the 10th century and were religious in content, relating two different forms of general confession, and a homily about sin and penitence.

The father of literary Slovene is Primož Trubar (1508-1586), a Protestant reformer and the first Slovenian writer who published his first book, *The Catechism*, at a printing house in Tübingen, Germany, in 1550. He was followed by Jurij Dalmatin who translated the Bible and published it in 1584.

Among other well-known Slovenian writers are the world-acclaimed poet France Prešeren (1800-1849), whose poems have been translated into the major world languages. Josip Jurčič and Ivan Tavčar are two of the best Slovenian representatives of literary realism. The works of Ivan Cankar (1876-1918), a great Slovenian playwright, are also translated into many languages.

Slovene is spoken in Slovenia by almost two million people, and in the countries where Slovenians have migrated, including the USA, Canada, Argentina, Brazil and Australia. It is also spoken by Slovenian minority groups in neighbouring countries. It is a uniform and rich language which has developed as a national tool of communication, and which, therefore, has a unificational and representative task.

Slovene uses Roman characters. Apart from singular and plural forms of words, Slovene also has a dual form, a rare characteristic in linguistics. The dual is used when referring to two persons or objects. The dual form has a special ending, for example:

one child	otro**k**
children	otro**ci**
two children	otro**ka**

I go	g**rem**
we go	g**remo**
we two go	g**reva**

PRONUNCIATION

No sounds in Slovene are difficult for a speaker of English to learn. The Slovenian alphabet consists of 25 letters. Each letter has only one sound, with very few exceptions.

Vowels

a	as the 'u' in 'cut'
ê	as the 'a' in 'hat'
e	when unstressed, as the 'er' in 'opera'
é	as the 'e' in 'hey', but slightly longer
i	as the 'i' in 'ink'
ó	as the 'o' in 'or'
ò	as the 'o' in 'soft'
u	as the 'oo' in 'good'

Consonants

c	as the 'ts' in 'cats'
č	as the 'ch' in 'chocolate'
g	as the 'g' in 'gold'
j	as the 'y' in 'yellow'
r	a rolled 'r'
š	as the 'sh' in 'ship'
ž	as the 's' in 'pleasure'

SLOVENE

Stress

Slovene has free stress, which means there's no general rule for which syllable is stressed. It simply has to be learned.

SUBJECT PRONOUNS		
SG		
I	yus	jaz
you	tee	ti
he/she/it	on/o-nah	on/ona
PL		
we	mee	mi
you	vee	vi
they	o-ne/o-nei	oni/one

GREETINGS & CIVILITIES
Top Useful Phrases

Hi.	poz-drahw-lyei-ne/ poz-drahw-lyan	*Pozdravljeni/ Pozdravljen* (inf).
Goodbye.	nahs-vee-dan-yea	*Nasvidenje.*
Please.	pro-sim	*Prosim.*
Thank you (very much).	hvah-lah (le-pah)	*Hvala (lepa).*
You're welcome.	dob-ro-dosh-le!	*Dobrodošli!*
Yes.	yah/dah	*Ja./Da.* (inf/pol)
No.	na	*Ne.*
Maybe.	mo-gho-chei	*Mogoče.*
Excuse me.	do-vo-lee-tei me, pro-sim	*Dovolite mi, prosim.*
Sorry. (Forgive me.)	o-pro-stee-tei/ o-pro-ste	*Oprostite.* (pol)/ *Oprosti.* (inf)

Forms of Address

Mr	ghos-pod	*Gospod*
Mrs	ghos-pah	*Gospa*
(to a young woman)	ghos-po-deech-nah	*Gospodična*

SLOVENE

SMALL TALK

Good day.	do-bur dahn	*Dober dan.*
What's your name?	kah-ko vum jei e-me?	*Kako vam je ime?* (
	kah-ko te jei e-me?	*Kako ti je ime?* (inf)
My name's ...	yus some ...	*Jaz sem ...*
Where are you from?	ot cought stei?	*Od kod ste?*
I'm from ...	some ez ...	*Sem iz ...*
Australia	ahws-trah-le-yea	*Avstralije*
the USA	ah-mair-re-kei	*Amerike*
UK	ve-le-ke	*Britanije Velike*
	bre-tah-ne-yea	
Do you like ...?	ah-le e-mah-tei	*Ali imate*
	rah-de ...?	*radi ...?*
I like it very much.	e-mahm za-lo rut	*Imam zelo rad.*
I don't like ...	nei mah-rahm ...	*Ne maram ...*
Just a minute.	sah-mo tran-noo-tehk	*Samo trenutek.*
May I?	ah-le luh-ko?	*Ali lahko?*
No problem.	braz prob-le-mah	*Brez problema.*
How do you say ... ?	kah-ko sei ra-chei ...?	*Kako se reče ...?*

Occupations

What's your profession?
  cuy stei/se po pock-leet-soo?   *Kaj ste* (pol)/*si* (inf) *po poklic*

I'm a tourist/student.
  some to-reest/shtoo-dent   *Sem turist/študent.*

businessperson	po-slow-nash	*poslovnež*
doctor	zdrahw-neek	*zdravnik* (m)
	zdraw-nee-tsah	*zdravnica* (f)
manual worker	de-lah-vats	*delavec* (m)
	de-lahw-kah	*delavka* (f)
computer	rah-choon-nahl-	*računalničar*
programmer	nee-char	
teacher	oo-cheat-tell	*učitelj* (m)
	oo-cheat-tell-lee-tsah	*učiteljica* (f)

waiter	nah-tah-car	*natakar* (m)
	nah-tah-car-ree-tsah	*natakarica* (f)
writer	pee-sah-tell	*pisatelj* (m)
	pee-sah-tell-lee-tsah	*pisateljica* (f)

Family

Are you married?
| | stei po-row-chan-ne? | *Ste poročeni?* |

I'm single.
| | sahm-ski some | *Samski sem.* (m) |
| | sahm-skah some | *Samska sem.* (f) |

I'm married.
| | po-row-chan some | *Poročen sem.* (m) |
| | po-row-chan-nah some | *Poročena sem.* (f) |

I have one child.
| | e-mahm ann-nag-gah ot-raw-kah | *Imam enega otroka.* |

I have two children.
| | e-mahm dvah ot-raw-kah | *Imam dva otroka.* |

I have three children.
| | e-mahm tree ot-raw-kei | *Imam tri otroke.* |

SLOVENE

brother	braht	*brat*
daughter	khchee	*hči*
father	ow-chei	*oče*
husband	mosh	*mož*
mother	mah-mah	*mama*
sister	sas-trah	*sestra*
son	sin	*sin*
wife	zhan-nah	*žena*

BREAKING THE LANGUAGE BARRIER

Do you speak English?

go-vo-ree-tei ahn-glesh-ko? *Govorite angleško?*

I understand.

rah-zoom-mam *Razumem.*

I (don't) understand.

(nei) rah-zoom-mam *(Ne) razumem.*

Could you repeat that, please?

luh-ko po-no-vee-tei? *Lahko ponovite?*

BODY LANGUAGE

Generally, Slovenes don't gesticulate when talking as much as the neighbouring Italians do. Slovenes nod for 'Yes', shake their heads for 'No' and shrug their shoulders for 'I don't know'. Beckoning is done with the pointer finger, palms up and other fingers folded.

SIGNS	
INFORMACIJE	INFORMATION
IZHOD	EXIT
ODPRTO/ZAPRTO	OPEN/CLOSED
POSTAJA	STATION
PREPOVEDANO	PROHIBITED
STRANIŠČE	TOILETS
VHOD	ENTRANCE
ŽELEZNIŠKA BLAGAJNA	TICKET OFFICE

SLOVENE

PAPERWORK

date/place of birth	dah-toom krahj royst-vah	*datum/ kraj rojstva*
given name	e-me	*me*
male/female	mosh-ke/zhen-skah	*moški/ženska*
nationality	der-zhahw-lyahn-stvo	*državljanstvo*
passport	pot-ne leest	*potni list*
surname	pre-e-mack	*priimek*

GETTING AROUND

I want to go to ...	zha-leem ee-te ...	*Želim iti ...*
What time does the ... leave?	k-die pel-yea ...?	*Kdaj pelje ...?*
bus	ahw-to-boos	*avtobus*
train	oo-lahk	*vlak*
boat/ferry	lahd-yah/trah-yect	*ladja/trajekt*

Can you tell me when we get to ...? me luh-ko po-ves-tei, k-die preed-dam-mo ...?	*Mi lahko poveste, kdaj pridemo ...?*
Stop here, please. oos-tah-vee-tei too-kai, pro-seem	*Ustavite tukaj, prosim.*
How long does the trip take? kah-ko dow-gho trah-yah po-to-vahn-yea?	*Koliko dolgo traja potovanje?*
Do I need to change? ah-le mo-rahm prei-se-ste?	*Ali moram presesti?*

SLOVENE

THEY MAY SAY ...

oo-lahk e-mah zah-moo-do/
oo-lahk prei-he-te-vah
   The train is delayed/early.
oo-lahk pre-hah-yah prah-vo-chahs-no
   The train is on time.
vozh-nyah jei od-po-ve-dah-nah
   The train is cancelled.
prei-se-ste mo-rah-tei/mo-rah-tei
   You must change trains/platforms.
   nah droo-ghe pei-ron

SIGNS

AVTOBUSNO POSTAJALIŠČE	BUS STOP
CARINA	CUSTOMS
ODHODI	DEPARTURES
PRIHODI	ARRIVALS
ŽELEZNIŠKA POSTAJA	TRAIN STATION

ticket	car-tah	*karta*
one-way (ticket)	an-no-smer-nah	*enosmerna*
	(vo-zow-ne-tsah)	*(vozovnica)*
return (ticket)	pow-raht-nah	*povratna*
	(vo-zow-ne-tsah)	*(vozovnica)*
I'd like to hire a ...	rud be nah-yew ...	*Rad bi najel ...*
bicycle	ko-lo	*kolo*
car	ahw-to	*avto*
guide	vo-dee-chah	*vodiča*
horse	con-yah	*konja*
motorcyle	mo-tor-no ko-lo	*motorno kolo*

SLOVENE

Directions

How do I get to ...?
 kah-ko pree-dam do ...? *Kako pridem do ...?*
Is it near/far?
 ah-le yea blee-zoo/dah-lach? *Ali je blizu/daleč?*
What town/suburb is this?
 kah-te-ro mes-to/ *Katero mesto/*
 prad-mest-yea yea to? *predmestje je to?*

What ... is this?	kah-te-rah ... yea to?	*Katera ... je to?*
road	tses-tah	*cesta*
street	oo-le-tsah	*ulica*
street number	oo-lich-nah shtei-veel-kah	*ulična številka*

(Go) straight ahead.
    (poy-dee-tei) nah-rahw-nost   *(Pojdite) naravnost*
    nah-pray   *naprej.*

(Turn) left/right ...	(o-bur-nee-tei)	*(Obrnite)*
at the ...	le-vo/des-no pre ...	*levo/desno pre ...*
traffic lights	sei-mah-for-you	*semaforju*
next/	nah-sled-nyam/	*naslednjem/*
second/	droo-gam/	*drugem/*
third corner	tret-tyam o-veen-koo	*tretjem ovinku*

behind	zah (zah-die)	*za (zadaj)*
opposite	nahs-pro-te	*nasproti*
here/there	too/tum	*too/tum*
everywhere	pow-sod	*povsod*
up/down	zgho-rye/spo-die	*zgoraj/spodaj*
north	se-vur	*sever*
south	yoog	*jug*
east	ooz-hod	*vzhod*
west	zah-hod	*zahod*

ACCOMMODATION

I'm looking for a/the...	eesh-chehm ...	*Iščem ...*
camping ground	kahm-pingh	*kamping*
guesthouse	ghos-teesh-chei	*gostišče*
hotel	ho-tell	*hotel*
manager/	de-rect-or-yah/	*direktorja/*
owner	lust-nee-kah	*lastnika*
youth hostel	po-cheet-nish-ke dom	*počitniški dom*

SLOVENE

What's the address?
    kah-ko yea nah-slow?   *Kako je naslov?*
Please write it down.
    pro-sim, nah-pee-she-tei   *Prosim, napišite*
    nah-slow   *naslov.*

Do you have a ...?	ah-le e-mah-tei pros-to ...?	*Ali imate prosto ...?*
bed	post-al-yaw	*posteljo*
cheap room	po-tse-ne so-bo	*poceni sobo*
single/	an-no-post-al-no/	*enoposteljno/*
double room	dvo-post-al-no so-bo	*dvoposteljno sobo*

How much is it per night/person?

ko-le-ko stah-ne zah an-no noch/o-se-bo?	*Koliko stane za eno noč/osebo?*

Is breakfast included?

ah-le yea zy-turk ook-lyoo-chan?	*Ali je zajtrk vključen?*

Is service included?

ah-le yea post-rezh-bah ook-lyoo-chan-nah?	*Ali je postrežba vključena?*

Can I see the room?

luh-ko vee-dim so-bo?	*Lahko vidim sobo?*

Where's the toilet?

kye yea strah-neesh-chei/ve-tse?	*Kje je stranišče/WC?*

I'm/We're leaving now.

dah-ness od-hi-ahm/od-hi-ah-mo	*Danes odhajam/odhajamo.*

Requests & Complaints

Do you have a safe (where I can leave my valuables)?

e-mah-tei sef (kyer luh-ko poo-steem drah-go-tsen-nos-te)?	*Imate sef (kjer lahko pustim dragocenosti)?*

Please wake me up at ...

pro-seem, zboo-dee-tei mae ob ...	*Prosim, zbudite me ob ...*

Do you have (a) ...?	ah-le e-mah-te ...?	*Ali imate ...?*
clean sheet	chees-to ur-yoo-ho	*čisto rjuho*
hot water	top-lo vo-do	*toplo vodo*
key	klooch	*ključ*
shower	toosh	*tuš*

SLOVENE

AROUND TOWN

Where's the/a ...?	kye yea ...?	*Kje je ...?*
bank	bahn-kah	*banka*
city centre	srei-deesh-chei mes-tah	*središče mesta*
consulate	con-zoo-laht	*konzulat*
embassy	ahm-bah-sah-dah	*ambasada*
exchange office	man-yahl-ne-tsah	*menjalnica*
post office	posh-tah	*pošta*
restaurant	rest-tau-rah-tsee-yah	*restavracija*
telephone centre	tel-lei-phon-skah	*telefonska*
	tsan-trah-lah	*centrala*
tourist	to-rees-tich-ne	*turistični*
information	in-for-mah-tseey-ski	*informaci*
office	oo-raht	*jski urad*

Post & Telecommunications

I want to make a telephone call.
rud be tel-lei-phon-near-ahw   *Rad bi telefoniral.*
How much is it for three minutes?
ko-leek-ko stah-nei-yaw   *Koliko stanejo*
tree me-noo-tei?   *tri minute?*
Where can I get Internet access?'
kye luh-ko pree-dam   *Kje lahko pridem*
doh inter-net-tah?   *do interneta?*

airmail	let-tahl-sko	*letalsko*
registered mail	pre-po-ro-chan-no	*priporočeno*
surface mail	nah-vahd-no	*navadno*

At the Bank

I'd like to change	rud be zah-men-yahw	*Rad bi zame*
some ...	ne-kai ...	*njal nekaj ...*
money	dan-nahr-yah	*denarja*
travellers cheques	po-to-vahl-nih	*potovalnih*
	che-kow	*čekov*

SLOVENE

Can I have money transferred
here from my bank?

   luh-ko pran-ness-sam some   *Lahko prenesem sem*
   dan-nahr z moy-yea bahn-kei?   *denar z moje banke?*

How long will it take to arrive?

   k-die bo pre-shlo?   *Kdaj bo prišlo?*

INTERESTS & ENTERTAINMENT
Sightseeing

What time does it open/close?

   k-die sei odd-pra?/zah-pra?   *Kdaj se odpre/zapre?*

Do you have a guidebook/local map?

   e-mah-tei vodd-neek/   *Imate vodnik/karto*
   car-to krah-yah?   *kraja?*

What is that?

   cuy yea to?   *Kaj je to?*

Can I take photographs?

   smem sleek-kah-tee?   *Smem slikati?*

abbey	o-pah-tee-yah	*opatija*
beach	plah-zhah	*plaža*
bridge	most	*most*
castle	graht	*grad*
cathedral	stol-ne-tsah	*stolnica*
church	tser-coo	*cerkev*
hospital	ball-neesh-ne-tsah	*bolnišnica*
island	o-talk	*otok*
lake	ye-zei-ro	*jezero*
main square	glahw-ne turg	*glavni trg*
market	turzh-ne-tsa	*tržnica*
old city (town)	stah-ro mes-to	*staro mesto*
palace	pah-lah-chah	*palača*
ruins	roo-shei-vee-nei	*ruševine*
sea	mor-yea	*morje*
square	turg	*trg*
tower	stolp	*stolp*

SLOVENE

Sports & Interests

What sports do you play?
   s kah-te-rim shport-tom
   se ook-vahr-yahsh?

S katerim športom se ukvarjaš?

What are your interests?
   kah-te-rah zah-nee-mahn-yah
   e-mahsh?

Katera zanimanja imaš?

art	oo-met-nost	*umetnost*
basketball	kosh-ahr-kah	*košarka*
chess	shahh	*šah*
collecting things	zbe-rah-tell-stvo	*zbirateljstvo*
dancing	ples	*ples*
food	hrah-nah	*hrana*
football	no-gho-met	*nogomet*
hiking	po-hod-nish-tvo	*pohodništvo*
martial arts	bo-reel-nei	*borilne*
	vash-chee-nei	*veščine*
meeting friends	sre-chahn-yah s	*srečanja s*
	pre-yah-tell-ye/	*prijatelji/*
	droo-zhan-yea	*druženje*
movies	feel-me/kee-no	*filmi/kino*
music	glahs-bah	*glasba*
nightclubs	noch-no zhiv-lyan-yea	*nočno življenje*
photography	pho-to-grah-fee-jah	*fotografija*
reading	brahn-yea	*branje*
shopping	nah-coo-po-vah-yea	*nakupovanje*
skiing	smoo-chahn-yea	*smučanje*
swimming	plah-vahn-yea	*plavanje*
tennis	ten-nis	*tenis*
travelling	po-to-vahn-yah	*potovanja*
TV/videos	tel-lei-vee-ze-yah	*televizija/video*
visiting friends	o-bis-ko-vahn-yea	*obiskovanje*
	pre-yah-tell-yew	*prijateljev*
walking	sprei-ho-de	*sprehodi*

SLOVENE

FOOD

Slovenian cuisine is very similar to that of Austria and Italy, due to the proximity of the two countries and their historical interaction.

breakfast	zy-turk	*zajtrk*
lunch	ko-see-lo	*kosilo*
dinner	va-chair-yah	*večerja*
Cheers!	nah zdrahw-yea!	*Na zdravje!*

I'm hungry/thirsty.
  lah-chehn/zhei-yehn some   *Lačen/žejen sem.*
Where can we get food?
  kye sei do-be hrah-nah?   *Kje se dobi hrana?*
I'm vegetarian.
  ve-ghe-tah-re-yahn-nets some   *Vegetarijanec sem.*
I don't eat ...
  nei yem ...   *Ne jem ...*
How much is ...?
  ko-lee-ko stah-nei ...?   *Koliko stane ...?*
I'd like the set lunch, please.
  luh-ko do-beem   *Lahko dobim*
  man-nee, pro-sim   *menu, prosim.*
Is service included in the bill?
  ah-le yea nah-pit-nee-nah   *Ali je napitnina*
  ook-lyoo-chan-nah?   *vključena?*
I'd like some ...
  rud be ne-kai ...   *Rad bi nekaj ...*
Another, please.
  shei an-krut, pro-sim   *Še enkrat, prosim.*
Waiter, the bill, please!
  nah-tah-car, rah-choon pro-sim! *Natakar, račun, prosim!*

hot/cold	to-puh/hlah-dehn	topel/hladen
restaurant	rest-tau-rah-tse-yah	restavracija
set menu	man-nee	menu
waiter	nah-tah-car/	natakar (m)/
	nah-tah-car-re-tsah	natakarica (f)
with/without	zeh/braz	z/brez

Typical Dishes

soup	you-hah	juha
roast beef	gho-vei-yah pat-chen-kah	goveja pečenka
roast pork	sveen-ska pat-chen-kah	svinjska pečenka
roast veal	tell-lech-yah pat-chen-kah	teleča pečenka
salad (mixed)	so-lah-tah (me-shun-nah)	solata (mešana)

Drinks

beer	pee-vo	pivo
fruit juice	sahd-ne sok	sadni sok
mineral water	me-na-rahl-nah	mineralna
	vo-dah	voda
tea	chai	čaj
wine	vee-no	vino

SLOVENE

SLURPING SLOVENES

The wine-growing regions of Slovenia and some of their better known products are:

- Podravje *Renski Rizling* a true German Riesling
  (in the east) *Beli Pinot* Pinot Blanc
  Traminec Traminer

- Posavje *Cviček* a distinctly Slovenian
  (in the south-east) light red

- (coastal) *Teran* a hearty red made from
  Refok grapes

At the Market

How much is it?
    ko-lick-ko stah-ne?   *Koliko stane?*
It's too expensive for me.
    pra-drah-gho yea zah-mae   *Predrago je zame.*
I'd like ... grams/kilos.
    rud þe ... grah-mow/keel   *Rad bi ... gramov/kil.*

Staples

bread	krooh	*kruh*
butter	mah-slo	*maslo*
cheese	seer	*sir*
chicken	pish-chah-nehts	*piščanec*
chocolate	cho-ko-lah-do	*čokolado*
coffee	kah-vah	*kava*
eggs	yai-tsah	*jajca*
fish	ree-bei	*ribe* (pl)
flour	mo-ko	*moko*
fruit	sahd-yea	*sadje*
ham	slah-nee-no	*slanino*
honey	met	*med*
margarine	mahr-gah-ree-no	*margarino*
marmalade	mahr-mel-lah-do	*marmelado*
meat	mas-so	*meso*
milk	mle-ko	*mleko*
olive oil	ol-leew-no ol-yea	*olivno olje*
pepper	pop-per	*poper*
pork	svin-yee-nah	*svinjina*
salt	so	*sol*
soup	you-hah	*juha*
sugar	slaht-cor	*sladkor*
yogurt	yo-ghurt	*jogurt*
vegetables	zal-lan-yah-vah	*zelenjava*

MENU DECODER

Soup

gobova kremna juha	mushroom soup
goveja juha z rezanci	beef broth with egg noodles
zelenjavna juha	vegetable soup

Meals

burek	sweet or savoury layered pastry
Dunajski zrezek	Wiener schnitzel
golaž	goulash
klobasa	sausage
kranjske klobase	sausages, usually served with *kislo zelje*
kislo zelje	sauerkraut (pickled cabbage)
njoki	potato dumplings
orehovi	walnut dumplings
paprikaš	chicken or beef stew
rižota	risotto
sirovi	cheese dumplings, a real delicacy
štruklji	dumplings
žlikrofi	ravioli-like dish

Desserts

gibanica	pastry filled with poppy seeds, walnuts, apple and/or sultanas and cheese, baked in cream
palačinke	thin pancakes filled with jam or nuts and topped with chocolate
potica	walnut roll
zavitek	strudel

SLOVENE

SHOPPING

How much is it?	ko-lick-ko stah-ne?	*Koliko stane?*

bookshop	knee-gahr-nah	*knjigarna*
delicatessen	dell-leek-kah-tess-sah	*delikatesa*
food stall	stoy-ne-tsah	*stojnica*
grocery store	sah-mo-post-rezh-bah	*samopostrežba*
laundry/laundrette	prahl-neet-tsah	*pralnica*
market	turzh-ne-tsah	*tržnica*
supermarket	tur-go-veen-nah	*trgovina*
newsagency	key-yosk	*kiosk*

I'd like to buy it.
  rud be coo-piw   *Rad bi kupil.*
It's too expensive for me.
  pra-drah-gho yea zah-mei   *Predrago je zame.*
Can I look at it?
  ah-le luh-ko pog-led-dahm   *Ali lahko pogledam?*
I'm just looking.
  sah-mo gled-dahm   *Samo gledam.*

I'm looking for ...	eesh-chem ...	*Iščem ...*
a chemist	chis-steel-ne-tso	*čistilnico*
clothing	o-blah-chee-lah	*oblačila*
souvenirs	spo-meen-kei	*spominke*
book	knee-gah	*knjiga*
newspaper	chah-so-pees	*časopis*

Do you take travellers cheques?
  ah-le oo-zah-mae-tei   *Ali vzamete*
  po-to-vahl-nei che-kei?   *potovalne čeke?*
Do you have another colour/size?
  ah-le e-mah-tei droo-gho   *Ali imate drugo*
  bahr-vo/val-lick-kost?   *barvo/velikost?*

Sizes & Comparisons

big/bigger	val-lick/vech-ye	*velik/večji*
small/smaller	my-hehn/mahn-she	*majhen/manjši*
more/less	vach/mun	*več/manj*
cheap/cheaper	po-tse-ne/tse-nay-she	*poceni/cenejši*

Essential Groceries

I'd like ...	rud be ...	*Rad bi ...*
batteries	bah-tear-ree-yea	*baterije*
cheese	seer	*sir*
chocolate	cho-ko-lah-do	*čokolado*
eggs	yai-tsah	*jajca*
honey	met	*med*
margarine	mahr-gah-ree-no	*margarino*
marmalade	mahr-mel-lah-do	*marmelado*
matches	oo-zhig-gahl-lee-tsei	*vžigalice*
milk	mle-ko	*mleko*
shampoo	shum-pown	*šampon*
soap	mee-lo	*milo*
sugar	slaht-cor	*sladkor*
toilet paper	toa-let-ne pah-peer	*toaletni papir*
toothpaste	zob-no cre-mo	*zobno kremo*
washing powder	prahl-ne prah-sheck	*pralni prašek*

SLOVENE

HEALTH

I'm sick.
ball-lahn some/bow-nah some   *Bolan sem.* (m)/*Bolna sem.* (f)

Where's the nearest dentist?
kye yea nahy-bleezh-ye   *Kje je najbližji*
zo-boz-drahw-neek?   *zobozdravnik?*

Where's the nearest
doctor/hospital?
kye yea nahy-bleezh-yah   *Kje je najbližja*
ball-neet-tsah?   *bolnica?*

I'm allergic to penicillin/antibiotics.
    ah-lar-ghe-chan some nah
    pan-ne-tse-leen/
    ahn-te-be-o-te-kei

Alergičen sem na
penicilin/
antibiotike.

I'm diabetic/epileptic/asthmatic.
    some de-ah-be-tick/
    ap-pe-lep-tick/ahst-mah-tick

Sem diabetik/
epileptik/astmatik.

I've been vaccinated.
    beew some tsep-lyan
    be-lah some tsep-lyan-nah

Bil sem cepljen. (m)
Bila sem cepljena. (f)

Parts of the Body

arm	rock-kah	*roka*
back	her-bat	*hrbet*
chest	per-see	*prsi*
ear	oo-ho/oo-shess-sah	*uho/ušesa* (pl)
eye	ow-ko/ow-chee	*oko/oči* (pl)
foot	sto-pah-law	*stopalo*
hand	dlahn	*dlan*
leg	nog-gah	*noga*
nose	nos	*nos*
skin	ko-zhah	*koža*
stomach	tre-booh	*trebuh*

Useful Words

antiseptic	ahn-te-sep-tick/ rahz-coo-zhee-lo	*antiseptik/ razkužilo*
aspirin	ahs-pe-reen	*aspirin*
condoms	con-do-me	*kondomi*
contraceptive	con-trah-tsep-tsey-sko sret-stvo	*kontracepcijsko sredstvo*
diarrhoea	dree-skah	*driska*
medicine	zdrah-veel-lo	*zdravilo*
nausea	slah-bost	*slabost*
sunblock cream	cre-mah zah sohn-chan-yea	*krema za sončenje*
tampons	tahm-pown-ne	*tamponi*

SLOVENE

TIME & DATES

When does (the) ... start?
k-die bo ...? *Kdaj bo ...?*

What time is it?
ko-lick-ko yea oo-rah? *Koliko je ura?*

It's ...	oo-rah yea ...	*Ura je ...*
1.15	chat-turt nah dve	*četrt na dve* (a quarter of two)
1.30	paul dvehh	*pol dveh* (a half of two)
1.45	tre chat-turt nah dve	*tri četrt na dve* (three-quarters of two)

in the morning	zyout-rye	*zjutraj*
in the evening	zva-chair	*zvečer*
all day	vuhs dahn	*ves dan*
every day	oo-suck dahn	*vsak dan*

yesterday	oo-chair-rye	*včeraj*
today	dah-ness	*danes*
tonight	no-tsoy	*nocoj*
tomorrow	you-tre	*jutri*
day after tomorrow	po-yoot-rish-nyam	*pojutrišnjem*

SLOVENE

Days

Monday	po-ned-dell-yack	*ponedeljek*
Tuesday	tor-reck	*torek*
Wednesday	sre-dah	*sreda*
Thursday	chat-turt-tack	*četrtek*
Friday	pe-tack	*petek*
Saturday	saw-bo-tah	*sobota*
Sunday	ned-dell-yah	*nedelja*

SLOVENE

Months

January	yahn-noo-ahr	*januar*
February	fab-roo-ahr	*februar*
March	mahr-rehts	*marec*
April	ahp-reel	*april*
May	my	*maj*
June	you-ney	*junij*
July	you-ley	*julij*
August	ahw-goost	*avgust*
September	sap-tam-bur	*september*
October	oc-to-bur	*oktober*
November	nov-vam-bur	*november*
December	dat-sam-bur	*december*

Seasons

spring	po-mlaht	*pomlad*
summer	po-let-yea	*poletje*
autumn	yea-sen	*jesen*
winter	zee-mah	*zima*

NUMBERS & AMOUNTS

1	an-nah	*ena*
2	dve	*dve*
3	tree	*tri*
4	shtee-re	*štiri*
5	pet	*pet*
6	shest	*šest*
7	se-dehm	*sedem*
8	o-some	*osem*
9	de-vet	*devet*
10	de-set	*deset*
11	an-nah-ist	*enajst*
12	dvah-nah-ist	*dvanajst*
13	tree-nah-ist	*trinajst*
14	shtee-re-nah-ist	*štirinajst*
15	pet-nah-ist	*petnajst*

16	shest-nah-ist	*šestnajst*
17	se-dehm-nah-ist	*sedemnajst*
18	o-some-nah-ist	*osemnajst*
19	de-vet-nah-ist	*devetnajst*
20	dvai-seht	*dvajset*
21	an-nah-in-dvai-seht	*enaindvajset*
22	dvah-in-dvai-seht	*dvaindvajset*
30	tree-de-seht	*trideset*
40	shtee-re-de-seht	*štirideset*
50	pet-de-seht	*petdeset*
60	shest-de-seht	*šestdeset*
70	se-dehm-de-seht	*sedemdeset*
80	o-some-de-seht	*osemdeset*
90	de-vet-de-seht	*devetdeset*
100	sto	*sto*
101	sto an-nah	*sto ena*
110	sto de-set	*sto deset*
1000	tee-soch	*tisoč*
one million	me-le-yon	*milijon*

SLOVENE

Useful Words

Enough!	doh-vaull!	*Dovolj!*
too much/many	pra-vach	*preveč*
a little	mah-law	*malo*
a lot	vell-leek-ko	*veliko*

EMERGENCIES

Help!	nah po-moch!	*Na pomoč!*
Go away!	poy-dee-tei strahn!	*Pojdite stran!*

Call a doctor/the police!
    pok-lee-chit-tei zdrahw-nee-kah/   *Pokličite zdravnika/*
    po-le-tsee-yaw!   *policijo!*

I've been raped.
    be-lah some po-see-lyan-nah   *Bila sem posiljena.*

I've been robbed.
    beew some or-rop-pahn   *Bil sem oropan.*

I'm lost.
    ez-goo-beew some sei/   *Izgubil sem se.* (m)
    ez-goo-bee-lah some sei   *Izgubila sem se.* (f)

Could you please help me?
    me luh-ko po-mah-gah-tei?   *Mi lahko pomagate?*

I didn't do it.
    te-gah nee-some nah-red-deew/   *Tega nisem naredil* (m)
    nah-red-deal-lah   *naredila.* (f)

I didn't realise I was doing
anything wrong.
    nee-some ved-do/ved-dell-lah,   *Nisem vedel* (m) *vedela* (f),
    dah dell-lahm nah-ro-bei   *da delam narobe.*

I want to contact my
embassy/consulate.
    ho-cham go-vau-ree-te z   *Hočem govoriti z*
    moy-yaw ahm-bah-sah-doh/z   *mojo ambasado/z*
    moy-yim con-zoo-lah-tom   *mojim konzulatom.*

SLOVENE

INDEX

GERMAN 85

I
N
D
E
X

374

SLOVAK 273

Phrasebooks

L onely Planet phrasebooks are packed with essential words and phrases to help travellers communicate with the locals. With colour tabs for quick reference, an extensive vocabulary and use of script, these handy pocket-sized language guides cover day-to-day travel situations.

- handy pocket-sized books
- easy to understand Pronunciation chapter
- clear & comprehensive Grammar chapter
- romanisation alongside script to allow ease of pronunciation
- script throughout so users can point to phrases for every situation
- full of cultural information and tips for the traveller

'...vital for a real DIY spirit and attitude in language learning'
– *Backpacker*

'the phrasebooks have good cultural backgrounders and offer solid advice for challenging situations in remote locations'
– *San Francisco Examiner*

Arabic (Egyptian) • Arabic (Moroccan) • Australian *(Australian English, Aboriginal and Torres Strait languages)* • Baltic States *(Estonian, Latvian, Lithuanian)* • Bengali • Brazilian • Burmese • British • Cantonese • Central Asia • Central Europe *(Czech, French, German, Hungarian, Italian, Slovak)* • Eastern Europe *(Bulgarian, Czech, Hungarian, Polish, Romanian, Slovak)* • Ethiopian (Amharic) • Farsi *(Persian)* • Fijian • French • German • Greek • Hebrew • Hill Tribes • Hindi/Urdu • Indonesian • Italian • Japanese • Korean • Lao • Latin American Spanish • Malay • Mandarin • Mediterranean Europe *(Albanian, Croatian, Greek, Italian, Macedonian, Maltese, Serbian, Slovene)* • Mongolian • Nepali • Papua New Guinea • Pilipino (Tagalog) • Quechua • Russian • Scandinavian Europe *(Danish, Finnish, Icelandic, Norwegian, Swedish)* • South-East Asia *(Burmese, Indonesian, Khmer, Lao, Malay, Tagalog Pilipino, Thai, Vietnamese)* • South Pacific Languages • Spanish (Castilian) *(also includes Catalan, Galician and Basque)* • Sri Lanka • Swahili • Thai • Tibetan • Turkish • Ukrainian • USA *(US English, Vernacular, Native American languages, Hawaiian)* • Vietnamese • Western Europe *(Basque, Catalan, Dutch, French, German, Greek, Irish)*

COMPLETE LIST OF LONELY PLANET BOOKS

AFRICA Africa on a shoestring • Cairo • Cairo Map • Cape Town • Cape Town Map • East Africa • Egypt • Ethiopia, Eritrea & Djibouti • The Gambia & Senegal • Healthy Travel Africa • Kenya • Malawi • Morocco • Mozambique • Read This First: Africa • South Africa, Lesotho & Swaziland • Southern Africa • Southern Africa Road Atlas • Tanzania, Zanzibar & Pemba • Trekking in East Africa • Tunisia • Watching Wildlife East Africa • Watching Wildlife Southern Africa • West Africa • World Food Morocco • Zimbabwe, Botswana & Namibia

AUSTRALIA & THE PACIFIC Auckland • Australia • Australia Road Atlas • Bushwalking in Australia • Cycling Australia • Cycling New Zealand • Fiji • Healthy Travel Australia, NZ and the Pacific • Islands of Australia's Great Barrier Reef • Melbourne • Melbourne City Map • Micronesia • New Caledonia • New South Wales & the ACT • New Zealand • Northern Territory • Outback Australia • Out to Eat – Melbourne • Out to Eat – Sydney • Papua New Guinea • Queensland • Rarotonga & the Cook Islands • Samoa • Solomon Islands • South Australia • South Pacific • Sydney • Sydney Map • Sydney Condensed • Tahiti & French Polynesia • Tasmania • Tonga • Tramping in New Zealand • Vanuatu • Victoria • Walking in Australia • Watching Wildlife Australia • Western Australia

CENTRAL AMERICA & THE CARIBBEAN Bahamas, Turks & Caicos • Baja California • Bermuda • Central America on a shoestring • Costa Rica • Cuba • Dominican Republic & Haiti • Eastern Caribbean • Guatemala • Guatemala, Belize & Yucatán: La Ruta Maya • Havana • Healthy Travel Central & South America • Jamaica • Mexico • Mexico City • Panama • Puerto Rico • Read This First: Central & South America • World Food Mexico • Yucatán

EUROPE Amsterdam • Amsterdam Map • Amsterdam Condensed • Andalucía • Austria • Barcelona • Barcelona Map • Belgium & Luxembourg • Berlin • Berlin Map • Britain • Brussels, Bruges & Antwerp • Brussels Map • Budapest • Budapest Map • Canary Islands • Central Europe • Corfu & the Ionians • Corsica • Crete • Crete Condensed • Croatia • Cycling Britain • Cycling France • Cyprus • Czech & Slovak Republics • Denmark • Dublin • Dublin Map • Eastern Europe • Edinburgh • Estonia, Latvia & Lithuania • Europe on a shoestring • Finland • Florence • France • Frankfurt Condensed • Georgia, Armenia & Azerbaijan • Germany • Greece • Greek Islands • Hungary • Iceland, Greenland & the Faroe Islands • Ireland • Istanbul • Italy • Krakow • Lisbon • The Loire • London • London Map • London Condensed • Madrid • Malta • Mediterranean Europe • Moscow • Mozambique • Munich • the Netherlands • Norway • Out to Eat – London • Paris • Paris Map • Paris Condensed • Poland • Portugal • Prague • Prague Map • Provence & the Côte d'Azur • Read This First: Europe • Romania & Moldova • Rome • Rome Map • Russia, Ukraine & Belarus • Scandinavian & Baltic Europe • Scotland • Sicily • Slovenia • South-West France • Spain • St Petersburg • St Petersburg Map • Sweden • Switzerland • Trekking in Spain • Tuscany • Venice • Vienna • Walking in Britain • Walking in France • Walking in Ireland • Walking in Italy • Walking in Spain • Walking in Switzerland • Western Europe • World Food France • World Food Ireland • World Food Italy • World Food Spain

LONELY PLANET

Series Description

travel guidebooks	in depth coverage with backgournd and recommendations
	download selected guidebook Upgrades at www.lonelyplanet.com
shoestring guides	for travellers with more time than money
condensed guides	highlights the best a destination has to offer
citySync	digital city guides for Palm TM OS
outdoor guides	walking, cycling, diving and watching wildlife
phrasebooks	don't just stand there, say something!
city maps and road atlases	essential navigation tools
world food	for people who live to eat, drink and travel
out to eat	a city's best places to eat and drink
read this first	invaluable pre-departure guides
healthy travel	practical advice for staying well on the road
journeys	travel stories for armchair explorers
pictorials	lavishly illustrated pictorial books
eKno	low cost international phonecard with e-services
TV series and videos	on the road docos
web site	for chat, Upgrades and destination facts
lonely planet images	on line photo library

LONELY PLANET OFFICES

Australia
Locked Bag 1, Footscray,
Victoria 3011
☎ 03 9689 4666
fax 03 9689 6833
email: talk2us@lonelyplanet.com.au

USA
150 Linden St, Oakland,
CA 94607
☎ 510 893 8555
TOLL FREE: 800 275 8555
fax 510 893 8572
email: info@lonelyplanet.com

UK
10a Spring Place,
London NW5 3BH
☎ 020 7428 4800
fax 020 7428 4828
email: go@lonelyplanet.co.uk

France
1 rue du Dahomey,
75011 Paris
☎ 01 55 25 33 00
fax 01 55 25 33 01
email: bip@lonelyplanet.fr
website: www.lonelyplanet.fr

World Wide Web: www.lonelyplanet.com *or* AOL keyword: lp
Lonely Planet Images: lpi@lonelyplanet.com.au